Doing Comparable Worth

Gender, Class, and Pay Equity

In the series
WOMEN IN THE POLITICAL ECONOMY
Edited by Ronnie J. Steinberg

Doing Comparable Worth

Gender, Class, and Pay Equity

JOAN ACKER

TEMPLE UNIVERSITY PRESS

PHILADELPHIA

Temple University Press, Philadelphia 19122
Copyright © 1989 by Temple University. All rights reserved
Published 1989
Printed in the United States of America

The paper used in this publication meets the minimum
requirements of American National Standard for Information
Sciences—Permanence of Paper for Printed Library Materials,
ANSI Z39.48-1984

Library of Congress Cataloging-in-Publication Data
Acker, Joan.
    Doing comparable worth : gender, class, and pay equity / Joan Acker.
    p.   cm. — (Women in the political economy)
    Bibliography: p.
    Includes index.
    ISBN 0-87722-621-0 (alk. paper)
    1. Pay equity—Oregon—Case studies.   2. Sex discrimination
against women—Oregon—Case studies.   3. Working class women—
Oregon—Case studies.   I. Title.   II. Series.
HD6061.2.U62O72   1989
331.2′1—dc19   88-26845
                                                      CIP

To my mother,
Frieda Steinmann Ellsworth

Acknowledgments

This book is an attempt to link the work of practical feminist action with the work of feminist theorizing. It owes a great deal to the existence of the United States women's movement, because that movement opened the space for feminist intellectual work and continues to produce innovative attempts, such as comparable worth, to alter and improve women's situations in our society. The dedicated work of Oregon women activists and their allies was also essential because their work resulted in the Oregon comparable worth project.

I am particularly grateful to Senator Margie Hendriksen and to Margaret Hallock. Senator Hendriksen gave me much information that helped me understand the pay equity efforts in Oregon. Margaret Hallock shared with me many of her experiences in doing comparable worth. I thank her for the long hours of discussion and the insights that were exceedingly important in developing my analysis. She has, of course, no responsibility for my interpretations.

I am indebted to many other people who worked on this project, including staff of the state's Personnel Division, other managers in the state's Executive Department, state employees who served on the benchmark job evaluation committees, Task Force members and staff, consultants from Hay Associates, and members of the Oregon Women's Political Caucus and the Women's Rights Coalition. In particular, I would like to thank Vicki

Lundmark, Betsy Apley, Darlene Hooley, Sara Lichtenstein, and Jean Atkins.

In the first phase of thinking through this book I worked closely with Melissa Barker. Her dissertation, which also uses Oregon comparable worth data, gives a different but complementary interpretation. Ronnie Steinberg contributed a great deal to my knowledge about the technical and political issues of pay equity, and, as editor of the Temple series on women and the political economy, encouraged me to write the book and provided essential criticism. I also appreciate the critical reading, advice, and support of Roslyn Feldberg and Joke Esseveld. Discussions with Dorothy Smith improved my analysis and Nona Glazer kept me alert to class differences among women. Finally, Michael Ames has been a perceptive and helpful editor.

The Center for the Study of Women in Society at the University of Oregon supported this work with two grants. The Swedish Center for Working Life, where I have been for two years, has provided me with an ideal working environment that has greatly facilitated my writing. My thanks to all my colleagues at Arbetslivscentrum.

Arbetslivscentrum, Stockholm
December 1988

Contents

Doing Comparable Worth

Gender, Class, and Pay Equity

CHAPTER ONE

Introduction

This is a study of a large comparable worth project and of how gender and class dynamics influenced its outcome. I have a double intent: first, to understand comparable worth as a practical effort, constrained by conflicting gender and class interests, and second, to explore theoretically the connections between gender and class, using the comparable worth project as a ground for making visible some of these connections.

Activists in the women's movement ask the practical question, What are the best strategies for increasing economic equality between women and men? Comparable worth, or equal pay for work of equal value, is, in the 1980s, the most visible answer to that question. Comparable worth argues for raising the wages of sex-segregated, female-dominated jobs on the grounds that this work has been historically undervalued (Aaron and Lougy, 1986; Treiman and Hartmann, 1981; Remick, 1981; Grune, 1980; Cook, 1983; Gold, 1983). The undervaluation is, proponents contend, a form of discrimination. Comparable worth projects determine the amount of undervaluation by comparing the complexity and responsibility of female- and male-dominated jobs, then institute pay increases to eliminate the identified discrimination.

Comparable worth is a recent strategy. In a few places, such as the state of Minnesota, the policy has been set and pay equity[1] has been implemented. In many others, delays and difficulties seem to slow down its acceptance (Cook, 1985). Accumulating experience suggests many questions (Hartmann, Roos, and Treiman, 1985). How does it actually work? Are there troubles and traps in doing comparable worth? Can sex bias in traditional job evaluation systems be reduced, as supporters recommend (Remick, 1984; Beatty and Beatty, 1984; McArthur, 1985)? What are the steps to transforming job evaluation rankings into wages (Schwab, 1985)? How easy, or difficult, is it to alter an established system of wage setting (Hartmann, Roos, and Treiman, 1985:17)? All of these are political questions.

The class and gender politics in comparable worth are evident in the identities of its supporters and its opponents. Employers are cautious, skeptical, or openly opposed to comparable worth (Bureau of National Affairs, 1984:9–12). Unions, particularly those with many women members, support it (Bureau of National Affairs, 1984:73–78). Women's advocacy organizations are probably the most active proponents. How do these potentially adversarial groups come together over comparable worth, as they must when there is an effort to put it into practice?

These questions are one focus of this study of the class and gender dynamics in comparable worth efforts in the state of Oregon from 1981 to 1987. The other focus is on a theoretical question raised by feminist social scientists (for example, Acker, 1973; Hartmann, 1976), and, increasingly recognized by others who study society, who now begin to see that women and gender must enter any discussion of human life (for example, Wright, 1985; Wilkinson, 1981). This is the question about the intersections of gender and class. Class has been the central concept for analyzing inequality in industrial capitalism, but feminist work has demonstrated conclusively that women's subordination and inequality cannot be understood solely through a class analysis (for instance, Dex, 1987; Crompton and Mann, 1986; Sokoloff, 1980; Acker, 1980; Hartmann, 1976). Gender, male dominance, or patriarchy—whatever term we use—has a determinate part in creating women's place. Yet, a central fact of women's situations in contemporary societies is their positions in the division of paid labor, or their positions in the class structure. Consequently, the issue becomes, How are these analytically different bases of inequality related?

The theoretical question is urgent, I think, because the economic inequalities between women and men are so persistent. Although reform efforts in the United States have been going on since the middle 1960s, sex segregation and the wage gap between the sexes have been only slightly altered. As women's positions improve in some, mostly middle-class, occupations, such as the law (Epstein, 1983), they are at a standstill or declining in others, such as the new computer occupations (for instance, Strober and Arnold, 1987). A central theme of this book is that gender inequalities seem to be so deeply embedded in social structures and processes that they are recreated even as we try to eliminate them. Differences between the sexes are reconstituted in new guises as part of the processes of restructuring, and technological and economic change also alter the manifestations of class.

How shall we develop an understanding of how this actually happens? Class and gender structures have often been studied at aggregate levels where broad pictures of labor markets, occupational distributions, and economic change can be drawn. Such data can be interpreted as the statistical traces of social actions that occur in specific and local natural settings (for example, Duster, 1981). This is not to argue that any local setting has as much power as any other in determining the larger patterns of inequality in a society, but only to point out that specific actions of particular people are involved in, for example, hiring decisions that produce sex segregation, or in decisions about what wages go with a certain job. A thorough understanding of how inequalities happen must include knowledge about what people do in local settings, what assumptions guide their actions, what images inform their decisions, what interests serve to locate them on one side or another. Such knowledge may be most accessible when the practices and images are under attack. An attempt to change the practices that produce inequality may bring to visibility some of the ways that these practices are embedded in the ongoing social life. This is my approach in this account of a comparable worth project.

In 1983 I was appointed to the Task Force that would carry out a comparable worth project in the state of Oregon. I saw this appointment as an opportunity to look inside the process of gender reproduction. Comparable worth deals with wage setting; the practice of setting women's wages lower than those of men is part of the process of creating gender inequality. I reasoned that an attempt to take apart even a small section of that process—the way that wages are determined—would tell me something about how the system works. I also thought that a detailed examination of a comparable worth project might reveal something about the intertwining of gender and class, for women's economic disadvantages in work organizations are products of the convergence of both class and gender processes (for instance, Hartmann, 1976; Cockburn, 1981; Acker, 1988).

In presenting this account of the Oregon project, I start from the assumption that gender is built into the class structure, that economically, culturally and socially constituted differences between women and men are the medium through which class processes are played out. Change is difficult, I will argue, partly because the connections are so pervasive and complicated, and efforts to change women's situations run up against entrenched class as well as gender interests. Through this case study and the insights and conclusions I draw from it, I also hope to contribute to the discussion on comparable worth as a strategy for changing women's situations. The kernel of the comparable worth idea is easily grasped, perhaps because it is deceptively simple. The much more complex and often problematic meaning of comparable worth emerges as people try to transform the idea and organizing slogan into higher wages for women.

What Is Comparable Worth?

Comparable worth is a strategy for raising the wages of jobs in which the pay is low, due, in part, to the predominance of workers who are members of low status groups, women, or discriminated-against minorities. The argument is that past and present discrimination by employers and male-dominated trade unions resulted in sex-segregated jobs and wage rates for female-dominated jobs that are systematically lower than wage rates for jobs of similar complexity usually held by white men. Considerable evidence exists to support these claims. For example, historically, employers often established separate wage scales for women and men, even when they were doing quite similar or identical work. The top of the female scale was often almost even with the bottom of the male scale (Treiman and Hartmann,

1981:57–58). In the United States this practice became illegal only in 1963 with the passage of the Equal Pay Act. As a consequence, inequities in pay for the same work have been decreased, although not eliminated. However, the wage gap between women and men remains fairly stable at the aggregate level (Steinberg, 1984:4). Attempts to explain the wage gap as a function of human capital factors or family demands consistently fail to account for a large part of the difference (Treiman and Hartmann, 1981:41–42). Some of the unexplained difference may be due to undervaluation of female-dominated jobs.

To pursue this possibility, comparable worth arguments have to define what is valuable and to whom.[2] As a practical matter, in comparable worth projects, the power to define is recognized as belonging to the employer, or to the employer and union together in the bargaining process. What is valuable is that for which the employer is willing, or forced, to pay. Undervaluation can be defined as Ronnie Steinberg suggests as a situation in which "wages paid to women and men engaged in historically female or minority work are *artificially depressed* relative to what those wages would be if these jobs were being performed by white males" (Steinberg, 1984:4).

Specification of the amount of undervaluation is central to the idea of comparable worth, but this requires comparing jobs that seem to have no common features. Traditional women's jobs, such as secretary or nurse, have different sorts of tasks than traditional men's jobs, such as electrician or engineer. Opponents of comparable worth often object that comparisons between such disparate occupations are impossible or meaningless (see Gold, 1983; Remick and Steinberg, 1984). Nevertheless, for many years management consultants have been earning fees from employers for making such comparisons. They use various systems of job evaluation to compare jobs on factors such as knowledge, complexity, and responsibility.[3] Each factor is scored and total scores are compared, often with the aim of establishing pay equity between jobs with similar scores. However, in the past, this technique was used primarily to compare jobs within similar job families and at similar hierarchical levels; administrators compared with administrators, engineers with engineers. But the method can be used to compare jobs with very different content and in different job families. The door to comparable worth was

opened when advocates for women recognized that this management tool could be used to establish the amount of undervaluation of female-dominated jobs as compared with male-dominated
jobs.

Comparable worth is a social movement as well as a technical strategy to reduce wage inequities related to sex, and race,
segregation of jobs.[4] Beginning in the early 1970s with a study of
comparable pay in the state of Washington (Remick, 1981) and
efforts of the International Union of Electrical Workers to gain
pay equity at Westinghouse (Hutner, 1986), the idea of comparable worth spread rapidly among activists attempting to improve
women's positions in the labor market. Eleanor Holmes Norton,
then Chair of the Equal Employment Opportunity Commission,
gave comparable worth a national presence in 1977 when she
identified it as a top issue for the 1980s. She commissioned the
National Research Council of the National Academy of Science
to form a committee to investigate the practicality of comparable
worth as a policy for equal pay. The reports that eventually came
out of that committee's work were instrumental in further spread-
ing the news about comparable worth and providing an expert
base for defending it (Treiman, 1979; Treiman and Hartmann,
1981; Hartmann, 1985).

In the federal government, states, cities, and counties of the
United States, women's groups and trade unions saw the possibilities of comparable worth and began organizing to achieve it in
the late 1970s. This is a grass-roots development, significant
in the history of the contemporary women's movement in the
United States. As it continues during a period of extreme conser-
vatism when the flow of officially sponsored welfare state reforms
has been cut off, comparable worth shows that the women's
movement is still very much alive and making new alliances with
organized labor.

Most comparable worth efforts took place, and still are
found, in the public sector. There are several reasons for this.
First, it is in government at all levels that the largest proportions
of women trade union members are located (Bell, 1985). These
are the women workers who are most likely to have some organized way to deal with wage issues. Second, the public sector is
more accessible to outside groups, such as women's organizations, than is the private sector. Legislators can be convinced that

it is in their interests to support fair and adequate wages for women workers. In addition, most public jurisdictions have merit systems that purport to set wages on the basis of merit alone (Bureau of National Affairs, 1984:95; Bell, 1985:292). Thus, they are vulnerable to charges that merit or value has been ignored. Finally, most states and many municipalities already had women's commissions charged with overseeing efforts to gain sex equality and, in many places, these groups gave essential support to comparable worth efforts. By 1983, such efforts were underway in at least 143 public jurisdictions (Cook, 1985), and by 1986, Cook (1986) estimated that comparable worth had been taken up as a policy issue in at least 156 jurisdictions.

Public sector comparable worth projects have a common pattern. First, through legislation or collective bargaining, a policy is established. Then, jobs are evaluated to determine the extent of wage disparities, or, in some cases, previously completed job evaluations are used. Next, a plan for equity adjustments is formulated. Finally, politics and bargaining are again involved in efforts to implement the plan. Using the Oregon case I will show that the process is not so easy as that, for it involves often severe conflicts over values and resources that originate in competing interests of class and gender.

The Oregon Project

The first Oregon pay equity effort took place in 1981 when an amendment to the state's Civil Rights Act was proposed, requiring all employers in the state to pay comparable wages for work of comparable value. This amendment received little support and was not approved, but the movement for comparable worth was on its way. In the spring of 1983, a feminist state senator introduced, and the Oregon State Legislature passed, a bill mandating the appointment of a Task Force on State Compensation and Classification Equity that was to carry out a study of the classification and compensation systems of the state and propose ways to reduce any gender-based inequities that it found. Great enthusiasm and high hopes surrounded the victory over the bill. The Task Force, of which I was a member, along with an outside consultant and the State Personnel Division, completed most of the project in the time specified in the legislation, between November, 1983, and January, 1985. The task was tremendous, and included collecting and analyzing job content data from 32,000 state employees, evaluating 2,000 job composites, determining wage inequities, developing new compensation and classification plans, and developing an implementation strategy (see Figure 1.1).

As directed in the 1983 legislation, the Task Force made a report to the 1985 Legislature with recommendations for a new bill to implement comparable worth. That legislation ran into great difficulties because it had provisions unions could not support and because the classification plan was not sufficiently developed. The 1985 Legislature, after much controversy, passed an amended pay equity bill which the governor then vetoed. However, for the next two years, work on comparable worth continued. In 1987, with a new governor, a new legislature, and new trade union strategies, another comparable worth bill was passed. The governor signed the bill and state workers began to get equity increases in October, 1987. My account of the process analyzes what went wrong in the first two years and what went right in the second two. I argue that the original study was marred, not only by ambitions that exceeded the allotted time resources, but also by failures to adequately understand and deal with the realities of conflicting interests of class and gender. The success after the second two years shows that pay equity can be won, but also reveals the limits of this reform, the potential again constrained by competing structural interests.

The Oregon experience is significant for a number of reasons. At the beginning of the project in 1983, Oregon seemed to have one of the most innovative and exciting comparable worth efforts in the nation. Feminist activists were in control of the Task Force and they were determined to do as much as possible to get wage raises for low-paid women. The confrontation between gender and managerial interests is, as a result, particularly clear. Another factor that makes Oregon especially interesting is that the state has full collective bargaining, with some nine unions bargaining wages and working conditions for state workers. Labor-management relations are complex and often adversarial, resembling those in the private sector. Therefore, in this context, it is possible to see class as well as gender processes, and to

Figure 1.1
Chronology—Oregon Comparable Worth History

1981	Spring	Comparable worth bill covering all employers in state fails to pass.
1981–82		Workshops, conferences, development of plans for new bill.
1983	July	Governor signs comparable worth bill.
	Sept.	Personnel Division sends out Request for Proposal to management consultant firms for classification and compensation study.
	Nov.	Task Force appointed. First Task Force meeting.
	Dec.	Hay Associates hired as consultants. Decision-data would be gathered on all positions.
1984	Jan.	Project begins.
	Jan.– May	Questionnaire development, pretest, distribution. Guide chart modification, job evaluation pretest. Policy discussions on all aspects of project.
	May	Implicit decision by Personnel to group all questionnaires by tasks, not current classes.
	July– Aug.	Benchmark job evaluations.
	Aug.	Discussion of concrete classification, compensation, and implementation decisions begins.
	Sept.	Anxieties about ability to complete project surface.
	Oct.	Job evaluations on all groups completed.
	Oct.– Dec.	Discussion of all issues continues.
	Dec.	Decision—Task Force recommends a single pay plan and a one-time intervention in collective bargaining. New classification plan is delayed. Legislation for 1985 is prefiled.
1985	Jan.	Data analysis linking wages and evaluated points for individuals and preliminary new class structure.
	Feb.	No satisfactory classification plan. Efforts to decouple classification and compensation begin. Legislative hearings begin.
	Mar.	No satisfactory classification plan. Pressure to release classification plan. Information released to agencies, unions, legislature. Reaction to plan negative. Task force modifies recommendations—decouples classification and compensation.

Figure 1.1 (*continued*)

	April	Amended bill introduced.
	June	Amended bill passed by House and Senate.
	July	Amended bill vetoed by governor.
	Aug.	New Legislative Task Force appointed.
	Dec.	Agreement reached by management and union to complete classification system and propose pay equity plan for 1987 legislature.
1985–86		Management, with cooperation of Oregon Public Employees Union, continues work on classification and pay equity.
1987	Jan.	Pay equity bill based on previous two years of work, with limited implementation of new classes introduced.
	Mar.	Management withdraws plan to implement new classes—pay equity to be for current classes.
	May	Management requires elimination of anti–red lining clause from bill.
	June	Pay Equity Bill passes. Equity increases to be bargained.
	July	Governor signs bill. Management and union at impasse in bargaining—no pay equity until contract is signed.
	Sept.	Strike—settled in 9 days.
	Oct.	Pay equity increases in paychecks.

examine the intersection of collective bargaining and job evaluation as two principles for wage setting, a ground for potential contradictions between gender and class interests. In addition, the Oregon case illustrates another possible gender/class conflict, in the sometimes opposed views of those supporting a feminist-legislative strategy and those supporting a trade union–bargaining strategy.

Coming after the experience in Washington and Minnesota, the state of Oregon was in a position to profit from the lessons others had learned. The study was to be, with the exception of the New York study, on a larger scale than others. Job evaluations would be done specifically for the purposes of pay equity, something no other project, had attempted at that time, again with the exception of New York, which used a very different methodology (Steinberg and Haignere, 1987). The Oregon project did not deal with wage discrepancies based on race because the state has a very small minority population and, as a result, they represent only about eight percent of state employees.[5]

The temporary failure of the project raises many questions about comparable worth. These are not only local and specific questions, for, with the notable exception of the state of Minnesota, no jurisdiction had implemented pay equity fully. Nor is it yet clear how to define "implemented fully." Questions include: How do you know when pay equity has been achieved? Why are projects so slow in implementation? How suitable is a management tool to the task of achieving a radical reform? Indeed, how radical is this reform? How much can comparable worth upset old patterns of inequality? Can the comparable worth approach to wage setting be used in concert with other ways of wage setting, such as collective bargaining or keying wages to the market? One avenue to answers to these practical questions is to look at comparable worth projects as attempts to alter some aspects of the gender/class structure.

Gender and Class: The Theoretical Issues

One motive for doing this study arises from my interest in the connections between gender and class (Acker, 1973; 1980; 1988). Although gender inequality and class inequality have often been seen as separate phenomena, they are obviously related in practical experience. For example, most low-waged women are employed in female-dominated and working class jobs. Their place in the hierarchy of wages is the result of the interaction of processes that create low wages (class) and sex-segregated women's jobs (gender). Such a clean analytic divide is, however, misleading, for sex segregation and low wages are created in the same series of actions.[6] Understanding these gender-class connections is important for our comprehension of the extraordinary persistence of women's secondary status (for instance, Hartsock, 1983; Hartmann and others, 1981). Moreover, as many feminist theorists have pointed out (for example, Zinn et al., 1985; Hooks, 1984; Jagger, 1983), the lives of women are as various as the lives of men, and this variation cannot be encompassed without including class and race differences in our analyses. To imply that only gender concerns us is to build our images of female existence around the experience of educated white women, since we are those with the time and money to theorize. Such images will inevitably be inadequate as representations of women in other social, economic, and cultural situations.

In spite of compelling reasons to join gender and class analytically, including the accumulation of research showing that women are in different situations than men in the overall structuring of exploitation and inequality in any society, feminist theorists have disagreed about how this might be done. One way is to talk about two systems of oppression, capitalism and patriarchy, analyzing each as an independent set of relations and looking at the ways that they intersect, reinforce, and contradict each other.

A Marxist perspective[7] on capitalism informs most of this work, primarily because its central focus is on oppression and exploitation and how systems of domination may be overcome. In this perspective, "class" refers to property relations that underlie production systems and to the cultural understandings and organizational forms that accompany them. These are relations between groups that are always unequal and exploitative, and contain an inner dynamic that carries the potential for change. Slaves have revolted, even if the workers of the world have never united. The property relations of capitalism, central to the process of capital accumulation, consist of the ownership and control of the means of production by a small group, and the selling of their labor power by almost everyone else. As capitalism has grown old, almost all those with money income have become wage earners, in a subordinate position in the property relations of this system.

But this bare schematic does not encompass the complexity of capitalist relations, particularly if the analysis is to apply to women. Highly paid managers and administrators are wage earners just as are nurse's aides and receptionists. Nothing in traditional class theory tells us why men dominate the first pair of occupations, while women dominate the second. Vast differences in power, pay, and prestige, patterned by gender, exist between different sectors of those who earn their income through wage and salary work. In addition, class theory cannot convincingly deal with the structural situations of women doing unpaid work in the home.[8] Obviously, the concept of class must be elaborated and even extensively revised if it is to serve us in understanding contemporary society.

Theories of patriarchy and capitalism,[9] rather than dealing directly with deficiencies in the theory of class, suggest that another structure embodies the dynamics of the subordination of women. This is patriarchy, a system organized around gender difference and male dominance. We can discuss how women's lives are affected by capitalist processes, but to understand how their experiences are different from those of men we must turn to patriarchy. There are a number of difficulties in thinking about gender and class in this way. One is that class, unrevised to include women, remains the central theory about societal-wide oppressions and inequalities, while gender and race still stand on the sidelines, the often forgotten "in additions" in theoretical discussions (Young, 1981). Another is that there are problems with patriarchy in locating the central underlying relations of domination, which must be done if patriarchy is to qualify as a system relatively distinct from capitalism. Are the roots of patriarchy in male control over female bodies and sexuality, or over female labor and its products? Or are they both, or are they located somewhere else? Perhaps they are ideological, perhaps they are material, or perhaps they are both. The penetration of the powers of gender has many sites, to borrow from Foucault (1980).

Feminist theorists working from Marxist foundations have recognized these problems, increasingly coming to the conclusion that a theory of one system, encompassing both gender and class, is what is needed (for example, Beechey, 1987). This has proved to be extraordinarily difficult to achieve. In spite of all the arguments in favor of a unifying theory, we continue to talk about the relationships between gender and class as though we assume two systems. As Cynthia Cockburn points out, "Unitary theory is, so far, self deluding" (1986:82). Yet, to me at least, the intractable problem of gender and class seems to be a barrier over which we must go if we are to make further progress in understanding the continuing re-creation, within widely differing and rapidly changing social and economic conditions, of the subordinate and disadvantaged position of women.

Two lines of approach to the problem are needed, I believe. One is a rethinking of both class and gender. The concept of class found in much of the American writing on patriarchy and capitalism cannot be accommodated to a unifying theory because, implicitly or explicitly, all concrete human beings—and thus gender—are absent. This view of class is a structural analysis focusing on economic relations at the most abstract level and deriving classes, class positions, and class boundaries from these relations. In this view, class structure consists of empty places, a structure of positions determined by abstract relations of production within an abstract mode of production. The structure is indifferent about who fills the empty places (for example, Wright, 1985). Into some positions go women, into others go men, and patriarchy determines these placements. Similarly, race or ethnicity may play a part in determining which actors turn up in which positions, but gender or race have nothing to do with the way the structure itself is constituted. Thus, gender is always an afterthought.

Another way of thinking about class in the Marxist tradition is more promising for an attempt to link class and gender.[10] This alternative emphasizes process, class formation and transformation, asking how class is produced and reproduced in concrete social practices. This approach makes no formalistic use of analytic levels, but understands that processes outside the control of individuals set the conditions for what actual (not abstract) people can do in particular, historical, economic-social-political situations. These structural determinants always include, as very important factors, the actively changing operations of the capitalist economy. E. P. Thompson (1963; 1978), whose work represents this direction, defines class as historical process in which "men and women, in determinant productive relations, identify their antagonistic interests, and come to struggle, to think, and to value in class ways" (Thompson, 1963:9).

This way of thinking about class is more congenial to the feminist project than is the structural view of class as empty places. Feminist questions are not about categories and their boundaries, but about how women's situations are historically produced and reproduced. Women are differently located than men in class processes and in order to understand this better, we need ways of thinking that allow us to see that ties to the central processes of capitalist development take multiple forms. We need ways of thinking that do not foreclose, through *a priori* definitions of the most fundamental relations, different ways of understanding.

Gender as a concept has a shorter history than class and does not have such well-entrenched meanings. It is a concept in the process of elaboration. The term was first used by feminists to differentiate between biological sexual differences and those produced through social processes. Its meaning has expanded and become more complex, referring not only to femininity and masculinity, but also appearing as a basis for organizing social life, a ground for establishing identity and interpreting experience, and a symbolic and material line dividing work, resources, power, and honor between the sexes. Gender has, through recorded history, meant organized systems of male dominance over females, but it has meant other things as well. As Scott argues (1986), it is a major symbolic form in which power is justified.[11]

Gender is now understood by feminist theorists as part of the basic processes that constitute social life. We now talk about gendered relations, gendered organizations, or gendered class structures. To say that an organization or class is gendered means that its fundamental structure of advantage and disadvantage, exploitation and control, action and emotion, meaning and identity are constructed through, and in terms of, distinctions between male and female, masculine and feminine. Gender is not an addition to ongoing processes, conceived as gender neutral. Rather, it is an integral part of those processes, which cannot be properly understood without an analysis of gender. Thus, we can explore class and gender as intrinsically linked processes, bound together within a dance of oppositions and contradictions in which each mediates the other (Lewis, 1985).

A creative rethinking of gender and class depends upon a second line of approach through empirical work, examining already completed research and going with a fresh eye to new kinds of data. I think that we already have a large amount of research that shows in concrete detail how class and gender are reproduced in the same processes. This study of comparable worth is intended to add to that store of knowledge.

The research that already shows the intrinsic connections between gender and class suggests, I think, that we still need to talk about a working class, several middle strata, and a ruling class, but to see these as internally stratified in complex ways, most importantly by gender and race. This stratification has developed through processes of technological change (for instance, Cockburn, 1985) and occupational and professional separation and differentiation (Larson, 1977; Goldman and Tickamyer, 1984). These are not inevitable or disembodied processes. The elaboration of multiple stratifications within the class structure is accomplished by people acting in what they take to be their own interests, which include gender and race interests. Many of these interests are rooted in organizational positions, consciously created by managers, as well as in occupations. This is important for the Oregon story.

The empirical grounding for a theoretical linking of class and gender comes, first of all, from historical studies of the changing situations of women in the development of industrial capitalism. This feminist reconstruction of history requires the linking of class and gender, and the recognition that the domestic arena has to do with class as well as gender. For example, the expansion of the wage relation itself was facilitated by the infrastructure provided by the gender-based division of labor. Production in emerging industrial capitalism was organized, with some rare exceptions, without regard to the living conditions of workers. Women, caring without pay for men and children, helped the working class family to survive. Women and men resisted the full integration of wives and mothers into the paid labor force (Sen, 1980), even as many women wanted or were forced to work for wages that were systematically created as lower than the wages of men. The family wage for men was posited on these arrangements of gender inequality. Thus, the wage has been, and is, a gendered social relation.

The sex segregation of work, paid and unpaid, and the wage gap between women and men are indications of the ways that gender mediates class in late capitalist societies. Women's class situations are characterized by, among other factors, sex segregation, low wages, intermittent employment, and subordination to men in the workplace and often at home. Men's class situations are characterized by, among other factors, sex segregation, higher wages, lifelong employment, and either dominance over women or little contact with them in the workplace and dominance in the home. An accumulation of studies suggest that these situations are experienced and understood through images and feelings about gender (for instance, Willis, 1977; Sennett and Cobb, 1973).

Sex segregation and the wage gap are continually recreated in the same process of technological change, reorganization, and restructuring that alters class structure (for example, Cockburn, 1985). This reproduction of gendered class situations is central to the ongoing subordination of women in late capitalist societies. Although gender and women's subordinate place are reproduced in many other locations—the family, the schools, the media— work organizations now have to be seen as extremely important. As larger proportions of women depend upon their own wages, as more and more women experience bureaucratic male-dominated organizations, the comprehension of what it means to be female, in terms of both material fate and consciousness, more frequently emerges here. Holter (1984) identifies this as part of the reorganized patriarchy of the welfare state. Another interpretation is that the reproduction of male dominance has become more and more integrated with the reproduction of class.[12]

In broad outline, these are some of the conclusions about the intersections of gender and class suggested by contemporary research. However, to understand how these relations are perpetuated and reproduced, a more concrete approach to process is necessary.[13] The work organization is one place to study these relations. Considerable research has been done, although with little sensitivity to gender, on class processes within work places as they affect men, beginning with work by C. W. Mills (1956) and Gouldner (1965), through Braverman (1974) and Burawoy (1979). Some have examined class processes as they affect women (Braverman, 1974), and more recently there has been a series of studies that look at the interlocking processes of class and gender at work (Glenn and Feldberg, 1979; Cockburn, 1984, 1985; Game and Pringle, 1983; Pollert, 1981; Westwood, 1985; Gamarnikow, Morgan, Purvis, and Taylorson, 1983; Knights and Willmott, 1986). These studies of the labor process have revealed a great deal about how gender, skill, technology, the organization of work and managerial strategies interact to produce a gendered class structure, bringing us closer to a unitary theory. However, the labor process is only one way to enter the topic of gender and class. Another avenue is through the wage-setting process, which, although related to the work process, has a dynamic of its own.

This study of comparable worth looks at wage setting. The wage is a central component of class relations in capitalist societies. It represents the proportion of the value created by labor that is paid to the laborer. Every time that a wage is set or paid, the fundamental relation of power between the worker and the employer is re-enacted. The wage is also the primary mode of distribution and of survival for most people in late capitalist nations; consequently it is the focus of a great deal of conflict and competition. Marxists have tended to see struggles over the wage as simply fights over how the pie is divided, and thus much less important than fights over the control of production, the making of the pie. However, I argue that class and gender processes cannot be understood without understanding how wages are set, and the pie divided.

Wage setting is accomplished through practical activities within organizations, often guided by bureaucratic compensation systems consisting of job classifications assigned to salary ranges.[14] Wages are set in daily life as various people make decisions, press their claims, argue and fight, or silently accept whatever is offered them. Where there are unions, the primary contests are between unions and management. The outcome of these encounters, whoever is involved, is that female-dominated jobs have consistently lower wages than male-dominated jobs. Observing an attempt to raise those low wages through intervention in wage setting, which is what comparable worth efforts do, should give some insights into the process, and thus into the ways that class and gender are linked and reproduced.

Comparable worth provides an excellent opportunity to observe the processual union of gender and class because it is both a gender issue and a class issue. It is a gender issue because it is an attempt to raise women's low wages by altering the wage-setting practices of employing organizations. Comparable worth argues that organizational practices incorporate and express historically created undervaluation of women's work relative to the valuation of men's work, and that undervaluation is based on a series of assumptions about differences between the sexes and their appropriate family and economic activities (Feldberg, 1984). Comparable worth aims to alter the relative valuation of women's and men's work, and, in the process, has to confront the assumptions about gender differences that support and legitimate the disparate valuation (Steinberg, 1986).

Thus, comparable worth challenges some elements in the ideology of male domination. Most directly it confronts the belief that men are worth more than women. By implication, it also takes issue with the notion that men deserve higher wages because they have families to support. One of the ideological supports for higher male wages has been that men need more than women; family responsibilities are one reason for that need. By arguing that the intrinsic value of the work, rather than the needs of the worker, should be the basis for wages, comparable worth undermines these old ideas.[15]

Ultimately, comparable worth intends to redistribute money, and perhaps power, from men to women (Steinberg, 1984:25). Although most comparable worth advocates do not support taking anything away from men, a change in the relative shares of wage income going to the two sexes will result in redistribution, unless women's wage increases are funded through higher prices, higher taxes, or lower profits.

Comparable worth is also a class issue. Pay equity adjustments are designed to go primarily to women with the lowest wages. These are women in working-class—clerical and service—jobs. Unions organizing such workers are using pay equity as an organizing tool. Pay equity may also affect the relative rewards going to other occupations and positions in the internal stratification of class groupings. In the process, established hierarchies of power and status, as well as of income, may be upset. For example, comparable worth may challenge long-existing advantages of certain workers over others, particularly advantages of men over women, and thus create difficult internal tensions in unions. There is also the possibility, as Feldberg (1984) points out, that comparable worth might increase class differences among women. For example, if the salaries of registered nurses were brought into line with those of engineers with comparably valued jobs, the differences between registered nurses and practical nurses might be increased. However, job evaluation could also reveal that practical nurses' tasks and responsibilities are very similar to those of registered nurses. The class effects of comparable worth are probably indeterminant, dependent upon the ways in which the comparable worth strategy is implemented and the relative power of those managing the implementation.

The challenge of comparable worth to the ideology of gender confronts class on another level. Employers have guarded their power to define what is valuable to them, and how valuable it is. Organized labor has challenged this monopoly over the power to define, but usually without questioning the systematic definition of women's work as less valuable than that of men. Now, unions with large numbers of women members are questioning these definitions. Comparable worth, adopted by labor unions as a strategy for attaining wage increases, extends the area in which employer control over the conditions of employment is contested. In addition, comparable worth takes issue with the theory that wages are set by the unseen hand of the market, or by genderless returns to human capital. These theories are major ideological justifications for the contemporary class structure. Comparable worth has the potential to expose such theories as ideology and thus, indirectly raises questions about the justification of present systematic class inequities.

Studying Gender, Class, and Comparable Worth

I have thought of this study as current history and political ethnography, as well as feminist sociology. I am convinced that the comparable worth movement will take an important place in the history of late twentieth-century feminism. As a strategy for change in many other countries than the United States (ILO, 1986; Hutner, 1986), it is part of the worldwide feminist movement. Looking at comparable worth gives us the opportunity to observe in the present the sort of process that historians often reconstruct by sifting through old documents, letters, and newspapers. Here, in immediate reality, is a reform effort as significant as the nineteenth-century efforts of women workers to organize. We can ask historical questions about it, and get our answers immediately. For example, we can ask who supports comparable worth. Are male workers encouraging wage equality for women, or are they part of the problem, as they sometimes were in the past (for instance, Hartmann, 1976)? Are women united around comparable worth, or are there divisions? Where does management stand? Is this a significant reform; does it make a difference? If so, what kind of difference and for whom? In other words, a comparable worth project presents the possibility of asking and answering questions about the politics of gender and class inequality in the United States in the 1980s.

My method contains some elements of ethnography, which has been defined as a description of a culture, a shared system of meanings (Spradley, 1979) accomplished through an intensive participation in the life to be described. My participation was intense and intensive for almost two years. Field notes of this participation, combined with the documents of the project and interviews, are the material for this account. The culture of the project, in the sense of an emerging shared understanding of comparable worth, is described. This was a political culture full of conflict.

However, I hoped to get at something more than the political meanings and process of doing comparable worth. I looked at the project, as I outline above, as a window into the inner workings of organizational practices which result in the unequal wages characteristic of both gender and class inequality. As the project participants discussed what should be changed and how to go about it, some of the dimensions of a culture and a set of social practices that sustain inequalities might be revealed. I hoped to decode the implicit meanings of the discourse through which change was either accomplished or impeded, as well as record the explicit reasons for actions that shaped the project. I believed analyses of moments of disagreement or opposition were likely to provide insight into underlying processes. While recognizing that any insights I might get would be partial, I thought that by carefully observing the project I could gain greater understanding of the connections between gender and class, and help to penetrate the mysteries of the persistence of gender-based inequalities.

As with any ethnographer, I had my loyalties. Although I am one of those who is convinced that the value-free, distanced observer is an impossibility (Acker, Barry, and Esseveld, 1983), I believe that a sociologist should make her values public and clear so that the reader can beware. I was on the Oregon Task Force, I am a feminist, and I was deeply involved in the project. Doing comparable worth was an intense emotional and intellectual experience, exciting, interesting, anxiety producing, and frustrating. I experienced it from my own standpoint in the process. An account written by anyone else, another Task Force member, someone from management, from one of the unions, by a consultant or by an uninvolved outside observer, would probably differ in some ways. However, some time elapsed between the project and the writing, allowing me to step back from the experience. I have tried to present a factual picture, taking as facts the actual public statements made by participants in the project and recorded in written minutes and on tapes. Every public meeting was tape-recorded and all quotes have been checked against those tapes. Most of the account of the second project stage from 1985 to 1987 is based on interviews, because I was not a direct participant during that period and attended only a few public hearings. I also had access to some of the documents for that phase of the project. Although I don't use names, anyone familiar with the Oregon scene can identify the players. While some may not agree with my interpretations of actions, we were all there as public performers, speaking for the record.

Most of what is reported here took place in the State Capitol Building and adjacent office buildings. Some of it occurred at other places around the state where workers were brought together to listen to discussions about the study and the questionnaire. Some of it occurred in restaurants, cars, and homes. The work of describing the jobs of state employees was done in hundreds of offices throughout the state. The Oregon Task Force on State Compensation and Classification Equity met approximately twice a month from November, 1983, to April, 1985. More frequent meetings occurred during certain periods. The project Advisory Group also had many meetings. In addition, there were subcommittees and work groups. In the spring of 1985, many legislative hearings took place and the project moved onto the Senate and House floors. All Task Force meetings, Advisory Group meetings, and legislative hearings were open to the public. Usually the Task Force sat at a table, each member with a microphone, while others sat in front as observors and participants. A representative of the state's Personnel Division attended every meeting and often there were trade union staff and state employees from other departments and agencies. Backstage a great deal was going on and, of course, there was much I did not observe and can only report second hand.

I was able to observe many manifestations of gender and class. The Oregon project was filled with conflicts originating in competing class interests that undermined the intended focus on women's wages. Images of gender were revealed as deeply entrenched in the job evaluation process. Technical issues were also complicated political issues, rooted in the ways that class and gender inequalities are built into organizational structures. Clashing political agendas shaped the technical work and ultimately resulted in the failure of the first Oregon comparable worth project. A more politically informed approach that negotiated between competing class and gender interests finally resulted in some significant pay increases for women.

In the following chapters I describe and interpret the comparable-worth process in Oregon. Chapter 2 discusses the construction of gender and class interests in the state organization and in its wage setting process. Coalescing and competing interests defined the series of problems this comparable worth effort had to face. These included the project's control, legitimacy, scope, and timing, the definition of the primary issue—pay inequity or an outmoded job classification system—and problems in combining collective bargaining and job evaluation in wage setting. A definition of "true comparable worth," a comprehensive equitable pay system based on gender-neutral job evaluation, emerged from the problem discussions and guided subsequent project development. True comparable worth became the center of class conflict in later project stages.

In Chapter 3 job evaluation is the topic. True comparable worth requires an unbiased, sex neutral system of job evaluation. I analyze the Hay Guide Chart–Profile Method of job evaluation, its structure and application, showing in detail how this method reconstructs hierarchy and how the protection of hierarchy affects the relative value placed on women's work. This examination reveals some of the ways that women's place is built into organizational structure in processes that also contribute to the maintenance of class relations.

Chapter 4 discusses building the comparable worth plan, which included a new job classification system and a new wage structure. The feminist image of true comparable worth became the ground for conflicts between management and unions as well as between unions themselves. These conflicts focussed around technical steps in doing comparable worth: data analysis, choosing a pay line, implementation strategies, and long-term maintenance of pay equity. Thus, technical issues were always political issues as well. I present the findings of the project—that at the entry level female-dominated jobs earned 25 percent less than male-dominated jobs, and at the skilled level female dominated-jobs earned 7 percent less than male-dominated jobs—and the Task Force recommendations to raise the wages of over 9,000 workers. However, severe problems with job classification, management's use of the project for its own ends, and contradictions between true comparable worth and collective bargaining damaged the project's legitimacy.

In Chapter 5, I analyze the fall of true comparable worth and the two subsequent efforts that led to partial achievement in 1987 of pay equity goals that had been frustrated in 1985. Two broad changes in approach brought success. First, the Oregon Public Employees Union (OPEU) worked for an implementation plan that did not undercut the interests of unions or their male members. Second, the mobilization of union women and their allies in the state women's movement and the legislature saved comparable worth at some critical points. However, it was only after a strike that pay equity was implemented. By 1987, the operational definition of comparable worth had been changed from an equitable pay system to poverty relief.

Chapter 6 presents the theoretical conclusions from this study. I look at class/gender in the political process of doing comparable worth and in the underlying practices, actions, and images that are revealed in the political process. I identify some of the dynamics of gender/class in the reproduction of hierarchy, the active creation of the invisibility of women's skills, the opposition to wage redistribution, the active creation of the marginality of women's interests, and in a gendered logic of organization that is part of our taken-for-granted reality. I conclude with a discussion of the possible effects that comparable worth may have on gendered class formation. In the short term, better wages for low-wage women will ease the poverty problem. In the longer term, its most important consequence may be that it will draw women into labor union activity and push unions into realizing that women's issues are important labor issues. Comparable worth also has the radical potential to question what our society really values and who has the power to set those values.

CHAPTER TWO

Competing Interests, Multiple Goals

Class and gender interests, whether in conflict or coalition, helped to shape Oregon's comparable worth project from its inception in 1983. The comparable worth legislation was sponsored by the leading feminist state senator, in close cooperation with women staff of the state's largest labor union, the Oregon Public Employees Union. Within that union there was some gender-based disagreement, as the male leadership was ambivalent about strong comparable worth wording in the bill. The class interests of the Republican state executive were reflected in their initial opposition to the bill. However, feminist leaders in the legislature organized wide support and, recognizing that the bill would pass, management came over to the winning side and labor dropped its reservations. Both management and the Oregon Public Employees Union supported the comparable worth bill more because it mandated a revision of the state's job classification system than because it mandated pay equity. Thus, even at the moment of passage, potentially competing interests were evident.

Although the bill became law in June, 1983, the Task Force that was to carry out the project was not appointed until late October, a serious delay. When they were finally made public, the appointments reflected the class alignments in state government—the labor-backed Democratic leaders of the state Senate and House of Representatives had appointed four women identified with the women's movement and trade unions while the

business-identified Republican governor chose three representatives of business and management. This created a task force in
which conflicting interests mirrored long-simmering distrust between labor-oriented legislators and a conservative state executive. Moreover, the feminist domination of the task force meant
that, at least temporarily, the legislature had taken some power
over wage setting out of the hands of management and unions,
both male dominated, and placed it in the hands of women
committed to women's interests.

Because the concepts of class and gender interests are used
so frequently in the following, I want to point to complexities in
defining these terms, and make clear that I use them loosely. I
define interests as aims, or as what benefits or advantages a
particular group, recognizing that group members often disagree
about this. Interests are linked to power, which can be partially
defined as the ability to promote or secure interests.[1] Class interests refer to management aims within state government as well as
to management perspectives from outside government as they
confronted worker interests usually, but not always, represented
by unions. Management did not have a unitary set of goals, nor
did labor present a united front, and there were often conflicts
within these two general camps. By gender interests I mean the
sometimes conflicting interests of men and women workers. I
have difficulty separating the gender and class interests of working women and men. Often, what is good for the working class is
defined as what is good for working men. If this goes against the
needs of working women, the resulting conflict may be seen as a
gender conflict. However, working women's (and men's) interests are based on class as well as gender, so that discussions of
conflicts rooted in gender may be simultaneously discussions of
conflicts rooted in class. Adding complexity, class differences
between women make it impossible to talk about women's gender interests as a single phenomenon. Task Force feminists, all
middle-class professionals who supported organized labor, intended to represent the gender interests of women, but, as we
shall see, at some critical points—usually when the issue had to
do with male-dominated unions—they disagreed with each other
about what the interests of working women were and how they
should be best supported.

Conflicting interests also had roots in the state's organizational structure and its system of wage setting. Oppositional interests were reflected in the identities of project participants as well as in a series of issues that appeared and reappeared throughout the project's life. These oppositions point to some of the underlying dynamics of the daily reproduction of class/gender relations. In this chapter I discuss these bases of conflict and describe the emergence of the issues central to this comparable worth project.

The State of Oregon as a Complex Organization

The state of Oregon, as any state government, can be conceptualized as a large bureaucratic organization, as well as a concrete location of class and gender processes. It is divided into three branches, the legislative, the judicial, and the executive. The executive, the largest branch, carries out the bureaucratic work of the state. Headed by the governor, the Executive Branch includes 32 state agencies, a number of boards and commissions, and a number of central divisions that control and coordinate from the state capital. State agencies, such as Human Resources, Higher Education, and Transportation, are large bureaucracies in their own right. They have a fair amount of autonomy, although they are dependent upon the legislature for their mandate and their funding, and are responsible to the governor and to his executive divisions. State agencies compete for scarce resources as they also, often, attempt to maintain autonomy.

Two of the mechanisms for central control by the executive are the job classification system and the wage system, which are constructed for the state as a whole and are used in all agencies. These systems are established by the legislature, which also seeks control through this means. These systems undergo constant negotiation and change, channeled through the legislature, through agency and central government personnel departments and through collective bargaining. These bureaucratic processes are part of the daily round of actions that replicate class relations. Women's low wages, one sign of their situation within class societies, are determined in that same series of decisions. This is a contested territory where class interests have long been at issue. Comparable worth, through an act of the legislature, intrudes upon this terrain and introduces gender interests.

Wage Setting in Oregon's State Government

The wage setting territory that comparable worth was intended to change was a complex set of practices involving approximately 35,000 people with varying and competing interests. To understand the issues with which the project struggled, a description of these practices is necessary. The state of Oregon, in common with most other public jurisdictions, has a job classification system and a system of wage grades keyed to the classification system. Wage setting is the process of assigning job classes to salary ranges, putting particular positions into the proper classes, and adjusting the wage rates. Major adjustment of wage rates for the salary ranges occurs every two years when the legislature meets and bargaining for new union contracts occurs.

The state of Oregon had 1,775 job classifications and 32 salary ranges, most divided into six levels, at the beginning of its comparable worth project.[2] The wage level for each class had evolved over time through a combination of legislative action, trade union bargaining, and administrative practices, including the use of salary surveys and a process of whole job evaluation. Some jobs in state employment, most notably the faculty in higher education, had salaries determined through individual negotiations. The overall system had not been restructured for over 40 years; it probably contained remnants of relative wage rates that were considered reasonable 40 years earlier, but would not look reasonable today. Some effects of sex discriminatory wages in existence before any equal pay legislation was passed probably survived in the contemporary wage rates.

Legislative actions and collective bargaining are the principal processes through which the wage system is adjusted. The Oregon legislature meets every two years and adopts a budget for the coming biennium. In that budget is the "wage package." The package contains proposals for raising wages of particular job categories, for establishing wages of new job categories, and for general or across-the-board wage increases. For jobs that are in collective bargaining units, the wage proposals are the result of union-management negotiation. Increases for unrepresented jobs are proposed by the Personnel Division in cooperation with the various state agencies. All these proposals go through the legislative committee system. There is a great deal of lobbying around the wage package and the final outcome is, of course, a political decision. The wage package is usually split into several separate bills and one or more of these may be vetoed by the governor of the state.

The legislature, anxious to set limits on state expenditures, continues its control over wages even when it is not in session through its Emergency Board, which sits continuously to make decisions between legislative sessions. The Emergency Board has the responsibility to approve or disapprove all requests for reclassification. That is, if the tasks of a particular position are changed so that a reclassification into a position in a higher wage bracket seems justified, this must be approved by the Emergency Board.

Both management and the unions have difficulties with this required legislative approval of reclassifications. It is a restriction that brings together the collective bargaining parties around a common goal: elimination of legislative approval of reclassification. An example may clarify the process. Mary's wage depends upon the job class to which her position is assigned. The job class is assigned to a particular wage group. Each group has six levels and Mary will reach the top level within six years if her performance is satisfactory. Then she will have no more increases, except across-the-board general increases. Mary may get a salary increase by qualifying for and being hired into a higher level job. However, she may like her present job, she may be doing new and more interesting tasks. If she wants to stay, she can only be rewarded for doing more and becoming more skilled by having her job reclassified—put into a new class which is in a higher wage group. The legislature scrutinizes such moves and Personnel must spend considerable time justifying in terms of content and available money its requests for reclassifications. Although management has the final say, unions may become involved, and often do, when members appeal to them for help. This is time, and staff, consuming for the unions too. The elimination of legislative approval would provide greater flexibility and much more rapid resolution of classification problems.

Wage setting in Oregon is complex because nine unions bargain separately with the state. The Oregon Public Employees Union, affiliated with the Service Employees International Union (SEIU), with over 17,000 members in some 700 job classifications, was the largest union in 1983. The American Federation of State County and Municipal Employees was second with approximately 1800 members. The Teamsters were third, and smaller unions represented registered nurses, parole and probation officers, engineers, graphic workers, and licensed practical nurses. Oregon has a particularly good collective bargaining law, from the perspective of organized labor, since unions bargain wages and workers have, in general, the right to strike. In principle, the union has the right to negotiate wages separately for each job class. The law is not so advantageous from management's perspective because bargaining a large number of contracts is time consuming and results in different wage rates for different bargaining units. Moreover, trade unions have more power than in many other public jurisdictions, with more participation in wage setting than is usual. Relations between management and unions are often contentious. Many legislators are sympathetic to labor, as I noted above, perhaps increasing the adversarial stance of management.

The state agency usually constitutes the bargaining unit. For example, the Oregon Public Employees Union bargains for university employees while the American Federation of State, County, and Municipal Employees bargains for the state prison. This arrangement contrasts with that of many other states. In Minnesota, for example, bargaining is by job classification instead of state agency. All secretaries, for example, are represented by one union and, in practice, there are not so many different unions organizing state workers.

In Oregon, various unions have different situations within the overall bargaining structure. The Oregon Public Employees Union, as noted above, had the largest number of members from the largest number of job classes, including blue collar, white collar, and professional jobs. This union was likely to settle for across-the-board increases that would benefit everyone, but this strategy would maintain any historically-existing wage differences between female-dominated and male-dominated jobs. The smaller unions usually follow the lead of the largest union and, in terms of an overall wage level, make the same settlement. However, some unions have workers whose wage claims go to binding arbitration, rather than to a strike, if no agreement is reached. Such unions could push wage negotiations to binding arbitration and take the chance that an arbitrator might give them higher increases than those negotiated by OPEU. That had happened in the past, with settlements that gave some workers higher wages than those of other workers doing exactly the same jobs, but represented by different unions. For example, the job classification Secretary 1 had four different wage scales.

Unions in Oregon, as elsewhere, are male dominated, with male leaders even when a high proportion of members are women. Anecdotal evidence indicates that often male workers are more active and insistent than female workers and manage to get their unions to negotiate higher pay for male-dominated job classes than for female-dominated classes.

The legislative process and collective bargaining occur at the same time, as noted above. For a few months every two years there is an intense process of legislative maneuvering and labor-management bargaining. The legislature must approve the wage package, partly determined through bargaining that is constrained by the budgetary limits set by the legislature. All of this is further constrained by the governor's budget proposals, which must be considered if a veto is to be avoided.

Under these conditions, the market appears to play a relatively minor role in wage setting. Nevertheless, the market enters wage setting in a number of ways. First, it is state policy to pay at a level low enough to prevent the state from drawing workers away from private industry. Thus, the present wage structure represents the accretion of the market over at least the last 40 years. The state is the largest single employer in Oregon and the wages it pays probably affect various wage markets, as well as being affected by them. Second, the state Personnel Division carries out a market survey every two years to guide it in setting the parameters of union bargaining and in setting its own wage proposals.[3] The state surveys private employers, other public employers in Oregon, and seven or eight other governments of states of similar size and industry mix. These surveys include data on salary and fringe benefits for a series of benchmark jobs, usually jobs with a large number of incumbents that are found in many organizations. Market information seems to be used within job groups as a guide, but not a rigid standard. For example, clerical jobs in state employment are compared with clerical jobs in the survey, blue-collar jobs with blue-collar jobs and so on.

Third, the market may enter when a new job is established, as the wages for that job will be set high enough, but not too high, to allow the state as an employer to recruit successfully. Computer-related jobs are, of course, the most recent example of this impact of the market on wage setting. In addition, a job applicant whose skills are in high demand might bargain individually for a wage at the top of a wage category rather than in the middle or at the bottom. In Oregon, a higher proportion of men are at the top of their respective wage categories than are women. It is not clear whether this is due more to seniority or to hiring at a higher initial level.

Prior to the comparable worth project job evaluation was a minimal factor in wage setting. Beginning in the 1970s, job evaluation was used for jobs at the upper management levels. Here point-factor job evaluation was employed to establish equity between managerial jobs. A kind of whole job evaluation was used for other jobs. This was a rudimentary process for a large proportion of female-dominated jobs. For example, four large clerical classes were graded on the basis of increasing complexity and responsibility of the job. These classes were assigned to low wage grades; in 1984 almost 54 percent of employees in female-dominated jobs were at salary range 9 or below, compared with 4 percent of employees in male-dominated jobs (Table 2.1). Individual clerical positions were assigned to one of these classes, again roughly on the basis of the complexity and responsibility of the job. Often, however, the assignment of a position and a person to a job class—and thus to a salary level—was determined by the amount of money available in the particular departmental budget, or by the amount of money a particular administrator thought was appropriate to commit to a particular position. In practice, this meant that an unknown number of clerical jobs with heavy responsibility were assigned to the lowest clerical class, clerical assistant, and thus pegged at a very low salary level. One-

Table 2.1
Employees in Gender-Dominated Classes, by Salary Range of
Current Actual Classes,
State of Oregon, 1984

Salary Range	Employees in Female-Dominated* Classes		Employees in Male-Dominated* Classes		Employees in Gender-Neutral Classes	
	N	%	N	%	N	%
1–9	7,640	53.7	481	4.1	1,058	17.0
10–14	3,149	22.1	2,723	23.1	719	11.5
15–19	2,951	20.7	3,742	31.7	2,216	35.5
20–26	435	3.1	3,548	30.0	2,051	32.9
27–42	65	0.5	1,317	11.2	197	3.2
Total	14,240	100.0	11,811	100.0	6,241	100.0

*Seventy percent or more of incumbents are of the same gender.
Source: Final Report and Recommendations, Task Force on State Compensation and Classification Equity, 1985, appendix 2C.

half of all women employed by the state of Oregon were, in 1983, in these four large clerical classes. Other nonmanagerial and lower managerial positions were assigned to job classifications in a similar way. The process was guided, of course, by an effort to match the tasks and responsibilities of a position to the description of the job classification, and to position the job classes in the wage structure consistent with a hierarchy of authority and responsibility. However, this method could hardly be called job evaluation and, over time, it had produced many inequities.

Overall, Oregon's wage setting process was pleasing to some parties and not so pleasing to others. Management wanted to simplify by reducing the numbers of negotiations they had to undertake. Labor liked the substantial rights they had been able to win with the help of a labor-oriented legislature. Labor and management had a problem in common, the old and unwieldy classification system, and the law that required all requests for reclassification to go to the legislature. Thus, within the structure of the wage setting system, there were the grounds for union-management cooperation while, at the same time, there were grounds for opposition. In addition, the system helped to structure conflict between labor unions. Nine different unions bargaining to get the best deal possible for their own members meant that they might take different and possibly opposing strategies at any particular time.

The interests of women were generally unattended in this structure, except for the nurses in the Health Sciences Center, the state medical teaching institution. Organized in an almost totally female union, the Oregon Nurses Association, these nurses had been able to win salaries above those of nurses in the state institutions as well as other concessions such as regular pay increases for those who wanted to stay in bedside nursing and not move on to administration or teaching in order to raise salaries and status. Other women workers were in male-dominated unions in which women's low wages had not become public issues until comparable worth had been taken up by feminist legislators. Thus there were many open conflicts over class issues, particularly those affecting men, but little open conflict over class issues concerning women or over gender issues. This then was the complicated process, with its many actors and gender/class interests, into which the comparable worth Task Force was to intervene.

Doing Comparable Worth: The Participants

Representatives of all of those who take part in wage setting for state government, plus some outsiders representing interested groups such as business and feminist organizations, participated in the project. Public identities of the participants were implicitly defined in class and gender terms. That is, it was clear who represented feminism, labor unions, and management. There were core participants, who spent most of their time for a year and a half working on the project, and peripheral participants, who came in to influence the proceedings at particularly eventful turning points.

Participants included the seven members of the Oregon Task Force on State Compensation and Classification Equity. Four were women, feminists and professionals, including the research director of Oregon Public Employees Union—a Ph.D.

economist; the state senator who had initiated the comparable worth bill—a founder of the Oregon Women's Political Caucus; an attorney experienced in sex equity cases; and a university sociology professor who specialized in questions of women and work. Three other members of the Task Force were professionals in personnel and employee relations. These included a woman who was the civil rights compliance officer of the State Board of Higher Education; the director of human resources of the largest industrial firm in the state, a man; and another man, an executive of an organization of county and local governments who was later replaced by a male state administrator.

The Task Force hired a nationally known expert on comparable worth to advise it in early project formulation. It also had a small staff of its own and an Advisory Group with representatives from management, unions, and the public. The state Executive Department was represented by the Personnel Division, whose Director and Assistant to the Director, both women and career employees in state government, spent almost full-time on the project. Personnel had other staff on pay equity work, a total of twenty-one at the peak of the effort. Twenty-one additional state employees were members of the Benchmark Job Evaluation teams. The project consultant was Hay Associates, with an experienced staff of three assigned to Oregon. Finally, there were all the others concerned, the 32,000 state employees who filled out questionnaires about their work, the state legislature, nine labor unions that organized state employees, the governor, and managers of state agencies. The feminist public in the state, represented by the Oregon Women's Political Caucus and the Women's Rights Coalition, were watching and acting when it was possible.

Points of Conflict and Resistance: Project Issues

The often conflicting interests and opinions of the array of participants were expressed in recurring issues that surfaced in early project stages. These issues remained as undercurrents, resurfacing later in new forms as major project problems. These issues also indicate some of the points of resistance to the project and some of the structural locations of the determination of the depressed wages of women's jobs. That is, the conventional patterns of distribution in which female jobs receive lower wages than male defined jobs are written into the structural processes of organizations, and are often invisible. When change processes are set in motion, the greatest opposition may be over exactly those processes that are most essential to the status quo. In the early project stages these issues were (1) What is the operational definition of comparable worth? (2) Who shall control the project? (3) On what basis can we establish the legitimacy of the change effort? (4) What is Oregon's problem—pay inequity or an outmoded classification system? (5) Can we combine collective bargaining and comparable worth? (6) What should be the scope and timing of the project?

Definitions of Comparable Worth

Comparable worth is a strategy and a social movement with a slogan that work of equal value should get equal pay. That principle has to be translated into practice if wage increases are to be achieved. The Task Force and Personnel began the translation process in their first meeting. Initially there appeared to be little conflict over the definition of comparable worth. The Oregon legislation had specified that it was public policy of the state "to attempt to achieve an equitable relationship between the comparability of the value of work performed by persons in state service and the compensation and classification plans within the state system." The bill further specified how comparable worth would be achieved.

The wording of the 1983 bill was very different from the bill that feminists attempted to get passed in 1981, which would have amended the state's civil rights act to prohibit any employer from compensating "any employe at a rate less than the rate paid other employes for work which requires comparable skills, efforts, responsibilities under comparable working conditions" (House Bill 2969, July 3, 1981). This bill did not pass, but it marked the beginning of new strategies for comparable worth. In the next two years feminist organizations and labor unions worked together, holding conferences and workshops, and deciding how to approach the next legislative session. One decision was to try for a bill that would cover only state employees; another had to do with the specific wording of the bill, that "a single, bias-free, sex-neutral point factor job evaluation system shall be applied to all jobs in state service, across job families to rank order jobs, to set salaries, and to create career ladders for advancement according to the value of work performed."

A staff member of the Oregon Public Employees Union first proposed the wording, an operational definition, to the bill's feminist sponsor in the Senate, attributing the definition to the published work of Helen Remick, a leading activist and writer on comparable worth from the state of Washington. Apparently no other definition of comparable worth was considered in the writing of the 1983 bill or in the hearings preceding its passage. The Oregon Public Employees Union favored this wording, although they preferred to keep any mention of comparable worth out of the legislation, fearing that using that term would impede passage.

Remick had proposed in 1981 to define comparable worth as "the application of a single, bias-free point-factor job evaluation system within a given establishment, across job families, both to rank-order jobs and to set salaries" (Remick, 1981). Remick argued that an operational definition is useful even in the absence of consensus on an abstract definition. More abstract definitions tend to raise arguments because of the difficulties in agreeing on what is valuable and to whom it is valuable. The problem of defining value is sidestepped by such an operational definition. Value becomes whatever is measured by the job evaluation system. Remick also recognized, however, that job evaluation schemes sold by management consultation companies "primarily measure how cultural values are compensated in the marketplace" (Remick, 1984:113). These are, of course, the values of male-dominated cultures, a problem recognized by Task Force feminists.

The definition written into the Oregon legislation created guidelines for the achievement of pay equity and Task Force members accepted those guidelines with little question. As the State Senator who sponsored the legislation said: "The law that was passed envisions a universal system of objective point-factor job evaluation in which dissimilar jobs are being compared, and then the compensation would be set from that point." The manager in the department of forestry was to be assessed on the same criteria as the kitchen aid in the institution for the mentally retarded. All job categories were to be considered in order to establish equity throughout state government employment. Thus, potentially the distance between wages at the top and at the bottom of the work hierarchy could be narrowed. This potential was limited by agreements made in back room negotiations to get the bill passed. Excluded from the study were doctors, lawyers, judges, board members, elected officials, college and university teaching faculty, top administrators appointed by the governor, and the state police. Thus, some of the possibilities for a radical attack on the organizational class structure were cancelled at the beginning, and some comparisons, such as that of doctors and nurses, that might have shown extremely large wage gaps, were never made.

The Oregon bill, SB 484, also required that job evaluation be used to set salaries. The Task Force interpreted this to mean that evaluated points would be transformed into a dollar figure. Exactly how this would be done was to be determined after job evaluation results had been analysed. The concrete interpretation of this mandate became a major issue in later project stages. Another question was, whose salaries were going to be set by evaluated points? In the first weeks of the project, disagreements surfaced over whether or not comparable worth should deal only with women's salaries. Is it right, Task Force members asked, to raise wages only for women, or should men with undervalued work also be included in the definition? All agreed that men working in female-dominated job classes should get any increases going to that job category. After all, these men suffered low salaries because of discrimination against women. But what about job classes in which men predominated or that were not sex segregated but that still had wages significantly below those of other classes with the same points? Feminists initially supported a definition that would not include such groups in a pay equity plan. Management-oriented Task Force members argued for the fairness of including undervalued male and mixed classes. The Task Force finally agreed on their inclusion, as the understanding emerged that job evaluation points should influence the wages of all jobs included in the study. Only in this way could we get an equitable *system*, as contrasted with equity for certain female-dominated jobs.

Another provision of the Oregon operational definition was

that the job evaluation system should be "bias-free, sex-neutral." Management was uneasy about this part of the definition. The personnel director contended that no one really understood what a bias-free, sex-neutral system was and, further, that bias probably would only be brought into the process through biased judgments of those collecting or evaluating data (Task Force minutes, Nov. 18, 1983). Task Force feminists disagreed and focussed their attention on "bias-free, sex-neutral" requirements. Sensitivity to sex bias in job descriptions and job evaluation became a criterion on which potential consultants were assessed.

Task Force feminists implicitly defined sex bias as the failure to give evaluated points to arguably important job characteristics that are specific to female-typed jobs, and failure to give points to female jobs for characteristics that are also found in male-dominated jobs, where they are properly rewarded. Bias might be imbedded in job descriptions, definitions of factors, or in the job evaluation process (Remick, 1984; Steinberg and Haignere, 1987). Thus, the operational definition began to focus on collecting good job descriptions, generating "good" or unbiased factors and factor weights, and applying these consistently in job evaluation. As the Task Force advisor on hiring the consultant said, "These are the bases by which the classification system perpetuates cultural bias" (Task Force minutes, Dec. 13, 1983:13). An unarticulated agreement emerged in the Task Force during long sessions with its advisor on the hiring of a consultant that if good, unbiased technical work were done on job evaluation and restructuring of job classes, the next step to determining the degree of wage inequality would be relatively simple.

An implicit definition of "true comparable worth" emerged by the completion of the full work plan in January, 1984. True comparable worth, a concept that shaped the Oregon project, was a wage setting system in which wages are pegged to unbiased, sex-neutral evaluated points, with some flexibility to respond to market forces, but with controls to keep inequities from creeping back over time. A true system includes all jobs, guaranteeing that new inequities are not created by leaving out undervalued mixed sex or male dominated jobs. "True" comparable worth implied broad changes in the long-established wage and classification system, as well as changes in the process of structuring and restructuring that system. In this system was embedded the ongoing reproduction of women's low wages and the comparable worth goal was to change it. However, as subsequent conflicts showed, such broad changes threatened the balance of power between management and labor and other bureaucratic and individual interests, creating unanticipated difficulties.

The Right to Define or the Struggle for Control

The appointment of a Task Force composed of people from outside the Personnel Division, and primarily from outside of state management, was an incursion into fiercely protected territory. The inclusion of feminists and trade unionists on the Task Force meant that the dominant Task Force perspectives were at odds with the views of the state Executive Department led by the conservative governor. Task Force feminists wanted to control the project to assure a positive outcome for women workers. According to the State Senator who had sponsored the bill, "The bill clearly puts the Task Force in charge and the Task Force sets the direction." However, the Personnel Division had considerable power over the project, gained in the legislative compromises necessary to pass the comparable worth bill. Personnel was to carry out the staff work, and thus, would actually manage daily operations. In addition, much of the budgeted $355,000 would go for this purpose. Moreover, the project budget was channeled through Personnel. Although all expenditures had to be approved by the Task Force, Personnel had a certain amount of flexibility in handling the funds. Finally, Personnel had campaigned energetically for a reclassification study and the director was committed to achieving this goal. The stakes on both sides were high. Consequently a struggle for the right to define the scope of the project, the job description and evaluation process, the building of a new classification system, and implementation policies, began before the first Task Force meeting.

Weeks before the appointment of the Task Force, the Personnel Division, concerned about the delay in the appointments and aware of the short time allotted to the project, had sent out a Request For Proposals (RFP) to a long list of management consulting firms that did job evaluation. The RFP, written without Task Force consultation, outlined a classification and compensation study based on job evaluation. In the RFP there appeared no mention of discrimination against women, gender based inequities, or gender bias. The RFP went into great detail about the study of the classification system, job evaluation, and salary analysis, but the main point of the project to its feminist supporters—that the wages and evaluated points of female and male dominated jobs should be compared—was not there.

The Request For Proposal also described the role of the Task Force, the Personnel Division, and an advisory group. The Personnel Division had prepared an organizational chart of the project showing the Division in the center, coordinating position, while the Task Force was off to the side, in a peripheral position where it would be consulted from time to time, and from which it would give final approval to the project plan and the final report. The Advisory Committee was to provide technical advice and to make technical decisions, along with Personnel and the major consultant. As the personnel director said, "The Study Advisory group will be, technically, working with the Personnel Division as a part of that organization. The contractor will work with that group in formulating recommendations and these will be brought before the Task Force for discussion and approval."

The feminist-labor union majority on the Task Force would not accept such a subsidiary role. At first, they talked about rejecting the RFP, because Personnel should not, they argued, have gone ahead without the Task Force and, in any case, the RFP, failing to mention pay equity, was seriously deficient. They decided not to reject the RFP, but to amend it to put the Task Force in control and to specify that the consultant was to provide a comparison of the wages of female- and male-dominated jobs, as well as assistance in the development of a plan for achieving pay equity.

The first three meetings of the Task Force were tense as the question of control was fought out. The main protagonists were the Personnel Director and Task Force feminists. Other Task Force members sided with Personnel. Task Force feminists won, or at least it seemed to be so at the time. The Task Force was put in the center of the process, with Personnel in a staff position. Personnel would organize the actual work of studying the jobs in the state and producing a new classification structure. The Task Force would stay in close contact with the process and would make all decisions of a policy nature in open meetings. A project steering committee was appointed, consisting of the chair of the Task Force, the Director of the Personnel Division, and her deputy for job classification. Thus, a Task Force feminist and full-time trade union employee would be part of the group directing daily operations. She worked almost full time on the project for the next 18 months.

The Task Force majority won another hotly contested issue, the appointment of its own staff to handle information on the project and to document the process. Personnel as well as the management representatives on the Task Force objected to a separate staff for the Task Force. This was a waste of money, totally unnecessary, they said.

Feminists in the Oregon case were standing outside the administrative structure, although they had a base in the legislature. The feminist majority, attempting to overcome this structural exclusion from power, wanted the Task Force to have a separate identity, not to be swallowed by Personnel, which the majority perceived as potentially antagonistic to feminist goals. Appointed to the position of Task Force executive was the top legislative assistant to the feminist senator on the Task Force. A lawyer, she had been part of the group which had achieved the passage of the comparable worth bill; her appointment was a symbolic victory for the feminist side.

Conflict over control did not subside, however. The next issue was the hiring of staff for the technical work in the Personnel Division. Task Force members wanted to make these decisions, expecting to hire people with feminist convictions and research skills. However, the Director of Personnel was adamant. These people would be working under her and she had the absolute right of management to hire them. This became a moot point when she revealed that she had indeed already hired her staff. They were people with personnel administration backgrounds, not researchers. Feminist convictions had not been a hiring criterion. The director made clear that one of her concerns was to hire people who could remain after the project was completed and who would be able to keep the job evaluation system going. Task Force feminists were more interested in short term effectiveness in identifying and eliminating pay inequities than in the long-term maintenance of a new classification system. Here again was a conflict that had its roots in the definition of the problem and in a conflict of interests between management and feminists. The disagreements on this issue were bitter, with Task Force feminists feeling that the director had simply done what she wanted in the face of opposition by the Task Force majority.

The struggle for control of the project continued throughout the year and a half of work. Control was contested in public meetings and in the closed meetings of the steering committee. The conflict was not only over project decisions and work procedures, but over the rights of managers more generally. The passage of the bill and the setting up of the Task Force could be seen as an interference into matters that had always been the exclusive right of management to decide. Managers deal with the content of jobs. Managers construct classification systems. Managers decide on the value of jobs. These themes appeared in various forms as management representatives discussed the project.

Even closer to home, within the project itself, the Task Force was invading some of the Personnel Director's prerogatives by wanting to make hiring decisions and to actively supervise the project. The Task Force was upsetting the distribution of power within the organization in the name of organized labor and the feminist movement. Moreover, the legislation was an implicit criticism of the Personnel Division and of the personnel departments in state agencies. The people working in these units had always had the responsibility for classifying jobs, setting wages, and putting workers into the proper slots. The legislature had said, in effect, you have done this wrong, you have probably been discriminating against women workers. A less than enthusiastic response is not surprising.

The Search for Legitimacy

Some of the tensions resulting from clashing interests were held in check by the necessity to convince different publics that the project was well conceived and worthy of support. Change could not be achieved without at least the passive acceptance of diverse groups from feminist activists to conservative legislators. The Task Force, Personnel, and the Advisory Group all recognized that the project must appear to be legitimate and palatable to the central actors. As the Task Force's consultant on the hiring of the major job evaluation contractor said, "What is essentially being done is finding a systematic basis for legitimizing a wage structure that people with a particular work organization are going to have to live with and believe is legitimately derived" (Task Force minutes, Dec. 13, 1983:15).

This need to keep contending parties convinced that pay equity was a good idea affected some of the most fateful project decisions. The coalition that supported the enabling legislation consisted of advocates of a new classification system: OPEU and the state Executive Department, and advocates of comparable worth, legislators and feminists. To continue to hold that coalition together, the anxieties felt by many about comparable worth had to be kept in check. Management in state agencies was skeptical. The Personnel Division seems to have encouraged agency management participation by defining the project as a reclassification study, something that management wanted, rather than a study to decide about pay raises for clerical and service workers. A series of meetings with management was planned and at the first large meeting the governor's top aide endorsed the pay equity effort. In spite of such support, rumors from lower-level staff were that top managers said that comparable worth would never amount to anything. Whether accurate or not, the rumors pointed to opposition and anxiety.

Legitimacy concerns entered the discussions about what consulting firm to hire. The Task Force hired an advisor, a person with extensive experience with comparable worth, to help with this decision. With her participation, the Task Force and Personnel staff interviewed the four finalist firms. Each firm presented their proposals and the staff who would work on the Oregon project. Task Force feminists asked questions about how sex bias would be handled in the job evaluation process. Those from the management side were interested in the potential consulting firms' views on how the market should be considered in wage setting. Each side was speaking to the concerns of its particular constituents.

Hay Associates was the choice. The firm's reputation was excellent, making it most acceptable to management. Hay staff made a highly polished and professional presentation, convincing the Task Force that with their experience and skill "they could deliver a product." All those working on the project realized that time to the completion date was short, and that we needed a consultant who had a record of getting things done. The self-confidence and experience of the Hay representatives suggested that they would be the ones to best get the project through a tight schedule. Hay was at least minimally acceptable to Task Force feminists, who had read authors such as Donald Treiman (1979) and Helen Remick (1981) on the problems of possible bias in the Hay system. In their presentation, Hay consultants agreed that some alteration of their job evaluation factors could be done to build in more sensitivity to the particular aspects of women's jobs that often go unrewarded. This was reassuring, even though feminists outside the Task Force had grave doubts about Hay. There were some suggestions that Task Force feminists had sold out by hiring a firm that catered to top U.S. corporations. However, the project could not go forward without a consultant who inspired confidence. Hay was the only one that seemed to have the competence and on whom all members could agree.

Hay was also the firm with the most thoroughly elaborated and tested job evaluation methodology. If this methodology were carefully applied, they were prepared to help the Task Force argue that the project was technically adequate. Technical adequacy was an important peg on which to hang claims to legitimacy that we expected to have to make. Would we be able to convince the legislature, the governor, and probable critics from the business community that study findings were sound and objective? Hay consultants pointed out that no job evaluation system can be called objective, because job evaluation has to do with making value judgments. However, the Hay system assures the consistent application of the same set of values to all jobs. The Hay consultants had the experience of thousands of applications standing behind their claims for the reliability of their method.

The decision to include all undervalued jobs in equity raises was also made partly because of legitimacy concerns. How would people in male-dominated or mixed sex undervalued classes feel if they got no pay increases, while workers in female-dominated classes had bigger paychecks. The almost unspoken assumption was that such disadvantaged groups might oppose comparable worth, and that they would have some justice on their side. Thus, they should be included. Even the timing of the project was influenced by the overall aim of getting acceptance. The legislature had instructed the Task Force to return with recommendations to its next session, and this we intended to do, even though the Task Force advisor, the Personnel Director, and some Task Force members thought that a year might not be long enough.

Legitimacy concerns may have been most critical in mediating the ongoing disagreements between Task Force feminists and the Personnel Director. Because the director had the actual control over the study process, the project could not continue without her. As we shall see, the desire to prevent a major public explosion, which would bring into question the technical adequacy of the study and undermine support, may have played a major role in shaping the outcome that went contrary to women's interests by, among other things, delaying pay equity raises for over two years. Legitimacy was essential to project success, but as subsequent events showed, it was impossible to maintain in a reality of competing and unresolved differences of class and gender interests.

Pay Equity versus a New Classification System

Oregon's comparable worth bill called for a revision of both the compensation and classification systems of the state; the concept of true comparable worth was, in part, a response to this mandate. In practice, however, project participants had different agendas, some putting pay equity first and others placing a priority on classification. Feminist supporters of the bill and many of the legislators who voted for it saw the law as, first, a commitment to comparable worth. The problem to be solved was clear. Women working for the state of Oregon were, in 1983 and 1984, disadvantaged in pay and position as compared with men. Women working for the state earned a mean salary of $1,358 per month, while the mean salary for men was $1,846 (see Table 2.2). Thus, women earned 73 percent of the earnings of men.[4] Moreover, the state's labor force was highly sex segregated. In October, 1984, the Index of Dissimilarity for the state work force stood at 68, indicating that 68 percent of either men or women workers would have to change their jobs before women and men would be equally distributed across all jobs in the state's labor force. Moreover, the primary energy that got the bill passed was generated by a belief in comparable worth and years of work in organizing

Table 2.2
**Monthly Salary of State Employees, by Gender,
State of Oregon, 1984**

Monthly Salary	All Employees		Females		Males	
	N	*%*	*N*	*%*	*N*	*%*
$1,000 and less	3,155	11	2,693	18	462	3
$1,001 to $1,250	6,338	23	5,067	34	1,271	10
$1,251 to $1,500	5,775	20	2,912	19	2,863	22
$1,500 to $2,000	7,435	26	3,033	20	4,402	33
Over $2,000	5,671	20	1,340	9	4,331	32
Total	28,374	100	15,045	100	13,329	100
Mean Monthly Salary	$1,589		$1,358		$1,846	

Note: For current actual job classes with 10 or more employees.
Source: Final Report and Recommendations, Task Force on State Compensation and Classification Equity, 1985, appendix 2C.

conferences on comparable worth, building networks in its support, and lobbying legislators had preceded the passage of the bill.

Nevertheless, there were indications early on that influential parties had a greater interest in classification than in women's wages. For example, as the bill was being written in 1983, a representative of Oregon Public Employees Union had urged the sponsoring senator not to put anything on gender into her bill, sending three women union members to tell her that. Although women on the union staff had helped to write the bill, the union leader seemed to be primarily interested in a new classification plan, because many problems that members brought to the union had to do with classification.

The actions of state management indicated that they concurred in putting classification first. The Executive Department was interested in a tighter, more consistent, and thus more controllable job classification system. Individual state agencies had, for years, had the primary responsibility for managing their own personnel systems, requesting new job categories or the reclassification of positions, and carrying out other personnel functions.

This meant that effective control over personnel resided in the agencies, not in the central Personnel Division. Many observers of the state bureaucracy believed that Personnel wanted a new classification system so that central control could be strengthened and the power of the Division increased. Thus, the Executive Department and the union supported the bill for reasons that had little to do with better pay for women workers.

With the appointment of the Task Force, the Oregon Public Employees Union seemed to have come over to the side of priority for pay equity. The union's research director, a feminist and an economist, was on the Task Force, and union leadership agreed that she should be the Task Force chair, on union time. However, the strong union commitment to a complete overhaul of the classification system remained and was a factor in the project design.

The Personnel Division continued to reveal that its main stake was in a new classification system, rather than in pay equity. The most obvious early indicator of this stand was the failure to mention pay equity in the Request For Proposal that Personnel sent to management consultant firms. As project planning continued, Personnel continued to interpret the project primarily in classification terms, arguing that a complete revision of the classification system was a necessary foundation for job evaluation and a comparable worth pay plan.

The current classification system was seriously deficient. Some classifications were so broad that they included jobs that varied widely in levels of knowledge and responsibility. Other classifications were too vague to be easily evaluated. Additional problems were the allocation of similar jobs to different classifications and the lack of accurate information about new technical aspects of jobs. As a result, a large but unknown number of classifications were so poorly structured and described that they could not be accurately evaluated. Task Force feminists were particularly concerned about the problems with the large female-dominated job classes. Four job classifications, clerical assistant, clerical specialist, secretary, and administrative assistant, contained 7,821 employees; the majority were women with low wages. Pay equity adjustments depended on the evaluations of these jobs, and it would have been impossible to evaluate a clerical specialist, for example, because there was no single set of tasks assigned to clerical specialists.

Thus there seemed to be compelling and logical reasons for putting the classification study first in the project time line. However, some Task Force feminists were worried about the amount of emphasis on classification that appeared in the project plans. The tangled mass of classification issues seemed to be technical, but their political nature surfaced repeatedly through the project's life. For example, as we shall see, the number of job classifications, a technical issue, influenced the number of employees identified as undervalued, an outcome with grave political consequences for women.

Collective Bargaining versus Comparable Worth

Potential difficulties in combining comparable worth and collective bargaining were raised in the first Task Force session by the Personnel Director: "I just feel that the Task Force needs to look at the bargaining process and the legislation which creates it to see whether comparable worth will exist in the state of Oregon if the bargaining process continues." Although as yet the Task Force had no position on collective bargaining, several members assumed that actual amounts of increases would be bargained. Union officials testified at the second meeting, voicing their concerns over the impact of comparable worth wage setting on collective bargaining. Wages have to be negotiated, they all said. Implied but unarticulated was the fear that an outcome of the study would be a legislated wage plan, leaving unions to bargain over only the general level of wages, not the wage rates for particular jobs. Task Force feminists tried to decide whether this was, indeed, a problem by talking with people in Minnesota, where comparable worth had been implemented through bargaining. Minnesota was reassuring. They had identified inequities using job evaluation data developed by Hay Associates (Cook, 1984). The Minnesota legislature approved two pots of wage funds—one for regular salary increases and one for comparable worth. Pay equity money was allocated to the bargaining units with salary inequities, and bargaining of the exact increases was going forward successfully. At that point in the Oregon project, in spite of anxieties, most Task Force feminists expected to work out a similar solution.

Management Task Force members took a different tack, raising questions about the long run effect of collective bargain-

Figure 2.1
Oregon Comparable Worth Work Plan

1. Job Documentation—January to August, 1984.
    Develop and pretest job content questionnaire, January–April.
    Develop data collection plan, January–April.
    Distribute questionnaires to all employees, April–May.
    Sort and group returned questionnaires, May–August.
    Do desk audits as quality control of questionnaires, May–August.
    Write job composites from grouped questionnaires, May–August.

2. Job Evaluation—March to September, 1984.
    Review and modify guide charts, March.
    Pretest evaluation process, April.
    Assess pretest results, April.
    Approve guide charts, May.
    Select bench mark job evaluation teams, June.
    Select bench mark jobs for evaluation, June.
    Bench mark evaluations, June 16–August 24.
    Hay Associates quality assessments of evaluations, September.
    Using bench marks as a frame, evaluate remaining jobs, September–October.

3. Communication—January to December, 1984.
    Develop newsletter, January.
    Meetings with managers and unions, February–November.
    Questionnaire distribution meetings with all employees, April–May.

4. Classification and compensation system construction—May to December, 1984.
    Sort and group job content questionnaires, May–August.
    Note that this was part of job documentations also.
    Re-sort evaluated job groups into new classes, October—December.
    Assign new job classes to new salary ranges, December.

5. Compensation analysis for comparable worth—November to December, 1984.
    Analyze point scores and salaries of current individual employees and proposed new classes, November–December.

Decide on pay policy, December. This policy is the basis for new salary ranges.

6. Write comparable worth legislation—October to December, 1984.

7. Write comparable worth project report—December, 1984 to January, 1985.

Source: This work plan is reconstructed, much simplified, from Task Force, Personnel Division, and Hay Associates documents.

ing on the continuity of the comparable worth system. Nine unions bargaining 16 or 17 contracts could, over time, erode the pay equity achieved by a comparable worth study. What was to prevent that from happening? Later this became a major issue in the study.

Scope and Timing of the Project

The project plan agreed upon by January, 1984 (see Figure 2.1), contained the conflicts and contradictions of class and gender that had already formed the subtext of discussions. These were, for example, conflicts between feminist aims to control the project in the interests of women, and managerial aims to control in the interest of their (class) rights to define the structure of work and wages. For unions, there were contradictions between their support for comparable worth and their need to hold on to the right to bargain wages. Internal to the project itself were contradictions between the goal of a new classification plan and the goal of pay equity. The two goals were interdependent, but the pursuit of one might sacrifice the other.

The scope of the project was huge and represented a victory for management and Oregon Public Employees Union top leadership, whose main interest lay in a new classification system. The victory was achieved because the feminist majority was won over by arguments that appealed to the ideal of true comparable worth and the necessity of a rational, logical, and systematic approach to its realization. The Task Force, convinced that an adequate comparable worth plan could not be achieved without a thorough renovation of the classification system, agreed to study all positions in state employment. Because the probability was high that many employees were in inappropriate job classes, every position had to be examined. Because existing job descriptions were so inadequate, new descriptions had to be written before job evaluation could take place. Thirty-four thousand employees would fill out questionnaires about the content of their jobs to provide the basis for these descriptions.

These decisions locked the Task Force into a two-stage process in which the first stage would have to be finished before the second—pay equity—could occur. Thus, feminist goals depended upon the successful completion of the part of the project to be carried out primarily by Personnel. This was risky business given the conflicts that had already emerged. On the other hand, there seemed to be a common interest in a successful project. In any case, the compromises that facilitated passage of the bill, particularly the agreement to do both a classification and compensation study, had structured this somewhat uneasy alliance and there was nothing to be done about the legislation.

The timing of the project was also apparently dictated by the legislation. However, here too, conflicting interests coalesced to produce a project time line that was extremely tight for a project of this scope. Although almost everyone involved in the first few meetings of the Task Force expressed some worry about the lack of fit between size and time in the plan, these concerns had little effect. There were political reasons for having a report ready for the next legislature. A certain momentum had been built behind the pay equity issue and supporters were anxious to request comparable worth action from substantially the same group of legislators that had passed the enabling bill. A delay might mean that a comparable worth proposal would go to an entirely new set of senators and representatives who would have less interest. The increasingly conservative direction of the political scene seemed to confirm the anxieties of pay equity supporters. The time was right for action. The Personnel Director also favored going back to the legislature with a plan in 13 or 14 months. Her motives may also have been political and possibly rooted in career concerns. The Republican governor was approaching the beginning of his last two years in office. A successful renovation of the personnel system of the state would be a positive achievement for the Republicans and a personal career achievement for the Personnel Director. Hay Associates' support for the decision to complete the study by early 1985 seemed to confirm that, although strenuous, the effort to do this could be successful.

The size of the project and the time frame represent a temporary coalescing of interests of the diverse parties to this comparable worth effort, a coalition that was to break down as deadlines on the technical work could not be met. These time and scope decisions, once taken, were not easily reversed, and they constituted very restrictive boundaries for the project.

Discussion: The Politics of Gender and Class

Pay equity, it was clear from the beginning, was a political question. I use the term politics broadly to stand for contests over power, in this case power to define and power to control the comparable worth project, and ultimately the classification and compensation system of the state. The project was a political attempt by the legislature to insert women's interests into a wage setting system that had been the province of management and unions, who in their negotiations, conflicts, and agreements had, for many years, made decisions, whether intended or unintended, that resulted in women's relative wage disadvantage. This legislative intervention aimed to, at least temporarily, take some power over wage setting from management and unions and put it into the hands of a Task Force dominated by feminists. Management was the most threatened by comparable worth because the project encroached upon management rights to control job description, job classification, and job evaluation. But, of course, management, and to a much lesser extent unions, still had most of the power, and this was represented in the Task Force by people with a dual labor-feminist allegiance, and by management oriented representatives. Thus conflicting interests of gender and class were built into the composition of the Task Force, and the loyalties of Task Force members.

A number of issues that were to plague the project throughout its life emerged in the first few weeks. First was how to give an operational definition to comparable worth. The legislature provided the Task Force with directives on how to go about doing comparable worth. These the Task Force elaborated in an operational definition of "true comparable worth" as a comprehensive wage determination system with sex-neutral, unbiased job evaluation scores as central criteria for both wages and job classifications.

There were potential contradictions between this definition and a wage determination system based primarily on collective bargaining, another ongoing project issue. Although some labor unions supported true comparable worth, others began to voice concerns over this issue early in the project, asking for clarification on the implications of the section of the legislation that linked salary setting to evaluated points. What would this mean for collective bargaining, they asked. Would wages be set in the job evaluation process rather than at the bargaining table? The reply that unions could still bargain for overall increases even if they could not bargain the relative distances between the wages of different jobs did not allay the fears of some union staff.

The Personnel Director and others on the management side also began raising questions about the integration of collective bargaining and comparable worth from the earliest project meetings. Their central argument was that it would be very difficult to maintain pay equity over time if nine different unions continued to bargain different wage rates. The solution they favored was coalition bargaining, which would have simplified management's tasks considerably by reducing bargaining to one process. The executive seems to have seen comparable worth as an opportunity to strengthen its power and to rationalize its dealings with organized labor. Thus the gender issue, the question of equitable pay, was from the beginning tangled with a class issue, the question of who shall have what power in the process of wage setting.

A struggle for control between Task Force feminists and state management as embodied in the Personnel Director marked the beginning of the Oregon project. Although the director was a woman, her loyalties seemed to be to a business-oriented state executive that, while not openly opposing comparable worth, did not put pay equity high on its list of goals. Perceiving the comparable worth bill as inevitable, this state executive intended to use the project to achieve a long needed reform, a new classification system. Divisions were complicated. Management and the labor unions were at odds, but there was also a management coalition with the Oregon Public Employees Union on the need for a new classification structure. Task Force feminists clashed with management while receiving sympathetic support from organized labor. Task Force feminists wanted to focus on pay equity, but became convinced that an overhaul of the classification system was necessary to achieve the comparable worth goal.

Technical decisions about the steps in the project, its scope, and timing, as well as staffing, were all affected by the underlying conflicts rooted in contending class and gender interests. Out of an intense series of meetings in which these issues were confronted came an ambitious project work plan (see Figure 2.1). The desire to create legitimacy for the project in the eyes of legislators, state employees, state management, businessmen, and community feminists acted to focus much concern on technical questions. The implicit drive was to overcome difficult issues of class and gender through creating a technically superior analysis that would convince everyone of the soundness of a comparable worth wage system. Hay Associates was chosen for its high technical competence as well as for its outstanding reputation in the business community. Both qualities would contribute to the legitimacy and the success of the project.

Project participants did not ignore the politics of class and gender, which continued to be played out each day, although the possible difficulties were not well understood by all participants in the early project phases. When the issues that plagued the first phases of the project re-emerged at later stages in even more complicated and conflictual form, it was often too late to take adequate corrective action. Politics were also an integral part of the development of the job description and job evaluation segment of the project, in which Task Force feminists attempted to minimize sex bias in the evaluation process. This is the topic of the next chapter.

CHAPTER THREE

Reproducing Hierarchy
—or Job Evaluation in Oregon

With the hiring of Hay Associates the State of Oregon purchased a complete job evaluation system based on "traditional organizational designs." According to one member of the Hay team, "The Guide Charts were developed over time by working with a number of different managers in different organizations. The Guide Charts represent a composite of the value systems of managers from various organizations. They are reflective of traditional organizational designs" (Task Force minutes, April 25, 1984:8). Traditional organizational designs emerged with the development of the large corporation and the search for better ways, more scientific ways, to manage production, as any history of management or of organizational theory attests (see, for example, Clegg and Dunkerley, 1980; Mouzelis, 1967). These designs are intended to provide control over work and workers; they can be seen as instruments used by capital in the continuing conflict between classes (Edwards, 1979).[1] Thus, in the job evaluation stage, the project moved to an arena already defined in management terms.

The focus was on technical work during this phase of the project and much of it went on with little public conflict. The crux of doing good comparable worth, many of us thought, was in producing unbiased, sex-neutral job evaluations. To that end, project participants were committed to doing the best technical work possible and this required cooperation. Backstage, in the continuing discussions of other issues such as control of the

61

project, collective bargaining, and how a new classification system would be structured, class and gender tensions were alive. These could be detected in meetings of the steering committee, in meetings between management and union representatives, and in rumblings from state agencies and male employees questioning the aims and the justification for all this work.

Some technical issues did, however, become major open political arguments, focussed around the questionnaire, the relative weighting of factors, the definition of factors, and the evaluation process itself. As could be expected, management and consultants tended to side together against Task Force feminists. These conflicts revealed how deeply embedded are both gender and class inequalities in organizational hierarchies. Observations of the job evaluation process also revealed how job evaluation reproduces hierarchy, a feature of organizational structure that was, with a minor and unsuccessful exception, unchallenged by any project participant. I will argue, as do Hay consultants, that the central accomplishment of job evaluation is the recreation of an acceptable hierarchy, a believable system of inequality.[2] The meaning of acceptable and believable will be discussed below. Such a legitimate system of inequality can tolerate the raising of some wages, but the demands of hierarchy also limit the degree to which this method can reduce the wage gap between women and men.

In this chapter I discuss in some detail the process of job evaluation and how it structured a somewhat revised system of inequality. Although the material is detailed, even technical, it is important to an understanding of comparable worth and of the intertwining of class and gender. The Hay system and similar ones, such as the Willis system, have been used in a number of successful comparable worth efforts: Hay in Minnesota and San Jose, Willis in the state of Washington. Although they tend to reproduce a traditional hierarchy, and can be accused of gender bias, these job evaluation methods still usually show that female-dominated jobs are paid less than male-dominated jobs with similar scores. Detailed knowledge about how these systems work can provide a basis for developing evaluation schemes that better reflect the content of women's jobs. Moreover, knowledge about the internal structure of job evaluation instruments and the process of their use can reveal ideology and image that help to produce hierarchy and wage inequality in work organizations.

The work at this stage was complex, including the development of a job content questionnaire, reviewing and modifying the Hay guide charts, pretesting the questionnaire and the guide charts, training state employees to fill out the questionnaire, distributing and collecting the questionnaires, analysing the questionnaires and writing job descriptions, selecting and training job evaluation teams, carrying out the job evaluations, and assessing their quality. All of this was accomplished in nine months, and by the end of August, 1984, 32,000 state employees, filling every position included in the study, had completed questionnaires, and evaluations of 350 benchmark job groups had been carried out. Other parts of the project were overlapping and the grouping of jobs was part of the later classification work as well as a preparation for job evaluation.

The Hay Guide Chart–Profile Method of Job Evaluation

The development of elaborate bureaucratic systems, including personnel departments, job descriptions, and job evaluation, began before World War II. It accelerated during and after the war as a consequence of government regulations that required certain kinds of accounting about employees, and of the rapid development of a profession of personnel experts that actively promoted its products, as well as of an interest in control of labor (Baron, Dobbin, and Jennings, 1986). The Hay Guide Chart–Profile Method of Job Evaluation was a particularly successful part of this development. According to Oregon consultants and published descriptions (McAdams, 1974; Treiman, 1979; Bellak, 1982; Farnquist, 1983), the Hay method developed over many years beginning in the 1940s, in an inductive process aimed at helping employers to establish internal equity within their firms.[3] Working with Hay consultants, employers identified the factors most important to them in jobs within their organizations. These were the knowledge required by the job, the thinking required to solve the problems the job faces, and the responsibility assigned to the job. Jobs could be ranked on these factors. Later, a system for determining the distance between ranks was worked out and the whole complex of decisions on the factors was put into Guide Chart form (Barker, 1986; Bellak, 1982).

This system "is used by more than 4,000 profit and non-profit organizations in some thirty countries with Western or westernized cultures" (Bellak, 1982:1; Bureau of National Affairs, 1984). For example, a 1976 survey of British employers found that 79 percent used job evaluation. The Hay Guide Chart–Profile method was the most frequently used specific scheme (Thakur and Gill, 1976:18). The International Labor Office (1986:107) reported that the Hay method was used to evaluate technical, professional, and managerial jobs in two-fifths of U.S. enterprises. Without doubt, this is an important tool for rationalizing managerial judgments about work positions. As Hay consultants emphasize, this method focuses on characteristics of the job, not on characteristics of the job holder, such as education, skill, or pay. Thus it is a system for constructing a structure of empty places, and in that sense, could be seen as defining the locations in the internal stratification of a class structure.

As a management technology originally devised to produce a consistent ranking of jobs, it is not surprising that hierarchy is built into the charts. As Treiman notes (1979), this hierarchy is also the managerial hierarchy. The managerial slant of the Guide Charts (Barker, 1986) worried Task Force feminists because, given that few women are in upper managerial positions, a weighting toward managerial tasks would underemphasize other—and more female—functions. An examination of the structure of the factors shows in detail how this occurs.

The Guide Charts are matrices which measure components of each major factor. There is a separate chart for each factor, Know-How, Problem Solving, Accountability, and Working Conditions. Each major factor has subfactors, so that a total of 11 decisions must be made about each job (Figure 3.1). Each level of each component is defined in generic language and in language specific to a particular employer. The evaluation process starts with qualitative decisions about, for example, the amount of technical knowledge, managerial knowledge, and human relations skills involved in a job. These qualitative decisions come together to indicate the particular, quantitative, location of the job within the Know-How matrix. Similar judgments are made for the other factors and the scores on the three factors are summed. Working conditions are scored and added, particularly when blue collar jobs are among those being evaluated.

Know-How is composed of (1) practical procedures, specialized techniques, and knowledge necessary to perform the job, (2) managerial knowledge needed to integrate and harmonize diversified functions, and (3) human relations skills, "active, practicing person-to-person skills" (Bellak, 1982:1). Eight levels of knowledge are arrayed along the left side of the chart, while four levels of managerial skills are along the top. Human relations skills are arrayed as subscales to Managerial Know-How, with—in most Hay Charts—three levels of Human Relations within each Managerial level.

Technical knowledge and skill potentially contributes the most points to the Know-How score. This includes knowledge about things, people, and management. Managerial Know-How is the application of the managerial knowledge already scaled under Technical Know-How; it is measured primarily by the diversity of functions to be integrated. For example, the hospital manager responsible for personnel, billing, and supply would have to integrate more functions than the manager in charge of only one of those departments. Managerial Know-How often parallels hierarchical position. Human Relations skills add the smallest number of points to the total Know-How score. The three levels of Human Relations skills start with a basic level where common courtesy is needed for normal contacts and providing information. At the next level such skills are important for understanding, influencing, or serving people and causing action or understanding. At the third level such skills are critical for successful job performance. Taken as a whole, the Know-How chart emphasizes managerial skills and knowledge and thus favors male-dominated jobs.

The numbering system is complex. Numbers in the charts rise by 15 percent increments as complexity increases. Each cell in the matrix contains three numbers. In using the charts to evaluate a job, first the appropriate cell is determined, then the appropriate number within the cell is identified. Both Technical and Managerial Know-How judgments are more significant than Human Relations judgments for arriving at the Know-How factor score. A change in judgment on Technical or Managerial Know-How from one cell to another changes a score by 32 percent, while movement from one cell to another on a Human Relations judgment alters the score by only 15 percent. Thus, a dimension that may have particular importance in female-dominated jobs

Figure 3.1
Job Evaluation Factors,
Hay Guide Chart–Profile Method

1. Know-How——Knowledge and skills, however gained
    Technical
    Managerial
    Human Relations* – *negotiation*

2. Problem Solving——Complexity and autonomy of problems
    Thinking Environment (autonomy)
    Thinking Challenge (complexity)

3. Accountability——Levels of responsibility for outcomes
    Freedom to Act
    Magnitude—in budgetary or program impact terms
    Impact—how directly the job affects organizational goals

4. Working Conditions†
    Hazardous working conditions
    Physical effort
    Physical environment

*Oregon modifications to Human Relations Skills and Knowledge——four
levels instead of three.
†Oregon modifications to Working Conditions:
Sensory effort, such as having to pay close attention to electronic monitoring
devices, added to physical effort.

Work Demands subcategory added:
    Time Demands—extreme time pressures in job
    Role Loading—conflicting and contradictory expectations
    Emotion Loading—heavy involvement with people who are violent, dis-
        oriented, psychotic or responsibility for action in extreme, life-
        threatening situations.

has the least possibility of adding points in the basic structure of
the charts. Other problems with Human Relations are discussed
below.

The second factor, Problem Solving, is scored as a percentage of Know-How because it is defined as an application of Know-
How: "You think with what you know" (Bellak, 1982:1). Problem
Solving has two dimensions, Thinking Environment and Thinking Challenge. Thinking Environment is defined as "freedom to
think," the degree to which the job allows or requires indepen-

dent problem solving. The scale goes from little freedom, jobs that are constrained by strict rules and procedures, to a great deal of freedom, jobs that are not even constrained by the most general organizational policies and goals. The levels seem to rise in parallel with usual organizational hierarchies.

Thinking Challenge refers to the degree of complexity in the problems to be solved. Complexity rises from simple jobs with a few delineated tasks to highly complex jobs. Again, the procedure is to choose a cell in the matrix and a number, in this case, a percentage, within the chosen cell. Two percentages are presented in each cell, giving evaluators a chance to carefully modulate their estimate of the problem-solving complexity demanded by the job.

Accountability is the third factor. It measures the "effect of the job on end results of the organization" (Bellak, 1982:3). Accountability is a more complex concept than responsibility. It has three subfactors. First, Freedom to Act refers to the extent of control the job has over its main goal. Second, Impact measures the "extent to which the job can directly affect actions necessary to produce results" (Bellak, 1982:3). Magnitude, the third subfactor, has to do with the proportion of the total organization affected by the primary emphasis of the job. Accountability is also presented in matrix form and, as with Know-How, three separate judgments are necessary to locate a job within a cell of the matrix. A final judgment picks one of the three numbers in the cell. As with Know-How, both Problem Solving and Accountability replicate in their construction the hierarchy of most organizations.

Working Conditions is the final factor, added to the others where jobs to be evaluated have physical demands or environmental hazards.

Factor weighting in the Guide Charts is not immediately evident because of the complex structure of the charts.[4] That is, weights are embedded in the internal structure of the charts. Know-How appears to have the heaviest weight. However, in different jobs factors may be weighted differently. Most obviously, Problem Solving is a proportion of Know-How, but it is a varying proportion, consequently the relative weights of the two factors vary. Some jobs are heavier on Accountability and some are heavier on Problem Solving. According to consultants, Know-How tends to have a heavier weight for lower level jobs, with

Problem Solving and Accountability contributing proportionately more to scores for higher level jobs. When Working Conditions is used, it has a heavier weight and contributes more to the total score of lower level than of higher level jobs. Analyzing total Hay scores for 355 benchmark jobs in the Oregon study, Barker (1986:261) found that the average contribution of each factor to the total score was Know-How, 60.9 percent; Problem Solving, 17.3 percent; Accountability, 20.4 percent; and Working Conditions, 1.4 percent.

In sum, the structure of the Hay Charts and the definition of factors is heavily weighted toward Technical and Managerial Know-How. These dimensions of the Know-How factor, both reflective of images of the male worker, whether a skilled craftsman, an engineer, or a manager, contribute the most to the Know-How score. Know-How is counted again in the Problem Solving factor which is calculated as a percentage of Know-How. Some elements in Accountability are closely related to knowledge and may actually be tapping the same dimension again. Each chart is arranged in a hierarchical manner, evoking images of bureaucratic structure. Images of class are also imbedded in the Managerial dimension and in the Accountability factor. This was the system Task Force feminists wanted to alter.

Modifying the Guide Charts

Gender issues were uppermost in the minds of feminists involved as the Task Force and the Advisory Group discussed with Hay consultants modifications of their Guide Charts to better reflect the values "bias-free, sex-neutral." Task Force feminists had a heavy investment in achieving these modifications. One of the unique features of the Oregon project was that it was the first one in which consciously feminist values would be applied in the job evaluation phase. As one Task Force member put it, "The critical aspect of the study, whether it is a success or a failure, will depend on whether bias can be eliminated" (Task Force meeting, Dec. 7, 1983).

Task Force feminists and their feminist constituency were aware of the contradictions imbedded in the use of a management tool to attempt to counteract inequities caused by years of management—and union—business as usual. A method to consistently apply managerial values would be employed to upset some of those values. Criticisms of *a priori* systems, such as Hay Associates' Guide Chart–Profile Job Evaluation System, had pointed to some of the problems and Task Force members had read these analyses (see Treiman, 1979; Schwab, 1980; Remick, 1979, 1981, 1984; Treiman and Hartmann, 1981).

According to Remick (1984:110), "Job evaluation systems are designed to reflect prevailing wages in their choice of factors, weighting of factors and salary setting practices." To the extent that prevailing wages reflect historically produced discrimination against women, point-factor scores may also reflect this discrimination. As Treiman and Hartmann (1981:81) suggest, "It is possible that the process of describing and evaluating jobs reflects pervasive cultural stereotypes regarding the relative worth of work traditionally done by men and work traditionally done by women."

In spite of the high probability that *a priori* job evaluation methods contain an inbuilt cultural devaluation of women's work, these systems have consistently demonstrated, as discussed above, that female-dominated jobs are underpaid when compared with male-dominated jobs with similar point scores. This consistent result reveals one type of devaluation: job elements that are rewarded in male-defined jobs are not equally rewarded when these same elements are found in female-defined jobs. For example, a certain level of knowledge and skill in a nursing job may earn fewer dollars than the same level of knowledge and skill in an engineering job. Consistent application of a measurement of knowledge and skill to both the nursing job and the engineering job, and a comparison of the scores and salaries of the two jobs, should reveal the magnitude of this type of discrepancy.

Another type of devaluation discussed in the literature is probably not tapped so well by *a priori* systems (Remick, 1984). This devaluation occurs when aspects of women's jobs that are valuable for organizational functioning are not evaluated, either because no factor captures these job components, or because operational definitions of factors refer only to components of male jobs. For example, Remick (1984:107; see also Barker, 1986; Steinberg and Haignere, 1987) points to a number of dimensions along which male-typed and female-typed jobs differ. Some elements characteristic of female jobs, such as responsibility for persons rather than for property, may not only be absent from job evaluation systems, but may actually be negatively rewarded in salary setting (see, for example, Pierson, Loziara, and Johannesson, 1984).

Task Force feminists wanted to make sure that our job evaluation system would give points for these hidden and undervalued dimensions of women's jobs. This was one way of meeting the legislative requirement to produce a bias-free, sex-neutral evaluation. Hay had agreed to some modifications of their instrument along these lines, as noted above. All other parts of the project would also be scrutinized for bias. One of the best protections against bias, we thought, was to do all of the technical work as carefully and systematically as possible, with ongoing review of the quality of the work.

The structure of the Hay charts presented formidable difficulties to Task Force feminists who were committed to modifying them to remove gender bias. Feminists pushed the consultants on the question of sex bias and identified places in the charts that could be altered, the Human Relations subscale, Working Conditions, and the definitions of criteria for the Technical Knowledge and Accountibility scales. However, changes to this complex system would have to be minor, we understood. As one consultant put it, they would be glad to build us a completely new system starting from the values of the state of Oregon, but that would cost far more than the $104,000 that Hay had bid, and take far longer than the scheduled 13 or 14 months.

In a large public work session devoted to modifying the charts, the consultant defined the goal of the meeting as "fine tuning, to address and resolve problems," to customize the charts for Oregon. Some feminists disagreed with this notion of the meeting's goals. They saw the task as the rooting out of sex discrimination. As one Advisory Group member said, "Over the past 40 years in our culture there has been discrimination against women in setting salaries. If so, one could argue that the Hay system, if it is a good system, if it has accurately captured the values of the culture, it is likely to be a sex discriminating system, because the culture has sex discrimination in it" (Advisory Group meeting, March 14, 1984).

Although the consultants had agreed to cooperate in the task of slightly modifying the charts, they reiterated with conviction that their system contains no bias and that it is only discriminatory pricing of jobs that introduces unjustified wage differences between the sexes. "It is our experience that the point spread (within the clerical series and within the blue collar series) is identical . . . but the employers for a variety of reasons have chosen to put a lower dollar value on a 150-point clerical job than they put on a 150-point blue collar job. So the issue is not the point evaluation, but that the employer is paying very differently for the same content in different occupational areas" (Advisory Group, March 14, 1984).

The feminist majority on the Task Force and feminists on the Advisory Group were not convinced, and they pursued the matter of the Human Relations Scale, pushing for alterations that would increase its weight, or its contribution to the total score. There were two issues, the number of levels in the scale and the definitions of the levels. As one Advisory Group member pointed out, Human Relations had only three levels in the Guide Chart as compared with Freedom to Act which had 26 levels.[5] The possible variation, and thus, the possible impact on the total score was much higher for Freedom to Act than for Human Relations.[6]

Feminists proposed that the number of levels in the Human Relations Scale should be increased from three to five. This would give some additional weight to the Human Relations subfactor. Feminists also proposed modifying the definition of Human Relations. They wanted to include skills needed in mediating relationships with coworkers, supervisors, and the public, as well as maintaining cooperative processes with irate clients and disturbed patients. They were particularly concerned about the definition given by a consultant to the first level of human relations, "overt friendliness or common courtesy." With a three-level scale, most workers, including most clerical and human service aide jobs, would fall in this lowest slot. But this would undervalue the skills needed to maintain common courtesy in the face of anger, fear, and hostility, and it would make it impossible to distinguish between jobs with such demands and those without them.

Hay definitions of Human Relations seemed linked to levels of bureaucratic function, focussing on supervisory and managerial tasks of motivating and training. Some consultants pointed out that asking whether a job has the power to reward and punish may help to place the job on Human Relations. According to the consultants, the first level requires personal interaction dealing essentially with facts. The second and third levels require different intensity of use of skills to cause behavioral changes in individuals or groups. Task Force feminists, while not denying that managers and psychotherapists need Human Relations skills, held out for definitions that would give more recognition to those skills involved in lower-level jobs.

This was not an idle exercise. Two full days of meetings were devoted to this and the issue of Working Conditions, in addition to significant parts of other lengthy meetings. Hay consultants argued against increasing the number of levels for a number of reasons: (1) Human Relations were never undervalued in the Hay system, (2) evaluators cannot make distinctions between more than three levels of skill, (3) increasing Human Relations to five levels would result in overcounting relative to managerial skills, and (4) it would reduce the point difference between managerial and nonmanagerial jobs, leading to problems in management recruiting.

The consultants went to great lengths to convince the Task Force. For example, they devised an exercise for the Task Force and the Advisory Group. In this exercise, all were invited to take part in the evaluation of two jobs, those of a social worker and an engineer. The only difference between the locations of the two jobs on the charts was that the social work job was given a "3" on Human Relations, while the engineering job got a "1". This high location on Human Relations, argued the consultants, would result in a ripple effect through other factors, producing for the social worker a score 35.5 percent higher than the score for the engineer. The Hay system, they said, compares one job with another and asks, "Does this difference make sense?" Most organizations, they continued, were unwilling to pay a 35 percent difference for human relations skills. Some feminists were angry with this exercise because it contained the unexplored assumption that assigning a "3" on Human Relations must lead to increasing scores on Technical Know-How and Problem Solving. Thus, they argued, the consultants had been deliberately misleading. Tensions were very high during this controversy, marking its significance in the conflict between management interests and women's interests.

A related issue had to do with the internal numbering of the charts. Expansion of Human Relations from three to five levels would require reordering the numbers within the cells. Because Human Relations is a subscale of Management Know-How, this reordering could reduce the point differences between management and nonmanagement jobs. The consultants felt that this was the most damaging probable outcome of enlarging Human Relations. In spite of the consultants' warnings, the Task Force majority voted to compare a five-level and a three-level scale in the pretest of the evaluation process. The pretest showed that use of a five-point scale altered the rank ordering of some jobs, as the consultants had predicted.

The battle over three or five levels of Human Relations continued in the Task Force and Advisory Group meetings. Management representatives sided with the consultants. Union people and feminists were on the other side. This was an emotional struggle. Clearly, important interests were embedded in a minor technical issue: Should there be three or five levels in a subscale? Finally, in a close Task Force vote, a compromise of four levels was passed. The consultants reworded the descriptions, but not as much as Task Force feminists had intended. There were some modifications in wording for the two highest levels in the scale, but no recognition of skills such as mediating, conciliating, and supporting necessary in many clerical and service jobs. Comparison of the Human Relations definitions offered by Hay at the beginning of the project and those finally used show little difference (see Figure 3.2).

Controversy also arose over Working Conditions. Hay definitions of Working Conditions, as in most systems, were developed to evaluate blue collar jobs (Remick, 1979). In the Working Conditions chart, physical effort was defined by such things as lifting heavy weights, and the work environment was defined as unpleasant or hazardous only when heat, cold, rain, or exposure to such dangers as toxic chemicals or speeding cars were necessary job components. The ordinary office environment was defined as normal, essentially benign. Such definitions were not peculiar to the Hay system; they were and are simply part of the

Figure 3.2
Hay Associates Human Relations Definitions
Comparison of Scales

3-Level Scale Suggested at Beginning	4-Level Scale Used in Oregon Project
1. Basic: ordinary courtesy and effectiveness in dealing with others through normal contacts, and request for, or providing information.	1. Incidental: Communication skills are incidental to the nature of the job duties performed.
2. Important: Understanding, influencing, and/or serving people are important considerations in performing the job; causing action or understanding in others.	2. Basic: Skills in communicating factual information are necessary in the job.
3. Critical: Alternative or combined skills in understanding, developing and motivating people are critical to successful job performance.	3. Important: Skills in understanding and influencing, motivating, counseling or training people are important job components.
	4. Critical: Skills in motivating, developing, understanding, persuading, and/or counseling people are critical for effective job performance.

taken-for-granted understanding of work. Feminists on the project were unwilling to accept this common understanding. They wanted to include frequent lifting of smaller weights, continuous hand motions, and concentrated staring at a computer screen as physical effort. Sitting continuously in one place and being confined in a poorly ventilated and noisy office were other Working Conditions feminists tried to include in the definitions.

Task Force feminists also argued that many state jobs involve a great deal of stress, that stress is frequently a component of lower-level women's jobs, and that it should be compensated, or counted in job evaluation. Hay consultants answered that job stress is picked up in factors such as Know-How. Part of the knowledge base of the psychologist position, for example, is how to deal with people who are emotionally disturbed. They emphasized the importance of avoiding double counting particular aspects of jobs in the evaluation process. In addition, the consultants countered, we must distinguish between characteristics of jobs and characteristics of the people who fill the jobs. Job evaluation has to do with jobs, not with their occupants. One person might find a job stressful, while another would simply love the challenge of the same set of tasks. State management voiced other concerns. Stress can be a basis for workers' compensation claims. Management worried that if we were to admit, by including it in the job evaluation process, that stress exists in certain jobs, this might put the state in greater jeopardy.

The Task Force finally decided to measure stress by including something called "Work Demands" in the working conditions factor. This terminology, suggested by the consultants, seemed neutral enough to avoid the implication that the state was putting its workers in danger of psychological damage. The content of Work Demands also seemed to capture some of the elements in female-dominated jobs that feminists had identified as hidden and undervalued. For example, secretaries frequently have to follow the orders of several bosses or answer telephones and meet typing deadlines at the same time; psychiatric aides do much of the face-to-face work with severely disturbed patients. Work Demands were defined as "mental alertness and mental energy required by the intensity, continuity and complexity of work being performed." They were further specified as "Time Demands: the build up of work that must be accomplished under generally inflexible timelines. Frequent interruptions, if characteristic of the job, may contribute to work demands. Role Loading: having to perform in multiple, critical roles, or two or more incompatible roles, and Emotion Loading: the provision of direct services to individuals experiencing physical or emotional distress" (Task Force minutes, June 27, 1984).

Management members of the Task Force and Personnel were solidly opposed to Work Demands; however, this factor was included in the charts by a majority vote. Again, the clear taking of sides on this issue and the time and energy devoted to it hint at a significance for maintaining existing hierarchical relations.

In the arguments over Human Relations and Working Conditions factors, the consultants concerns focussed on legitimacy: what makes sense, what is believable. The consultants seemed particularly sensitive to the reactions of managers and professionals, opposing changes that might decrease the point differences in the hierarchy as well as changes that might alter the rank order assumed to make sense. For example, changes that could place people-caring jobs higher than some technical jobs were impossible on the grounds that such changes were not rational, not in accord with what any person could see was sensible.

Task Force feminists, on the other hand, were facing competing legitimacy claims of a sophisticated local and national feminist community. This community shared a literature critical of systems such as Hay and a goal of eliminating deeply imbedded sex bias. The importance of these competing claims is underscored by the amount of time and effort the Task Force, the Advisory Group, and Hay consultants spent on working out relatively minor variations in the Guide Charts. Given the complex internal stratification of organizations such as the state of Oregon, the consultants' concerns were well founded, for as the project unfolded perhaps the greatest threat to its legitimacy turned out to be changes that upset the existing internal stratification structure. Thus, legitimacy was on the side of the status quo, creating a contradiction for feminists working for change. To be successful the project had to be accepted by diverse groups, but the means to acceptance undermined the possibility for change.

The final modifications to the Hay Guide Charts were modest: four rather than three levels of Human Relations skills, a Work Demands subfactor in Working Conditions to measure some aspects of job stress, the inclusion of continuous and rapid movements in the definition of muscular effort, and the addition of sensory effort to Working Conditions (see Figure 3.1). In addition, the Working Conditions chart was restructured by the consultants to include the new subfactor. This was not the end of it; as we shall see, the consultants achieved their aims to minimize changes in their system by giving operational definitions to the changes that made them almost impossible to use in the actual evaluation process.

Reproducing Hierarchy:
Job Evaluation Training and Practice

Job evaluation itself is the core of the process of reproducing the (on paper) hierarchy. What is actually evaluated is a job description and preparing the job description is called job documentation. This step in the process is discussed in the literature as a possible source of bias. The completed Oregon questionnaires were, on the whole, of high quality—workers seemed to describe their jobs fully and without bias. Although it was a tremendous undertaking, it was the least conflict ridden part of the project. I discuss it briefly here as a necessary prelude to job evaluation.

Job Documentation

Job classes had to be described before they could be evaluated. A job class is an aggregate of similar positions. Some job classes, such as secretary, contain several thousand positions. Others, such as ship's cook, contain only one. In order to describe the job classes, information on each position had to be obtained and composite descriptions based on the position information had to be written. To get this basic information, we developed and pretested a questionnaire, using a prototype provided by Hay as a beginning point.

The questionnaire was designed to elicit the information necessary to use the Hay method. Items included a listing of all job duties, types of contacts with clients, public, and coworkers, position in the organizational structure, problems and difficulties on the job, and characteristics of working conditions.

The going was smooth until we got to the question of supervisory review of workers' questionnaires. Here the management point of view differed from the trade union and feminist perspective. Feminists and trade unionists were concerned about confidentiality and the possibility that workers might feel constrained to answer the questions the way they thought the supervisor would approve. Thus, we thought, the validity of the data was in jeopardy with supervisory review. Unions were also afraid that the questionnaires might be used in a punitive way if available to supervisors.

Personnel advocates, although they agreed that supervisors should not be allowed to alter workers' answers, argued strenuously that supervisory review was essential if management support of the project were to be preserved. Supervisors have the responsibility to assign tasks; therefore, they have the right to review the adequacy of workers' descriptions of their tasks, was the argument. Another worry motivated Personnel's insistence on supervisory review. "The supervisor assigns the work and yet what often happens is either the supervisor doesn't know what the employee is doing or the employee has taken on responsibilities which are not immediately obvious to the supervisor. Sometimes you will find a situation where the employee is running the office and the supervisor is not" (Personnel Director, Task Force meeting, Feb. 1, 1984). Such a situation, according to Personnel, might have to be resolved by higher management in order to get a description of duties appropriate to the position. This suggests that Personnel may have expected to use the study to identify and rectify deviations from an orderly, rational model. The aim seemed not to be to identify and reward workers who were doing more skilled and responsible work than their positions required, but rather to police and clean up the system. This was an indication that the goals of pay equity and upgrading the status of women's work were subject to displacement by other agendas, such as the control goals of management.

Hay consultants sided with Personnel. As far as they were concerned, supervisory review was a quality check; supervisors were most likely to add tasks that workers had forgotten, rather than to challenge or criticize the workers' job descriptions. Moreover, they argued that confidence in the study would be damaged if supervisory authority were undermined. With the weight of these legitimacy arguments, Task Force feminists and union representatives went along with supervisory review, with the important proviso that supervisors were not to change any answers on workers' questionnaires.

In fact, workers had few problems in completing the questionnaires. Supervisors, on the whole, agreed with workers' views of their tasks. No supervisors were found to have abandoned their responsibility to underlings. Hay consultants were right. The success of this stage of the project was largely due to a tremendous educational effort by the Personnel Division, whose staff held 459 information and training sessions throughout the state. Every state employee was given time off to attend such a session, which included an explanation of comparable worth and detailed information about how to fill out the questionnaire. Some unions held separate meetings with their members to further instruct them in accurately describing their jobs. In addition, every state employee was given two hours of work time to fill out the questionnaire. In sum, state management had committed considerable resources to the study.

The Job Evaluation Process

Job evaluation is the process of applying the values expressed in the evaluation instrument, in this case the charts, to actual jobs. It is the transformation process that links the charts' complex imagery of work to the living hierarchy of workers. Thus, knowledge about how it is done provides some additional understanding about how hierarchies of power and reward are reproduced in contemporary large organizations. I will briefly describe the Hay job evaluation method, as it was used in Oregon, to set the context for the discussion of the ways in which training for job evaluation and the process itself reinforced the managerial hierarchy already evident in the structure of the charts.[7]

To do job evaluation using this method, several people sit down around a table. Each has in front of her a job description and a set of guide charts. To the side is a blackboard. There is a team leader or facilitator and a recorder who takes detailed notes on all decisions. Each person reads the job description and then makes a preliminary decision about where to place the job in the Technical Knowledge scale of the Know-How chart. The team leader begins the discussion on the placement of the job in the chart and discussion continues until there is agreement, or failing that, a vote. One person stands at the blackboard and writes the decision there. Each scale in each chart is, in turn, similarly considered until all are done and a total score determined. Once the total has been achieved, the relationships between the factor scores are scrutinized to see that they make sense, that the factors have the proper relationship to each other, as I discuss below. The charts are daunting, but it is possible to learn to use them efficiently; one evaluation may take from 15 to 45 minutes.

Evaluations are done through a consensus creating method. Learning the method and developing the ability to apply job content information to the charts takes four or five days of intensive work with a trainer. There is a continuous monitoring of the process by team leaders who are in touch with consultants. Con-

sultants returned for several additional sessions with the evaluators. In a sense, training is a constant process. Hay consultants
emphasized that there were no right or wrong assessments, of
course always within the implicit limits of what makes sense. The
training was to assure that evaluators were consistently making
judgments based on the values of the organization.

Legitimacy concerns structured the composition of the
teams and the choice of the evaluators. Although I emphasize the
political legitimacy issues, technical quality was also important
and linked to legitimacy, for believable evaluations could not be
attained with work of poor quality. Three teams of six evaluators,
a team leader, and a recorder met four days per week for five
weeks in the summer of 1984 to do the benchmark evaluations for
the state of Oregon. Team members were experienced workers
from a variety of agencies and a variety of levels within the
agencies. Nominated by management and unions and appointed
by the Task Force, they represented the best: people who had
broad knowledge, intelligent and energetic, respected by supervisors and coworkers alike. Their evaluations of a representative
benchmark group of state jobs would provide the framework
within which Personnel Division staff would evaluate and rank all
other jobs. Their reputations in state employment would lend
credibility to the scores. This approach was recommended by
Hay consultants as their usual method of doing the initial, or
benchmark, evaluations.

The consultants also recommended the distribution of types
of jobs and evaluators among the three teams. Each team had
equal or nearly equal numbers of women and men. Team 1
members were clerical and blue collar workers and they evaluated clerical, blue collar, and lower level service jobs. Team 2 was
made up of middle-level professionals and supervisors whose
assignment was to evaluate supervisory jobs. On Team 3 were
professionals and paraprofessionals with a strong representation
from health and care agencies. They evaluated jobs from these
areas and some other professional jobs. This division made sense:
The evaluators were examining types of work with which they
were familiar.

On the other hand, this division had consequences in regard
to class and gender cleavages. Women and men confronted each
other over the differences between working-class jobs, clerical,

and blue collar. Sharp differences emerged, but also some mutual support across gender lines. Clerical workers, however, did not have the opportunity to compare clerical jobs with management jobs higher than the first line supervisor. Therefore, no confrontation with structural anomalies at this level was possible. That is, instances in which there might be a blurring of responsibility across the clerical-management divide could not become visible and problematic. As I discuss below, this division of labor did not avert a rather disturbing compression of professional, supervisory, and management scores, an outcome that the consultants steadily warned would be potentially disastrous.

Doing job evaluation is an intense experience because it requires making clear distinctions between jobs on levels of complexity within each factor and subfactor. Evaluators make multiple judgments using qualitative criteria. It is exacting and demanding work, analogous to coding qualitative data in research. Moreover, in the Hay process, as in many others, the decisions are group decisions. Hay consultants structure the groups to facilitate the achievement of consensus. Each group facilitator keeps the work going along, sums up and sometimes mediates disputes. Group recorders make systematic notes on the bases for all decisions, creating a detailed record of the process which can be used as a basis for a quality check, or for reconsidering an evaluation if that is necessary. Other elements in the group process contribute to reaching agreements.

Most evaluators, according to my experience and observation on the Oregon project, come to feel an internal pressure to assess jobs fairly and consistently. At the same time, there is a push toward conformity that may be in conflict with the internalized commitment to fairness. When team members disagree strongly about where to place a particular job on a particular factor, tensions within and between evaluators may rise. Reluctance to seem contentious, as well as a desire to meet the quota for expected numbers of evaluations for the day, may push toward capitulation, while the pressure to be fair may push toward holding out. Differences of opinion may be resolved by getting more information on a job, looking at its organizational chart location, or consulting the description of the knowledge and experience required to enter the job. Sometimes the evaluators implicitly negotiated with each other on points for a factor or subfactor.

Sometimes consensus could not be reached and the team had to vote.

Agreement is facilitated by the emergence of decision rules within the group. For example, when the group has decided that all true supervisors get a "4" on Human Relations, that decision is made quickly and routinely. The more decision rules, the faster the evaluation. Evaluators comment on their skill in using the rules, saying "we're on target" or "I was out of line." However, decision rules cannot be made for many job dimensions and team members may disagree on what the rule should be even if, in principle, a rule could be made.

Sore-thumbing, an important part of the Hay system, serves to correct errors in the evaluations. When evaluations are completed and total scores are ranked, some jobs may stick out like a sore thumb. Thus, sore thumbing involves comparing scores for different jobs to see if their relative placement makes sense. Inconsistency in application of evaluation criteria will turn up in total or subscores that appear to be either too high or too low in relation to what evaluators and consultants know about how the job compares with others. In sore thumbing, the shape of jobs is also examined. Shape refers to the relative scoring on the three main factors. So, for example, if a research job had an Accountability score higher than its Problem Solving score, this shape would alert evaluators to an error. Research jobs should be higher on Problem Solving than on Accountability because their main function is to supply information to the organization, not to make operational decisions. Hay uses a final, independent check of the quality and consistency of evaluations called correlation. This involves a detailed comparison of scores from a particular customer, such as the State of Oregon, with scores arrived at in other applications of the Hay method, and an examination of the decision-making process that resulted in any scores that seem inconsistent or at great variance with other scores for similar jobs.

The production of consensus and sore thumbing can be seen as methods of attaining validity and reliability. These processes help to assure that female-dominated jobs are evaluated consistently on the same criteria as male-dominated jobs, but, at the same time, they help to assure that rankings do not unduly upset organizational hierarchies. One of the tests of validity is whether or not the scores reflect the established hierarchy within job or occupational families. Validity in another sense is established as team members discuss the placement of jobs on the charts, putting jobs with similar degrees of complexity in the same chart locations. At the same time, consistency of judgment or reliability is also established. The process has results similar to those of the process of establishing inter-rater reliability. Differing judgments are reviewed, discussed, and resolved, producing a consistent interpretation and application of criteria.

This part of the process accounts for some of the success in using job evaluation to locate and remedy undervaluation of women's work. My observation indicates that, within the confines of the values it represents and replicates, job evaluation is what it purports to be: a systematic, consistent, and open process of applying a set of values in the assessment of the content of jobs. Making qualitative decisions about values is a difficult process, but it can be done. The important question is, What are the values (Remick, 1984)? It is to this that I now return.

Methods of Reproducing Hierarchy

Managers' values, encoded in the Guide Charts, appear to be so carefully ranked that hierarchy itself emerges as a predominant value. The job evaluation training and process further assured the replication of a managerially oriented hierarchy in several ways, through operational definitions given to factors, through instructions about avoiding overcounting, through the use of organizational charts, and through insistence on consistent relationships between factors.

Operational Definitions

Training began with the instruction that evaluators would measure the value to the organization of one job class as compared with another along a range from the most complex and most valuable to the least complex and least valuable. Operational definitions of levels of complexity were partially established through illustrating the types of jobs found at a particular level. For example, Level B on Technical Know-How might fit a chauffeur or a production typist. Another example comes from training to use the "Impact" subscale of the Accountability factor. Impact was a difficult concept, referring to the importance of the job to the end result intended, or the overall reason for the existence of the job. The illustration of the levels of impact replicated an established hierarchy of jobs:

Level of Impact	Job
Remote	Data entry operator
Remote/contributory	Computer operator
Contributory	Programmer
Contributory/shared	Systems analyst
Primary	Head of electronic data processing

Depending upon the specific set of choices made on the Accountability Guide Chart, and one was the Impact choice, there could be a 150- to a 200-point distance between the data entry operator and the head of electronic data processing on this one factor. Thus, the structure of the charts and the decision rules learned in training both helped to insure that a believable hierarchy would emerge in the process. All these examples meant that some jobs were pegged at particular levels even before evaluation began.

Impact was also interesting because it contained one level that could have reflected a democratic organization of work. This was the "Shared" level, defined as "participating with others (except own subordinates and superiors), within or outside the organizational unit, in taking action." "Shared" could have been used to describe—and give points for—jobs that functioned within a team approach in a work unit. However, by definition sharing of decision-making could be conceived as happening only between equals in the organizational structure, and these were held to be rare occurrences.

Managerial Know-How was defined in terms of the specific managerial location of particular jobs. To manage is to carry out an integrative function, such as coordinating the work of the Welfare Division and the Corrections Division, but jobs that were not managerial in the organizational chart could not be evaluated above the lowest level of Managerial Know-How. Thus, the coordination of services that a ward clerk might carry out, or the program coordination assigned to many professional jobs could not be recognized with extra points for an integrative function. Such jobs are often held by women.

Operational definitions preserved hierarchy in another way, in making distinctions between supervisors and nonsupervisors and between custodial and treatment personnel. An implicit assumption in evaluation was that a supervisor should have a higher point score than her subordinates. Even though the supervisor's technical Know-How might be at the same level as that of the supervisee, greater knowledge about management might push the supervisor's technical Know-How score higher. In addition, Problem Solving and Accountability would probably add points to the supervisor's score. Also, supervisors motivate other workers, and this aspect of the job would place them higher on the Human Relations scale than other workers. Therefore, deciding who was or who was not a supervisor was important for the emergent ranking.

The problem for the job evaluators was that not all supervisory functions are located in jobs titled "supervisor." There are lead workers who organize work and motivate coworkers. There are secretaries who supervise clerical assistants. There are professional workers who supervise one or two other workers. In addition, in the universities, there are many clerical workers at various levels who hire, fire, and supervise work-study students.[8]

The evaluation teams, with the help of the consultants, developed rules to deal with this complexity: a lead worker gets a "3" on Human Relations. A "true supervisor" supervises five or more workers and 75 percent to 80 percent of the job's activities have to do with supervision. A true supervisor also hires, fires, and disciplines. Such a supervisor gets a 4 on Human Relations. However, if fewer than five workers are supervised, the Human Relations score may be lower. The secretary who supervises part-time student workers, even if she oversees 15 to 20 workers, is seen simply as a lead worker and does not get extra evaluated points above the "3" on Human Relations that went automatically to lead workers. Nevertheless, there was some accommodation in the evaluation process to the organizational reality that the supervisory function is partially distributed into nonsupervisory jobs. Many of these jobs are female-dominated and adding some extra points for supervision may be one of the sources of scores that show that these jobs have been undervalued.

The distinction between custodial and treatment jobs also

arose in the process of operational definition. This distinction was confounded or cross-cut by the distinction between supervisors and nonsupervisors. Again, the distinction has implications for point scores given to primarily women's jobs. It also has implications for the maintenance of class differences in the organizational hierarchy.

Custodial jobs are those low-level positions in state institutions, homes for the mentally retarded, mental hospitals, prisons, that have the responsibility for minute-by-minute care of inmates. These positions are nonsupervisory and seen as unskilled and routine. A decision about whether or not a position was "just custodial" was critical for deciding the level of complexity on the Technical Knowledge dimension of Know-How, and thus was critical for determining the total number of points assigned to a job.

The assumptions imbedded in the distinction between custodial and treatment reflect the undervaluation of people-caring functions in some female-dominated jobs noted by Remick (1984). The distinction is also rooted in a particular medical model. One assumption of this model is that treatment is separate from routine care and something that is applied in particular times and places by people other than the routine care-givers. Occupational status, reinforced by advanced training, becomes linked to the distinction between treatment and custodial care, with the knowledge and skill needed for custodial work being further devalued in comparison with the professional knowledge of treatment personnel.

This notion was widely challenged in the 1950s and 1960s by the movement to create therapeutic communities and by the recognition that unrelieved custodial care, as in some mental hospitals, could exacerbate and make chronic conditions that might otherwise have subsided after an acute phase (for instance, Jones, 1976). In the therapeutic community all who had any contact with a patient were part of the treatment team, and every moment of the patient's stay became part of the process of treatment. The aides who spent their days with patients were to be part of the treatment team, participating in team planning of therapeutic approaches, and developing skills on the job. This new ideology of care had an impact in Oregon, as elsewhere. The survival of the notion of custodial care in job-evaluation defini-

tions may simply reflect the failure of attempts to create therapeutic communities. Perhaps routine care is still the insensitive
and unresponsive management of human bodies. On the other
hand, the Oregon job evaluation process suggests that the term
"custodial" may inaccurately convey what some employees actually do, and may be required to do, in these sorts of jobs.

For example, kitchen aides and laundry workers often have
to work with mentally retarded inmates who are assigned to the
kitchen or laundry to learn some basic skills. These low level,
"unskilled," workers have considerable "responsibility in practice" for encouraging and monitoring the performance of the
inmates. Yet, skills needed to carry out these tasks are not reflected in the knowledge and experience requirements of the
jobs, in the organizational level of the job, or in its rewards. In the
actual job evaluation process, such jobs were given some points
for the Human Relations skills needed in supervising inmates, or
students, as they are called, but there was little recognition in
Technical Know-How points for the knowledge that this required.

The most significant example of the use of operational definitions in the reproduction of hierarchy is the undermining of the
major Task Force effort to eliminate sex bias in the Guide Charts
through changing Human Relations and Working Conditions. In
spite of the many hours of discussion in Task Force and Advisory
Group meeting, and in spite of the majority decisions in both
groups that a broadening of the Human Relations scale should be
the policy of the state of Oregon, in the benchmark evaluations,
the consultant's definition of three levels of Human Relations
skills prevailed.[9] The consultants achieved this outcome through
the training for the use of the four-level scale. They defined
Level One to include only those jobs in which practically no
human contact occurs. This level was called "Incidental" and
referred to the person who sits in a room all alone and gets
direction from pieces of paper shoved under the door. Of course,
there are practically no jobs that are so isolated, so that the
Incidental level was rarely used by the evaluators. This left a
three-level scale that did not allow a distinction between, for
example, a clerical worker who must interact with several bosses
in the office, and a highway maintenance worker who must get
along with others on the work crew.

The three-level scale was frustrating to the job evaluators who tried to recognize the caring and mediating tasks in many female-dominated jobs. I discuss this in some detail below. Several Task Force feminists observed the consultants' training sessions and were aware of this maneuver to save the consultants' three-level scale. The Task Force members did not interfere, primarily from considerations of legitimacy. Hay had been hired partly to give respectability and authority to the project. Initial training took place in a large public room with a number of observers. An open challenge in that setting would, we felt, undermine and slow down the process. Consequently, no challenge was made.

The consultants also shaped in the training process the use of the revised Working Conditions factor. Work Demands were interpreted as a way to add points for only the most severe conditions. For Time Demands, the criterion, in general, was, "Is this a drop dead situation?" For example, a hostage negotiator in a prison riot would experience Time Demands. Role Loading was defined in private sector, managerial terms as, for example, a job in which the incumbent was required to do long-term planning for a company and at the same time be responsible on a daily basis for production. The suggestion that many workers in human service jobs experience role loading or conflict when they have to act as enforcers of laws for the state and supportive helpers for the client was not adopted in the definition of role loading. Emotion Loading was defined as only applying to jobs in crisis medical care or treatment of extremely difficult psychiatric problems. Thus, the potential for altering the hierarchy of jobs through evaluating often hidden aspects of women's work was subverted by the actions of the consultants.

Double Counting

The predetermined hierarchy was also maintained through avoidance of overcounting or double counting. Trainers frequently emphasized the dangers of overcounting. For example, Emotion Loading, a component of the Work Demands subfactor of Working Conditions, could be used to double or triple count some aspects of jobs. Emotional stress might be implicitly accounted for under Human Relations, in Problem Solving, or even in the Technical Know-How subfactor where knowledge about psychological problems would be credited. Evaluators were warned that giving points for the same content under different factors could distort the rankings. As I have discussed above, double or triple counting on managerial tasks appears to be clearly built into the Guide Charts, but this was not seen as problematic. The stricture against double counting on the new subfactors or the redefined subfactors, therefore, acted to preserve the hierarchy, with its managerial slant, already built into the Charts.

Use of Organizational Charts

When in doubt about the complexity of a job, there were precedents set in the training to refer to the organizational chart. The charts were especially helpful when there were numerous bureaucratic levels and little apparent difference in job content between levels. For example, an agency might have district supervisors deployed geographically and a supervisor of these supervisors; the two job descriptions might look quite similar. Location in the organizational hierarchy could then help to peg the appropriate number of points for the factors, keeping in mind that supervisors ought to have more points than those beneath them, and fewer points than those above them in the hierarchy. Place in the hierarchy could also indicate formal responsibility and thus contribute to assessment of the accountability factor. Other criteria, such as licensing and other laws, were used to locate accountability. Registered nurses, for example, are legally responsible for patient well-being, in contrast to Licensed Practical Nurses. Although LPNs might do substantially the same things as RNs, almost everyone agreed, they could not have as high ratings on any of the factors because of the differences in legal responsibility. Thus, we can differentiate between formal or bureaucratic responsibility and responsibility in practice. Responsibility in practice was never recognized in awarded points at a level equal to bureaucratic responsibility, although the evaluation teams discussed these differences extensively. Here is another way, then, that the replication of the organizational hierarchy was guaranteed in the practical process of job evaluation.

Relationships Between Factors

Just as there are usual rankings of jobs produced by the Hay system, there are also usual relationships between the factors for any particular job. Technical Know-How, as the trainers insisted, cannot be lower than Problem Solving (Thinking Challenge and Freedom to Think) or than the Freedom to Act dimension of the Accountability chart. These relationships were justified on logical grounds: Problem Solving and action cannot occur in the absence of knowledge about the problem and possible courses of action. Similarly, if the freedom to think is very constrained in a job, it is not reasonable to believe that the job has a high level of freedom to act. Action implies some prior thought in this context. However, as discussed above, factor inter-relationships are not uniform. Certain types of jobs have common internal patterns. Some emphasize accountability or results, others problem-solving or generating information; still others have a balance between requirements to produce results and to produce information. Thus, each job has a characteristic profile. Examination of this profile and comparison with other knowledge about a job provides a validity check on the evaluation.

Training included instructions in achieving the proper internal consistency. Sometimes Technical Know-How had to be adjusted to make it consistent with Problem-Solving or Problem-Solving had to be adjusted to make it consistent with elements in Accountability. Sometimes these relationships did not make sense to the evaluators. For example, some clerical worker evaluators insisted that certain clerical jobs had problem-solving demands far too high to be consistent with the Technical Know-How they saw in the job. The Hay trainers would not accept this job "shape," arguing that this represented irrational and defective job design. By force of argument they convinced the recalcitrant clerical workers that this aberration in their jobs should not be reflected in the evaluations. Thus, at least at this point, an organizational logic was imposed over the evaluators' perceptions of job content, possibly obscuring an important characteristic of some female-dominated jobs, that they have to deal with problems that in the formal structure are in the provinces of their supervisors and that they are not rewarded for this work. This push toward consistent relationships across factors and subfactors also, of course, was another strand in the tightly woven fabric of hierarchy. In sum, through careful and forceful instruction in defining and assessing job content in terms of evaluation factors, the consultants gave concrete meaning to the abstract words in the Guide Charts. The production of a conventional gender and class hierarchy was reinforced by the ideas about gender that evaluators revealed.

Gender Images in Job Evaluation

Images of masculinity and femininity are associated with sex-segregated jobs, as popular knowledge and a large body of recent research attest (for example, Cockburn, 1983, 1985; Game and Pringle, 1984). Writers on comparable worth identify such images as one source of bias in job evaluation (for example, Remick, 1984; Steinberg and Haignere, 1987). Gender images are part of the ideology that supports male dominance; at the same time, images of masculinity and femininity are part of the ideology justifying existing class relations, for they provide part of the rationale that makes life worth living.[10]

Efforts to combat this ideology in job evaluation take the issue to the table around which sit women and men contending over the worth of their work. When people argue about the content and difficulty of the work process, the terms they use suggest their assessments of the work and how they differentiate it from other work. In my observations of job evaluation I could see clearly some of the ways in which typical female work is undervalued. Disagreements in the team that evaluated clerical and blue collar jobs provide most of the data. On this team, several experienced clerical workers, two of whom were feminists, confronted some highly articulate blue-collar workers. Their clashes of opinion resulted in long discussions of job content.

These interactions between the women and men on the clerical-blue collar team revealed something about how jobs become gendered. Women and men often disagreed about the content of female-defined jobs, but usually, although not always, agreed about male-dominated jobs. An asymmetry in the process emerged early. Women were willing, on the whole, to accept the men as authorities on male-defined jobs. Women deferred to the men, asked them to explain and evaluate the content of male jobs. Consequently, men talked more than women and directed the evaluation of male jobs. Often they argued for higher scores on Know-How for male-dominated jobs. However, the men did not defer to the superior knowledge of the women about female-dominated clerical and service jobs. There was much more dialogue across gender lines about women's jobs. The men were skeptical and contentious. The women often responded by refusing to budge. Sometimes tensions escalated and everyone became uncomfortable. The women reported distress at having to be so combative and adamant with the men, but they usually stuck to their positions, both out of the belief in the correctness of their ideas, and out of dedication to representing the interests of all clerical workers.

Technical Know-How and Human Relations skills were contested areas in which cultural images were revealed. Contrasting pictures of male and female work were implicit in different language used to describe the jobs, both in the written job composites and in the group discussions. Low-level women's jobs were called entry-level positions, while such male jobs were apprentice positions. Women's jobs were more often described as simple, routine, repetitive, and detailed; men's jobs were more often tricky, intricate, broad, and strenuous. Women were described as making judgments, interpreting, resolving, and verifying. Men were troubleshooting, negotiating, installing, and repairing. Above all, male blue-collar workers were journeymen. The designation journeyman implied a certain basic level of Know-How. "This is a journeyman-level job" carried meanings of autonomy, respect, skill, and long apprenticeship or training. Also, journeymen are troubleshooters. In contrast, even the highest-level clerical jobs, Administrative Assistant or Management Assistant, had no such implications. Assistants, after all, are only assistants. Moreover, these jobs have no apprenticeship and little formal training. Even the job descriptions used in evaluation tended to devalue by prescribing for almost all but entry-level clerical jobs a minimum experience requirement of only two years, while four years' apprenticeship and several years of experience were often required for male journeyman-level jobs.

Men on the evaluation team saw clerical work in a much

different light than did the women. According to the male image, much clerical work is typing and checking for accuracy. This is only a repetitive production job, in their estimation. Anyone with a high school education can type and write letters, they thought. Women evaluators, in contrast, saw these jobs as much more complex. Workers who primarily did typing had to edit and proof-read, rather than just check for errors. They needed to know how to choose the format and to construct new formats. Often typing was combined with receptionist work, and the pressure of completing reports and manuscripts combined with answering the telephone and responding to people at the front desk required a cool head and the competence to do several things simultaneously. These were the arguments of the women evaluators.

The organizational knowledge that women could see in some clerical jobs was completely invisible to the men. A case in point is the institution unit clerk, the person who does the clerical work on a hospital ward (see Sacks, 1984). The women argued that the person in this job has "to be pretty well versed in the operations of the whole place to do the job." The ward clerk coordinates appointments for patients, often has to explain what is going on to a distressed family and to the patient, and is the only clerical person in the unit. In addition, this work can't be learned in a year or two, according to the women evaluators. The men countered that the work may seem complex, but it isn't. Doctors and nurses do the explaining and scheduling is not difficult. You just answer the phone and note down the times. The women won their point on Know-How; the men conceded finally that perhaps the ward clerk needs to know about the structure of the hospital. However, the women lost on their attempt to raise the scoring on Problem Solving and Accountability for this job. One woman evaluator, depressed as she left the day's evaluation session, said that she felt as though she had betrayed the people to whom she was committed.

The blue-collar workers also had difficulty in seeing the complexity of bureaucratic tasks. For example, the state has a number of jobs that process records, verifying information, applying eligibility rules, routing forms, answering questions about rules, explaining regulations. "I don't see them making decisions; if they make a mistake it just comes back to them," said a blue-collar man. The women contended that rules have exceptions—to apply rules one must have knowledge about the exceptions. Moreover, a broader knowledge about how programs work is necessary in order to apply rules intelligently. The men countered that situations dictate procedures and that records specialists just had to fit things into categories. Women do production, they don't troubleshoot. They don't have to solve problems and make decisions.

The most extreme example of this view emerged in the evaluation of the stenographic court reporter who makes a verbatim record of court proceedings. Evaluators agreed that the stenographic system involves a fairly high degree of knowledge. However, the application of that knowledge was interpreted as routine. The sounds in the courtroom are processed through the reporter's brain, coming out as symbols on a tape. Indeed, "this person is a sophisticated machine." Therefore, points on problem solving are minimized: "You don't have to understand it to write it down." Women evaluators objected to this interpretation of the court reporter's job, but the male view prevailed. Evaluators faced similar problems with the word processing job. Working at a word processor is not very complex, they decided, although more complex than doing ordinary production typing. Some argued that production typing is really more complex because with word processing the knowledge about formating, document style, and even spelling may be in the machine. This was a topic of some ambiguity, and it seems that in this Oregon group, the question of whether the new technology deskills or requires new skills had not been resolved.

The ambiguity of the technology, the difficulty in deciding about deskilling, reflect the social components in the definition of skill. The links between skill and masculinity have been demonstrated in a number of studies (Phillips and Taylor, 1986; Game and Pringle, 1984; Cockburn, 1983). Male workers act to preserve the perception of their own work as skilled work, even when the tasks have been simplified through technological change. The definition of male work as skilled is maintained by contrasting it with female work which is, often by definition, not skilled. The process of saving male superiority, in this job evaluation case, was two sided—arguing both for the complexity and difficulty of male jobs and for the simplicity of female jobs.

Comparing clerical jobs at any level with skilled blue-collar jobs, these male workers usually placed the female jobs lower in an implicit scale of complexity of knowledge and problem-solving. They were also highly skeptical about claims that many office jobs need high human relations skills to keep the flow of work going smoothly. The invisibility to the men of many aspects of women's jobs came out in heated exchanges over Human Relations skills in the course of lengthy discussions of higher-level office jobs. The women on the team maintained that such jobs require Human Relations skills above the level of "common courtesy" or basic effectiveness in relating to others. Office conflicts must be managed, often several bosses must be placated, information must be extracted from and given to the public, liaison with other departments must be established and maintained, and arrangements and decisions must be facilitated. The blue-collar men argued first that these functions were not the basic purposes of the jobs, so shouldn't be credited, and, second, that in any case, the level of Human Relations skill required was not greater than that required of a member of a bridge maintenance crew. After all, it is essential that bridge workers be able to communicate with each other; to talk with the public requires no greater skill. To the men, the women were only arguing that secretaries or administrative assistants had to be nice and polite for longer periods of time than the bridge worker, not that there was anything qualitatively different about the work. The men, in addition, could not see the levels of skill that the women could see and thus, could not differentiate between different levels and types of office work. As one said in this debate, "the skills are no more than you would expect on the street."

The disputes over Human Relations skills were related to the way that the consultants restricted the choices on the scales, which I have discussed above. With the first level effectively eliminated by defining it as involving no human contact, the second level became "common courtesy." Level three was used for lead workers and for jobs such as the ordinary Registered Nurse or the supervisor of small groups, and level four, "critical," was reserved for jobs in which most of the work was done through human relations, such as psychiatric therapy. Thus, the women on the team who were aware of the invisible work in many female-dominated jobs, had no latitude in the scale. The clerical worker evaluators attempted to use the numbering patterns in the Know-

How chart to recreate a four-level scheme in order to differentiate between types of clerical jobs and between clerical and blue-collar jobs. They did this by giving the maximum points possible, within the Guide Chart limitations, to jobs deemed to have heavy human relations obligations. This solution was not satisfactory, and most of the acrimonious debates centered around this strategy. The women were dedicated to the comparable worth goal and argued their points fiercely. The men were equally adamant and, indeed, never gave in. Their concern was that, in comparison with female jobs, the male jobs would be undervalued.

The women identified several components of Human Relations, qualities of behavior such as responsiveness and tactfulness, task components, such as facilitating and explaining, and actors in interaction, coworkers, the public, bosses. To the men, it was all the same. A file clerk's job was no different than a secretary's. The stance of the men in this part of the evaluation was constructed with reference to their own public, other blue-collar workers, and with reference to the symbolic value of the image of journeyman. As one said, "the men at work will never believe that an administrative assistant is at a journey level."

Working Conditions were another matter, for here the discussions and outcomes reflect class-based rather than gender-based disagreements. Male evaluators sided with female on the question of Working Conditions in the office, against the management-oriented advice of consultants. The consultants had defined the office environment as normal, and a normal environment gets no points, by definition. Even though many clerical workers had stated in their questionnaires that windowless rooms, windows that don't open, poor artificial ventilation, dust and fumes made their work environments at least unpleasant, the definitions on the physical environment dimension made it impossible to give points for this. Ironically, while evaluations were in progress, a state office building was closed for several days because workers had become ill from some unidentified fumes in the ventilating system.

The concept of the office as normal contrasts with the idea of an outdoor workplace as not normal, or at least as unpleasant. Thus, blue-collar work is likely to be given job evaluation points when it is located outside. Sensory-muscular effort descriptions are, similarly, more applicable to male jobs than to female jobs.

Typist jobs that required virtually full-time keyboard work qualified for points on muscular effort. Sitting in front of a video monitor for seven or eight hours a day was considered to involve sensory effort. However, very few jobs had these characteristics. The operational definitions from the consultants meant that working with arms and hands extended brought no points unless this position was almost constantly maintained. But, "you ache after awhile when using a keyboard," according to one clerical worker. She and others thought that Working Conditions points should be given for jobs that were primarily typing jobs even if the workers had other responsibilities that took them away for the keyboard for periods of time. But the consultants disagreed. Since the consultants were in a position of authority and they were guiding the job evaluation process, their position usually prevailed, as it did in this case.

Evaluators tried to give points for jobs that were extremely sedentary or extremely boring. This effort was led by a man on the team who, early in his working life, had been briefly a file clerk. He argued that extremely routine jobs require a high degree of focus and attention and that workers must find some way to play mental games that help to keep them at the tasks.[11] "Does the state of Oregon want to pay for boredom?" said one consultant. "No one is comfortable justifying to taxpayers paying for boredom." Of course, the routine jobs, such as file clerk, that stimulated this discussion were all female-dominated jobs. Again, evaluators were unsuccessful in their attempts to modify the Hay system.

The new dimension of Working Conditions devised for the Oregon project, Work Demands, faced the greatest difficulties in evaluation. The consultants' definitions had made Work Demands into a factor that would only rarely be found in any job and one that would primarily occur in only high-level jobs, such as top managers or executives of the World Bank, as one consultant suggested. Points for Work Demands were given to only 20 of the 346 benchmark jobs. These were primarily jobs dealing with people under severe physical or emotional strain. The stress inherent in many clerical jobs (Stellman and Henifin, 1983) did not appear as a compensable factor.

Evaluators, especially those looking at blue-collar and clerical jobs, spent a lot of time discussing working conditions. These deliberations had little effect on the final scores, since the points actually awarded in the evaluations of Working Conditions varied only from 1 to 16, as compared with the variation of points awarded for Know-How, which ranged from 56 to 400 points. These differences in awarded points are one reason for Barker's (1986) finding that Working Conditions accounted for only 1.4 percent of the average total Hay score. Thus, the relative weights of the factors in the Hay system vary as a consequence of the points awarded in the actual use of the scales, as well as in the range of possible points built into the scales. This is one of the additional ways that particular values are built into the process. To "overvalue" working conditions would be to reduce the distance between managerial and nonmanagerial jobs.

Results

At the end of the benchmark evaluation process, when Hay consultants examined the ranking of scores and compared it with other applications of their method, they found that Oregon scores were, on the whole, quite similar to those of other employers. The scores of some clerical jobs were too low when compared with blue-collar jobs, according to the consultants, suggesting that the gender images of the blue-collar men had prevailed in the evaluation process. Some of these scores were raised in the sore-thumbing process. Scores on Human Relations followed a conventional pattern: Level One was used for only 11 out of 355 job classes evaluated. Clerical jobs were all evaluated at Level Two, with the exception of the Executive Administrative Secretary, who was Level Three. Level Three on Human Relations was given to lead workers and many human service jobs. All higher-level managerial jobs and human service-professional jobs dealing with sensitive emotional problems rated a Level Four.

Preliminary analysis of job evaluation scores and wages showed pay differences between female and male-dominated jobs with similar scores, despite our failure to make even slight modifications in the Hay method to better reflect the content of women's jobs. For example, Laundry Worker 2, 78 percent female and with a point score of 95, earned an average salary of $973 per month. Laborer 3, 11 percent female and with a point score of 98, had an average salary of $1,214 per month (Table 3.1). Other

Table 3.1
Female- and Male-Dominated Jobs
by Point Scores and Average Monthly Pay, 1984, Oregon
(Selected Examples)

New Classification	Point Score	% Female	Monthly Pay
Laundry Worker 2	95	78.60	$ 973
Laborer 3	98	11.10	1,214
Administrative Specialist 4	125	90.14	1,030
Hospital Worker 3	127	81.25	1,069
Printer 1	124	28.57	1,299
Equipment Technician 1	125	0.00	1,507
Administrative Specialist 5	143	81.96	1,170
Dental Assistant 1	143	100.00	979
Bindery Worker 2	142	21.43	1,526
Secretary 1	165	100.00	1,218
Administrative Specialist 7	165	97.55	1,128
Locksmith	166	0.00	1,616
Equipment Technician 2	165	7.10	1,581
Administrative Specialist 9	203	60.87	1,475
Dental Assistant 2	203	100.00	1,127
Electrician	208	0.00	1,952
Carpenter	208	1.39	1,809
Registered Nurse 3	275	92.10	1,882
Engineer 3	275	3.70	1,886

Note: These job classifications are from the proposed classification plan. The Administrative Specialist series contained jobs that, in current classification terms, were Clerical Assistant, Clerical Specialist, and assorted other clerical classifications.

selected illustrations of benchmark scores for proposed new job classifications are given in Table 3.1 and a more detailed account of study results appears in Chapter 4. On the whole, the results were quite consistent with those in other studies. We have no way of estimating how much higher scores for female-predominant jobs might have been had we successfully modified the Hay process.

Discussion: The Technical Reproduction of Hierarchy and Gender-Class Politics

Job evaluation reproduced Oregon's job hierarchy but also revealed gender-based divisions within class processes. Many lower-level women's jobs had less pay than men's jobs with similar point scores. However, the resulting estimates of underevaluation were probably low because efforts to reduce sex bias in the Hay system failed. Political questions about what should be valued in women's jobs were confronted, in this stage of the project, in terms of the technical structure of the Guide Charts, the definitions of factors, and the process of evaluation. Evaluation requires detailed interpretations of the abstract definitions of job factors as these are applied to concrete definitions of actual jobs. Consultants teach and supervise the use of conventional definitions that reproduce hierarchy. Skills in verbal interpretation, complex experience-based knowledge, and the ability to convince are parts of a consultant's competence. Feminists, unfamiliar with job evaluations, attempting to intervene from the outside, were no match for the consultants on their own technical ground. The consultants knew their system and understood how certain technical changes could reverberate through the whole process, altering widely-accepted hierarchical relationships. Altering these relationships too much would threaten the legitimacy of the job evaluation system, which is built upon and expresses managerial values. The consultants could not let that happen, and used their technical knowledge and expertise to circumvent the threat.

It was the legitimacy of their system, its public appearance of reasonableness, that the consultants were protecting as they made virtually impossible the implementation of any of the modifications sought by Task Force feminists. The hierarchy was somewhat rearranged, but only as a consequence of consistent application of the evaluation method to both female-dominated and male-dominated jobs, not as a consequence of altering the method to reduce sex bias. The consultants were able to further insure, through their training of evaluators and their extensive quality control methods, that there was no basic disturbance of the conventional ordering. This was their responsibility to the project, not only a matter of the self-interest of consultants, as part of their task was to confer legitimacy on the Oregon comparable worth effort. The need for legitimacy placed Task Force feminists in a contradictory situation. They too needed legitimacy for the project, but legitimacy achieved at the cost of reducing sex bias in job evaluation conflicted with their feminist goals.

Feminists would have avoided this contradiction if there had been a commitment within the state administration to decrease overall inequality (Acker, 1987). No such commitment existed, as was obvious as management representatives sided with the consultants against increasing points for human relations skills and job stress in low-paid jobs. Moreover, in the process there was much discussion by consultants and managers about the need for more, not less, inequality. That is, managers in the public sector are paid much less than those in the private sector, and public sector professionals are also underpaid in relation to the private market. No support existed among such employees for even further increasing their disadvantage in comparison with other managers and professionals through a reduction of hierarchy internal to the state.

These are expressions of class interests, not simply interests in preserving status hierarchy. Thus, class processes are intrinsic to hierarchical processes, and the reproduction of gender inequality is also accomplished within these same processes. In the political contest over the technical reproduction of hierarchy, the class interests of the consultants and of state management prevailed over the gender interests of feminists and the gender/class interests of those working women they intended to represent.

The language used by consultants in explaining and defending their system reveals managerial assumptions about hierarchies and jobs. Hierarchy is natural and the test of whether a particular ranking is correct is common sense. Common sense is what any reasonable person can see is right. In all probability, it is close to the hierarchical ordering that exists. Jobs are abstract categories with no occupants, and job evaluation assesses jobs, not workers. Characteristics of workers, which vary, should not be confused with characteristics of jobs. For example, stress may be the reaction of certain workers, not an element in a job. Thus, such stress could not be evaluated. Such concepts of jobs and hierarchies contributed to difficulties in changing the valuation of women's jobs.

Examination of the job evaluation process suggests some of

the ways that specifically female- and male-class positions are reproduced, and thus, some of the concrete processes through which class structures are constituted as gendered structures. Cockburn (1983) has described the historical process through which the gendering of work was constructed in one industry, printing, as a defense against processes of deskilling that were threatening to devalue men's work and to deprive male workers of their gendered identities. In this comparable worth project, we have a brief glance at a related phenomenon, the verbal strategies male workers used to try to avoid a devaluation of their skills. Such a devaluation would come from decreasing the differentials between male skills and female skills. Although scores would eventually affect relative earnings, I do not believe that these job evaluators had money in mind when they fought against attributing knowledge and some degree of complexity to clerical work. They were concerned with respect, getting their due. Admitting that certain female jobs might be worthy of a similar respect seemed to be demeaning to them. Their refusal to believe the women evaluators probably also reveals something about their regard for female knowledge and about the invisibility of dimensions of women's jobs, which are seen as auxiliary, assisting, supporting, without any agency of their own.

Job content that is supervisory, coordinating, mediating, or therapeutic is often obscured, not only in male minds, but in the abstract ordering of positions and in the documentation that supports and legitimizes that ordering. The formal hierarchy specifies that managerial and supervisory functions are located at certain levels. Job descriptions used for job evaluations in Oregon indicate, however, that supervisory responsibilities are part of many nonsupervisory jobs. This observation is confirmed for Great Britain in a recent study which found that "those who are not classified as supervisors nevertheless perform a wide variety of supervisory tasks" (Rose, Marshall, Newby, and Vogler, 1987:17). Among the nonsupervisors, nonmanual employees had the highest proportion of supervisory duties. Although this British study does not give information on the exact jobs with these supervisory duties, it is probable that many of them are female-dominated.

The Oregon data also suggest that clerical work is much more various than is implied by the term, as indicated by the initial division of six job categories into more than 80. Knowledge and skill specifications for such jobs often do not fully reflect the variations in complexity in many lower-level female-dominated jobs. This observation is contrary to the idea, widely accepted by sociologists (for example, Glenn and Feldberg, 1979; Crompton and Jones, 1984), that clerical work has been deskilled. Some clerical work is certainly unskilled and deskilled; other clerical work is not. The hierarchical location of all clerical work obscures variation and the dispersion of supervisory tasks to lower levels. The theoretical question of what constitutes class boundaries and where they might be located becomes more complicated when the work of women is entered into the analysis, for if supervisory responsibilities are widely dispersed downward in organizations, the supervisor/nonsupervisor divide may not constitute a good indicator of class boundaries (Rose, Marshall, Newby, and Vogler, 1987).

The assignment of job-evaluation points to all job classifications and all individual positions in state employment, a profoundly political process in bureaucratic clothes, was the first step on the road to true comparable worth. Issues of sex bias in job evaluation were joined early, and the feminists and trade unionists lost. The hiring of Hay Associates, while it was the best choice given the limitations of time, money, and political legitimacy, abdicated the ground to a conservative management approach. Since even this approach revealed more undervaluation of women's work than the state administration was willing or able to deal with, the question of male and managerial bias in the evaluation system paled in significance in comparison with the difficult issues of building and implementing a new classification and compensation system. These steps were even more obviously political, as I discuss in the next chapter.

CHAPTER FOUR

True Comparable Worth
The Technical as Political

The principles of true comparable worth, a complete wage system based on evaluated points, were the taken-for-granted assumptions of the project as the Task Force, the consultants, and the Personnel Division went about developing and formulating a comparable worth plan for the state of Oregon. The development of the plan began with the first Task Force meeting, its form prefigured in the Personnel Division's Request for Proposal that preceded the Task Force appointments. Thus, job evaluation and the development of true comparable worth were simultaneous and interlocking processes. It is only in the telling that they can be separated.

Competing class and gender interests were from the beginning a recurrent, if often unacknowledged, theme. The issues outlined in Chapter 2—who shall control the project, how to ensure legitimacy, whether to focus first on pay equity or job classification, how to combine collective bargaining and comparable worth, and scope and timing—resurfaced as the implications of "true" comparable worth were spelled out in detailed policy decisions. The coalition of trade unions, employer, and feminists that had made the project possible at the start held together in the face of growing doubts about the possibility of doing both a classification and compensation plan within the time limits.

As the project deadline approached, conflict became more open and more difficult. The attention paid to eliminating sex bias from job evaluation receded, and difficulties with the new classification plan and implementation issues dominated the work. Pay equity for women was still the goal for feminists and unions, but women's issues were forced to the sidelines as management goals and trade-union conflicts took center stage. Feminists were eventually mired in a disagreement between the unions, as serious difficulties with true comparable worth became more evident, and the feminist position began to split in different directions. Technical questions were the arena for these political developments; to understand how the focus shifted and women's issues were subordinated, it is necessary to look at the development of the plan and its main provisions in some detail. The detail shows concretely how class/gender−based difficulties affected the plan for comparable worth.

The Plan for True Comparable Worth

Early decisions to carry out a two-phase plan, first classification and then compensation, with pay equity as the outcome, had already given some shape to the Oregon plan, as had the decision to survey every position in the state. These early decisions were fateful, but their full consequences were not publicly recognized until it was too late to go back. Each step along the way filled in the outlines. Detailed discussions with unions, management, and consultants were ongoing from December, 1983. Some important decisions, such as how to group questionnaires were made in April and May of 1984, and concrete Task Force planning for implementation began in late summer 1984 and continued through the rest of the year (see Figure 1.1).

Task Force members felt they were breaking new ground for comparable worth. The consultant confirmed that Oregon was trying something that had not been done before and that the eyes of the national comparable worth community were on Oregon. The sense of being in the forefront raised the level of excitement about the project, but it also meant that there were no clear guidelines to follow. So far as we knew, there were no other jurisdictions that had carried out a thorough classification study primarily for the purposes of comparable worth. In the state of Washington's ground-breaking 1974 study, a selected group of sex-segregated job classifications were evaluated based on questionnaires sent to 1,600 employees (Remick, 1984:102). There was no classification component in the initial study nor in the subsequent study updates. Minnesota had begun in 1982 the implementation of pay equity based on a previous Hay Associates job evaluation study. No new study was needed and the classification system was not altered (Cook, 1985:140–143). In New York, two studies were underway, one solely on pay equity and another on the classification system (Steinberg and Haignere, 1987). How the results of the two studies would be meshed had not been directly addressed (Cook, 1985:177–179). According to our information, Connecticut had tried to implement comparable worth without an adequate classification system and had had to backtrack to do a classification study, delaying comparable worth, probably for several years.

Only Idaho provided a possible model. There the legislature in 1975 mandated a job evaluation study of all jobs in state employ. The study, done by Hay Associates, was the basis for a new classification and compensation system implemented in 1977. Although pay equity was not a goal, considerable equity was achieved. According to Cook (1985:92–93), "With implementation, women's salaries increased an average of 16.2 percent, while men's increased an average of 6.8 percent. Secretarial salaries increased between 20 and 30 percent." Idaho was an attractive model for Oregon management, but not for unions. In Idaho there is no public sector collective bargaining, and their plan included a provision unacceptable to unions, freezing the wages in job classes with wage levels above the new compensation plan levels. Although we had no information on how many workers were affected, union representatives indicated that this was a serious problem. Oregon's collective bargaining law, providing for wage negotiation, strikes, and binding arbitration, created a different situation, one in which the contradictions between collective bargaining and the operational definition of true comparable worth became more and more evident.

Plan development had a number of components. All were part of a simultaneous process that included (1) the new classification system, (2) compensation analysis, (3) a new wage plan, (4) implementation, and (5) future maintenance of pay equity.

The New Classification System

Sociologists have only recently begun to pay attention to job classification systems. Yet, classification is at the heart of organizational structure, in the process of defining positions in a hierarchy specifying relations of authority and lines of control (Edwards, 1979; Thompson, 1983). Job classifications also help to control wages, as pay ranges are allocated to job classes. Job classification is the specification of internal labor markets and career ladders. These processes can also be seen as part of producing "sets of places within the social division of labor" (Crompton and Jones, 1984:40). Edwards (1979) argues that classification systems themselves are major instruments of bureaucratic control, fracturing and stratifying the work force within organizations. Others (Rubery, 1980; Thompson, 1983) point to the positive consequences of such systems which provide specifications of the work expected, rules that protect against arbitrary and paternalistic bosses (Crompton and Jones, 1984:213), and often, job security. On the other hand, recent research (Bielby and Baron, 1987) indicates that levels of sex segregation are higher in larger, more bureaucratized establishments than in smaller ones. "In short, instead of promoting universalistic standards in personnel matters,

Table 4.1
Job Classifications by Gender of Dominant Group,
Current Actual Classes,
State of Oregon, 1984

Dominant Gender in Class	Number of Classes	Percent of Classes	Average No. Employees per Class
Female-dominated*	406	22.9	35.0
Male-dominated*	1,084	61.0	10.9
Mixed gender	285	16.1	21.9
Total	1,775	100.0	18.1

*Classes are gender-dominated if 70 percent or more incumbents are of one gender.
Source: Final Report and Recommendations, Task Force on State Compensation and Classification Equity, 1985, appendix 2B.

bureaucratic rules, procedures, and job titles seem to have been implemented in a way that sustains the segregation of jobs and opportunities by sex" (Bielby and Baron, 1987:220). Women's jobs may be dealt with differently than men's jobs in classification systems. That is, male-dominated jobs are spread through more job classes than female-dominated ones; male jobs are often more specifically described than female-dominated jobs; female job classes tend to have more incumbents than male job classes (see Tables 4.1 and 4.2). These gender characteristics of classification systems are related to the undervaluation of female jobs.

Classification systems also specify the status positions that internally stratify the working class, middle strata, and managerial class sectors within organizations. These are status positions that may be desperately defended if attacked. As the Task Force, consultants, and Personnel went into the next phase of the study, hindsight suggests, there was too little recognition of the centrality of the classification system in the ongoing reproduction of status, of individual loyalties, and of system legitimacy.

Although, in principle, everyone working on the project agreed that we needed a new classification system as the basis of comparable worth, what that meant in practical terms was by no means clear at the start. How much change did this imply? Would

Table 4.2
Employees by Gender of Current Classification, State of Oregon, 1984

Dominant Gender in Class	Total Employees		Females Employees		Male Employees	
	N	%	N	%	N	%
Female-dominated*	14,241	44.1	12,990	75.2	1,251	8.3
Male-dominated*	11,811	36.6	1,103	6.3	10,708	71.2
Mixed gender	6,247	19.3	3,175	18.4	3,072	19.3
Total	32,299	100.0	17,268	100.0	15,031	100.0

*Classes are gender-dominated if 70 percent or more incumbents are of one gender.
Source: Final Report and Recommendations, Task Force on State Compensation and Classification Equity, 1985, appendix 2B.

every job classification be altered or only a few? The positions of some individual workers would have to be reallocated, but how many? Several Task Force members had worried from the beginning that the classification portion of the study would dominate pay equity and that we might not, for this reason, reach the comparable worth goal.

The ability of the Task Force to define the scope of the reclassification process was severely limited, although conflict over this issue between Personnel and Task Force feminists was frequent. Job classification and the assignment of tasks to jobs is a management perogative in Oregon, as elsewhere. Management was jealous of this right and held tight control. Once the benchmark evaluations were done, Task Force members found it very difficult to get precise information on what was going on in the technical work. The process was complex, and probably, most Task Force members did not have the technical knowledge to intervene successfully even if they had been fully informed. The size of the project also precluded intervention. With a staff of at least 20 people working full time on the classification process, control had to be located in the hands of full-time state staff.

Anxieties over what was happening were confirmed by an incident that occurred early in the project, in April, 1984. One of the consultants, meeting over dinner with some Task Force members, said that she thought we had gotten off the track of comparable worth and more on the track of reclassification. There was discussion about how to remedy this, perhaps abandoning questionnaire data and going back to the old job specifications as a basis for evaluation. The Personnel Director exploded when she found out about this discussion, because she thought we should not have had any such discussion without her. Clearly, the Director would not countenance any backtracking on the plan for a reclassification study. Changes in the plan, it seemed at the time, would be perceived as undercutting her authority and her position. As the following discussion indicates, the Task Force chairperson did attempt to restrict the scope of the reclassification effort, but was not successful. Later analysis shows much more clearly than was evident then that this was a critical juncture for the project.

Why didn't Task Force members who were aware of the dangers of too much focus on reclassification intervene more forcefully? Part of the answer is that they underestimated the changes that were even then under way. In addition, there was the issue of territory. Job classification belonged to management. Management, it was assumed, wanted to complete the task and was supposed to have the skills to do it. Another factor was that the largest union, Oregon Public Employees Union, wanted a thorough reclassification. Finally, the Task Force by that time was locked into the project. The Personnel Director's reaction to even a raising of the question suggested that a major row would have ensued had the Task Force attempted energetically to intervene. A major row could cause a major delay. And there was no certainty that a majority of the Task Force would have approved such an invasion of management territory. In sum, Task Force feminists did not have the power to intervene successfully. The particular consultant who had raised the question left the project soon after and the issue was not raised again by any consultant.

This was an instance in which a technical decision, the scope of classification changes, provided a battleground over a class issue, management's right to control the job structure. Personnel interpreted any attempt to discuss the issue as an encroachment. In this process, low-paid women's interests were marginalized.

The general outlines of the classification revision process emerged in the spring of 1984 in the pretest of study methods. There were several steps:

1. Reading and grouping job content questionnaires.
2. Writing descriptions of job content for job groups.
3. Job evaluation.
4. Regrouping jobs with similar scores and content into new job classes.

In the specification of these steps, particularly in the grouping and regrouping, the struggle for control of the project continued, and the focus on pay equity for women was distorted and undermined.

Job Grouping.   The grouping step was the critical one, another example of a technical problem with political implications. By the middle of May, 1984, job content questionnaires were flooding the Personnel Division. A questionnaire tracking system was in place; every questionnaire was logged into a computer record as it was received, it was then sorted into its old job-class location. Half of the questionnaires for each old class were read and grouped, the other half were later matched to the new job groups. The design called for grouping questionnaires on the basis of 80 percent similarity of duties. Job analysts were instructed to avoid using any preconceived ideas about the job or the job title. The old class descriptions, or specifications, were to be used only to orient the job analyst to the job content. An alternative approach, rejected by Personnel, was to use the old class specifications as the basis for grouping and to allocate only jobs that were clearly misplaced to other and possibly new classes.

The Task Force chair expressed her serious concerns about the chosen method at a Task Force meeting on May 23, 1984. "I became concerned for three reasons. First, completing the project. I'm assuming that freely grouping takes longer than starting with the specs. Second, we are instructed in the bill to analyze the current system and make recommendations. I began to get comments from agency employees about the magnitude of the change that would occur with free grouping. We are talking about a possibly major change in the classification structure. The project design was only to solve the problems of misallocation and inadequate specification. If we produce a different system, we won't be able to analyze present inequities. The third concern is that the bigger the change, the harder it will be to implement. The basic question is how to group. I would start with the spec. If it's a match, keep it there. If it's not a match, don't keep it there."

Hay consultants recommended grouping to the existing system as much as possible. One after another, Task Force members concurred that there should be no more change than absolutely necessary. However, "absolutely necessary" was open to definition. The Personnel Director indicated that no one could tell in advance which of the old class specifications might still fit. A preliminary analysis had suggested that only 125 class descriptions of the approximately 1,700 in the state system were completely current and accurate. Further, she revealed the extent of restructuring she had in mind. "In that 600 [job specifications that needed some, but not total, revision] we have 235 class specifications that are parts of series [for example, Social Worker

1, 2, and 3]. Every one is an absolute nightmare. That starts with clerical and goes up through civil engineers and highway engineers." Thus, she was intending to correct all the inaccuracies in hierarchical structure that had crept into the system over the years. She was also dedicated to eliminating horizontal anomalies in the interest of a rational system. For example, "We looked at highway maintenance worker, laborer, and equipment operator and they all talk about operating the same large equipment, so classes are crossing lines." The Personnel Director saw the real danger to the project in the possibility that the staff would force individual jobs into inappropriate classes. She was not so concerned about the magnitude of the changes or about the problem of analyzing inequalities in the existing system with data on a new, and unimplemented, system.

The Task Force made strong recommendations to limit the extent of change, deciding that questionnaires should first be matched to existing job specifications and that as much as possible of the existing class structure should be preserved in the job groups. When the grouping was completed in August, 1,623 groups had been created. Many old job classes had been subdivided into new groups. For example, the Clerical Specialist class had been divided into 85 job groups. Some subdivision of this classification was to be expected because the 2,608 clerical specialist positions included many types of jobs from file clerk to executive-administrative secretary. But other jobs with far fewer workers were also subdivided. One was the Heavy Equipment Mechanic job with 65 workers who had been allocated to 5 job groups. Overall, the job groups departed considerably from the old classification structure. The Task Force directive had not been followed; perhaps it had not been possible. Whatever the reason, subsequent information indicated that the job grouping must have been done with little regard to the old class categories, creating a large number of new groups which later had to be recombined into new classes. The magnitude of the regrouping, as we shall see, later became an important cause for the failure of the project, causing delays and resulting in employee complaints.

The serious underlying disagreement between the Task Force and the Personnel Director over the real goals of the project—pay equity or classification reform—had emerged again around the technical issue of how to group jobs. The conflict also concerned, once again, questions of power and control. At this juncture, all Task Force members agreed that this was where we were going to go off the track if that were going to happen. At the same time, there was the beginning of the sense that not much was to be done. As one Task Force member said, "We can talk all night and it won't have much effect, because we're not doing the work."

Writing Job Composites and Doing Evaluations. The 350 benchmark evaluations described in Chapter 3 constructed a framework within which to locate the evaluations of the remaining job groups. The additional composite writing and evaluation constituted a tremendous task. The Personnel Division staff completed 1,634 job composites and evaluations by early October, 1984. At that time the project still seemed to be on schedule and the completion of a new classification structure was projected for November 15. As we shall see, the November deadline was unattainable.

Regrouping for a New Structure. Regrouping the evaluated job groups to produce new job classifications began in October, 1984, after completion of the evaluations. The process seemed straightforward. Evaluated job groups would be combined again, following the old class structure as much as possible, to form new classes based on similar content and similar scores. First, however, the questionnaires that had not been read and grouped had to be put into the proper groups. And the allocation of all questionnaires to job groups had to be checked for accuracy. Often questionnaires were in the wrong groups or there was no appropriate group. To take care of this difficulty, new groups were created and evaluated. Ultimately the project produced 2,100 groups.

Constructing a new class system proved to be much more difficult than anticipated, and completion was repeatedly delayed. The first issue was whether to have narrow job classes containing small numbers of jobs with a high degree of task similarity, or broad classes containing large numbers of jobs with less task similarity. Job classes could be broad or narrow on a horizontal or vertical scale. Horizontal breadth was no problem. Jobs in the same job family and with similar complexity but with dissimilar tasks could be grouped together. However, vertically broad classes created a problem because they would contain jobs with similar tasks at dissimilar levels of complexity. Feminists had identified such broad groupings as one source of pay inequity. In the old system hundreds of clerical jobs had been grouped into a few low-paid classes. Some jobs were skilled while others were less skilled, but all were described in general terms that did not capture the variation, and all were valued and rewarded at the same low level. In contrast, many male jobs were concretely defined, with few positions in the job class, and with pay levels more clearly linked to skill and complexity. One of the main points of job evaluation was to create for all female-dominated jobs the basis for compensation for the actual level of work complexity. For this reason, Task Force feminists energetically favored narrow classes.

Personnel experts, on the other hand, saw advantages in broad classes. Broad classes allowed management more flexibility in moving employees to new duties, or in reconstructing jobs without having to go through a process of job reclassification. A peculiarity of Oregon law, discussed in Chapter 3, made re-classification difficult. The law gave to the legislature sole author-ity to approve upward reclassification of jobs, a strategy to hold a lid on wage increases through "classification creep." The system had a built-in impetus toward such creep because it contained no way to reward employees who reach the top of their salary range, except through reclassifying a job into the next highest job in a series. Under these conditions, broad classes would give man-agers a measure of greater flexibility, and management greatly favored this alternative.

Hay consultants, however, recommended using a relatively narrow difference, 11 percent or 15 percent, in point scores to establish the breaking points between job classes (Table 4.3). If this were not done, the pay equity principle would be put in jeopardy, jobs with different levels of complexity would be in the same class with the same pay range. So, "you would get equal pay for unequal work." Pay differentials for different assignments could be worked out, but that would be administratively cumber-some. Alternatively, pay structures for vertically broad classes could be set around a midpoint for a class, but that would create inequity for the more complex jobs. The consultants recom-

Table 4.3
Proposed Pay Structure, Selected Salary Ranges, State of Oregon, 1985

Salary Range	Point Spread	Minimum Monthly Salary	Maximum Monthly Salary
A	67–73	$1,037	$1,334
B	74–83	1,061	1,364
C	84–94	1,086	1,397
D	95–105	1,115	1,433
E	106–116	1,143	1,470
F	117–130	1,174	1,509
. . .			
K	198–219	1,392	1,790
. . .			
O	300–332	1,667	2,144
. . .			
T	505–560	2,223	2,859
. . .			

Note: Each range has 6 salary steps, 5 percent apart. The pay structure was not implemented.
Source: Final Report and Recommendations, Task Force on State Compensation and Classification Equity, 1985, p. 42, figure 19.

mended, in the interests of equity, narrow classes along with a change in the Oregon law to give administrators the right to reclassify jobs, rather than requiring that all reclassifications go to the legislature.

Personnel took this solution, building the new system of both classifications and their wage groups around 11-percent increments in point scores. However, linking pay to level of complexity seemed to be introducing rigidity that had not existed before. For example, social workers in Children's Services had two levels of pay determined by whether or not the workers had M.A. degrees, but all workers were flexibly assigned to similar work, based on agency needs. These workers had recently negotiated an agreement with the state to reduce their classification to one category with one pay scale. They were moving to more equality. However, job evaluation showed that there were really four levels of complexity in these social work jobs. If four classes were created, any one worker would be assigned to only one class and would have to be reclassed to take on different task levels. Equality among social workers would be decreased and managerial flexibility constrained.[1]

Other problems plagued the effort. In some cases, evaluated scores were obviously going to downgrade jobs. As regrouping progressed, it was clear that job groups were not recombined into their old classes, but were regrouped in new ways, often to create new generic series that cut across agencies. The Personnel Director presented some of these problems to the Task Force, not asking for solutions, but imparting information. Task Force members with personnel experience gave some advice about how to achieve flexibility and still use point scores in constructing a system. However, without an immersion in the work of recombining job groups, relating new classes to each other, comparing job families, and checking for accuracy and consistency, it was impossible to fully understand the process. Moreover, the Personnel Director did not present any overall picture to the Task Force. Job classification was still a management perogative and a management responsibility and management clearly resisted Task Force intervention. Hostility and distrust between Personnel and some Task Force members escalated, increasing the impossibility of an open process. Fundamentally, then, the new classification system remained a black box for the Task Force. An equitable pay plan rested upon a good classification plan, but the Task Force, which had the responsibility for both, lost any control over classification.

Control was supposed to be regained later when the Task Force, unions, agency managers, and employees would participate in a multistage review of the new system preceding implementation. Planning for the review started early. Because Task Force and Advisory Group members knew that massive changes would be a shock, they planned a process that would be open and fair, allowing a say to every individual working for the state. Such a review was a normal part of any classification system revision. First, a detailed list of the new classes, accompanied by lists of the allocation of individual employees to the new classes, would be sent to agency managers and personnel departments. They would review this structure and notify central Personnel about any problems. Unions would also be given the same information. Adjustments to the new plan would be made on the basis of these responses. Following that, information on the new wage structure and point scores for the new job classes would be made available to everyone. Experience in other states indicated that a large proportion, perhaps 10 percent to 20 percent of employees, would take issue with their place in the new system. Therefore, time for appeal and review would be necessary after the general release of study results and the proposed new system. The Task Force and Personnel anticipated that appeals and adjustments to the plan would continue for at least a year. Implementation was scheduled for July, 1986, allowing sufficient time to work through the inevitable problems and put in place a system that would satisfy at least the majority.

Hopeful that the review process would be successful, Task Force feminists, including the chairperson who worked for the Oregon Public Employees Union, were in the uneasy situation of collaboration with, and dependence upon, the actions of a management that they perceived as antagonistic to both trade union and feminist goals. This ambiguous relationship was a product of the structure of the project, as well as of the history of past confrontations. It was inescapable and unresolvable, given the political-economic orientation of the governor and his administration. This situation illustrates the class nature of relationships between management and labor in the public sector, as well as the coalescing of feminist and labor concerns. There is no question that the effective power to define was held tightly in the hands of management, while in a formal sense, representatives of those who might have been in an oppositional relationship had the responsibility for the outcomes of management's work. Thus feminists and labor were in great danger of co-optation in the form of having to take responsibility for some of management's functions. Some who represented the interests of labor and women were well aware of this danger and their anxieties began to rise outside the formal meetings long before they became public issues.

For the arena of feminist-sponsored reforms, this raises the question of the consequences of basically adversarial groups, representing the interests of women and men workers, being drawn into collaboration on territory dominated by management.

Affirmative Action, which in many places was instituted as a consequence of feminist organization, is an instructive case. Informal observation of several Affirmative Action efforts indicates that managements can find many ways to circumvent change efforts, if they so desire. Assessing the outcomes of a large number of Affirmative Action plans, O'Farrell and Harlan (1984) find that one of the most important ingredients for success is active support at the top levels of management. Without management collaboration, chances of success are slim because workplaces are dominated by management. With it, chances of being co-opted into approving policies that are more the form than the substance of change are high. When this happens, cynicism and disaffection are often the responses of members of adversarial groups. Moreover, active collaboration may blunt the force of a movement for change, and transform the change process into new bureaucratic procedures. This seems to have been the fate of Affirmative Action in many places. Nevertheless, examples do exist of management taking the lead, in cooperation with both feminists and labor, resulting in Affirmative Action successes.

The contradictory relationship of feminists and unions to management control of the classification plan is also an example of the identity of women's class and gender interests. The interests of women workers cannot be sliced into two pieces. Both as women and as workers they needed the new classification plan, once the tight links between classification and compensation had been forged, if they were to get pay increases. Unions as organizations of both women and men also might need an adequate plan, although on this point serious disagreement between unions began to have a larger and larger impact on the project. But that is discussed at a later point in the story.

A New Wage Plan

The new compensation plan was tightly linked to the new classification plan. According to the image of "true" comparable worth, pay equity would be achieved when every position was located in a job classification that contained similar positions with similar point-factor scores and all job classifications with the same scores had been allocated to the appropriate salary range in the new wage plan.

Two central policy issues would affect the structure of the new wage plan and the amount of inequity revealed in the study. These were further specifications of the meaning of pay equity: Where should the pay policy line—or the standard for equity—be located, and what, in a technical sense, is meant by a single pay policy. Each of these issues was full of import for relationships between male- and female-dominated jobs and for the efforts of central management to gain greater control over the structuring of work, potentially at the expense of agency management and of unions. The higher the standard of equity, the closer the average wages of female jobs would come to the average wages of male jobs. The broader the definition of a single pay policy, the closer management would come to achieving its goals of reducing uncertainty and variability in collective bargaining. But reducing management uncertainty in collective bargaining could also reduce labor's ability to use varying strategies.

Thus we encounter again, in the necessity to give operational definition to a provision of the comparable worth bill, a single pay policy, the conflict between at least one version of the feminist pay equity goal and labor's self-perceived interests. Just how conflictual these policy decisions were apt to be was differentially perceived by Task Force members. Most aware of the import was the Task Force chair who, sitting as a representative of organized labor and of feminists, received the most direct and forceful feedback on the project from many different directions. Nevertheless, the policy decisions had to be made if the project were to go forward.

The Meaning of One Pay Policy. Before the Task Force could chose the actual pay policy line, it had to decide whether one pay policy, as prescribed in the legislation, was feasible. Hay consultants warned that few employers had a single pay policy. Yet, this was central to the concept of true comparable worth. As indicated earlier, the use of more than one pay policy may be a primary mechanism of wage discrimination (Steinberg, 1984:22). Remick (1984) defines comparable pay partly in terms of a single policy. In Oregon, Hay Associates in defending their job evaluation system against charges of sex bias argued that bias only enters at the stage of defining pay policy when employers use more than one policy, pegging clerical wages to salaries in a clerical market and blue-collar wages to salaries in a blue-collar market. Management also supported a single pay policy as one of the ways that order and efficiency could be imposed on a complex and diverse collective bargaining system. Thus, commitment to one pay policy was strong.

However, the precise definition of a single pay policy had to be worked out. Did it mean, in practice, one formula for calculating wages based on evaluated points and applied uniformally to all jobs in state employ, across all agencies and bargaining units? Or could it mean that jobs with similar scores would have similar pay, leaving the question of the exact relation of points to dollars to bargaining or adminstrative adjustment? These issues were reviewed again and the earlier commitment to true comparable worth, one formula applied universally, was reconfirmed.

Choosing a Pay Policy. A payline, expressing the relation between evaluated points and dollars, summarizes the pay policy of the employer. A new payline can establish a new and more equitable policy. The policy question is how should the line be determined. Should it be based on the market, some summary description of what other employers pay for similar jobs? Management representatives on the Task Force favored an average or composite market line. However, as a Hay consultant pointed out, there is no real composite market of any kind, just a combination of multiple dispersions. Different pictures of the market can be created with different types of analysis, or with data selected in different ways, as several market surveys indicated (Rynes and Milkovich, 1986). The Oregon Personnel Division had done market surveys of in-state employers in both the public and private sectors, and of state governments of similar sizes in the western region. In general, Oregon paid somewhat more than other states and somewhat less than in-state employers. Salary survey data for western states provided by Hay consultants indicated that the state was considerably under the large private-sector firms represented, especially at the higher managerial levels (see Figure 4.1).

The Task Force majority decided that there was no logical basis for selecting one of these surveys as representing the market. In addition, an average market line, which continued to be the choice of the Task Force minority, would include in its cal-

Figure 4.1
Selected Market Lines and Proposed Pay Policy, Oregon, 1984

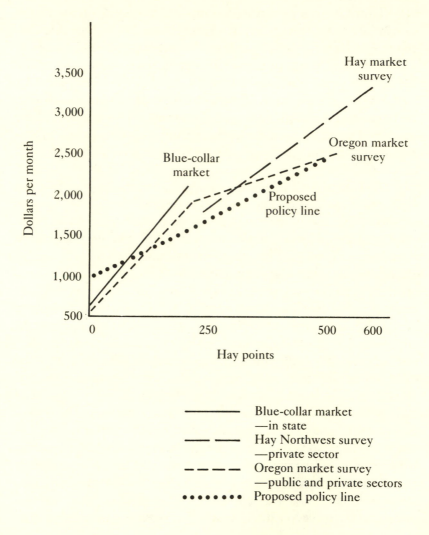

Source: Adapted from Final Report and Recommendations of the Task Force on State Compensation and Classification Equity, State of Oregon, March, 1985, p. 33.

culation female jobs and wages and would thus contain the legacy of historically existing pay discrimination against women. Moreover, the idea of comparable worth was to establish equity internal to the state as an employer. Indeed, part of comparable worth strategy was to explicitly argue that pay equity has to be achieved *within* employing organizations, not *between* them (for example, Remick and Steinberg, 1984). For these reasons, an external market payline was only briefly considered by the Task Force.

Comparable worth literature argues that a nondiscriminatory payline, one that does not contain the effects of sex, or race, based wage discrimination, can be calculated in two ways. One is the trend line based on male wages in male-dominated jobs. By definition, that line does not contain discrimination against women. The other approach uses a payline based on all wages with a statistical correction for the effect of gender composition of jobs (Steinberg and Haignere, 1987; Treiman and Hartmann, 1981). With some reservations, the consultants went along with the argument for using the male payline. Warning that pay for male blue-collar jobs is moving more slowly than pay for other jobs, they implied that blue-collar wages are too high and would provide an unrealistic standard. "It's being impacted by what's happening in the industrial midwest, negotiated paybacks and no increases. So, the logical question is, do you want to hop the whole structure up to a level at which everyone else is trying to control? But, if you have to pay those jobs at that level to recruit, then if you want pay equity, this represents what the market values without discrimination. You'd better pay at that level" (Task Force meeting, Dec. 18, 1984).

Other considerations entered the payline decision. The policy line could not be so high that the cost would exceed the ability of the state to pay. By this time in the discussion, December, 1984, the Task Force chairperson had already secured a preliminary commitment from the governor for $25 million for comparable worth in his next budget. As I discuss later, this was an amount that would allow a beginning implementation, using the male trend line as the standard for equity.

The ability of the state to recruit was another factor. What do you do when you can't hire an electrician? Some recruiting differential was essential. At the same time, balancing the cost concerns was the problem of how to place the line to minimize the number of male-dominated jobs with pay considerably above the male trend line. Oregon had a law that jobs with wages above the assigned wage range would have those wages frozen or red-lined until a rising wage structure caught up to that level. Poten-tially, some male employees could be adversely affected. The Task Force considered the issue while discussing the choice of a line, but only later did it become a serious problem for the project.

The Task Force majority favored using a male trend line, representing the actual wages of men working in male-dominated jobs. Analysis showed that the actual pay of men was higher than the male pay structure, indicating that men employed by the state earned near the top of their wage grades. The picture for women was different; they earned, on the whole, somewhat less than the female pay structure, defined as the fourth step of their respective wage ranges. Choosing a line close to the male practice seemed wise to everyone but those who held out for a market composite line. The male practice line would minimize possible negative reactions from male workers in well-paid jobs who might feel that a comparable worth pay plan set the policy-defining line too low. Such a consideration was important only because of the state's redlining law. In addition, this line would reveal the max-imum pay inequities and, therefore, allow us to go as far as possible toward removing wage discrimination.

Compensation Analysis. The exact meaning of a new pay-line, how it would be calculated and how much it would cost, depended upon compensation analysis, much of which was done in January, 1985.[2]

Analysis of the Oregon data presented a different and more complicated problem than had existed in other comparable worth studies. This was one consequence of the extensive regrouping discussed earlier. Old job classifications had been broken up for the purposes of job evaluation. Thus, there were no point-factor scores for most of the existing job classes. The 2,100 evaluated job groups had been collapsed into 593 preliminary new job classes. These new job classes had point-factor scores, but no set wages. The new comparable-worth wage plan would locate new job categories in new wage ranges. In the meantime, at the moment of compensation analysis, we could not compare the actual wages of existing job classes that had similar scores. Instead, the analysis was performed using individual data, comparing individuals' current wage rates with the evaluation score for their proposed new job classification.

Wages were measured in two ways, first—a structural measure—the wage *rate* at the fourth step of the current salary range of the job in which the individual worked, and second—the actual measure—the *actual* current wages of job incumbents. The Hay scores assigned to each individual were the scores of the 593 preliminary job classifications in which each individual position had been placed. Whether the job was in a female-dominated, a male-dominated, or a mixed-gender classification was also determined by the position's allocation in the proposed and unimplemented classification structure. As the Task Force Final Report (p. 17) pointed out, this produced "minimum estimates of gender based wage inequities." I discuss the reason for this in detail below.

The primary statistical tool in analysis was a simple regression of wages on Hay points, showing the degree to which wages rise with increasing Hay point scores. Using different estimates of wages, this produced a series of trend lines. Trend lines were calculated for employees in male-dominated, female-dominated, and mixed-sex jobs, and for all employees. In sum, estimates of undervaluation are based on a synthesis of current wage data, Hay scores for the preliminary proposed classifications, and identification of gender composition of job classifications for these still unimplemented groups (see Table 4.4).

Findings. How much wage inequity existed, and what jobs, which workers, were underpaid? Gender-based wage inequities, estimated from regression equations, were found primarily in the jobs evaluated below 250 points.[3] Workers in female-dominated, entry-level jobs (about 100 points) earned, on average, 25 percent less than workers in male-dominated entry-level jobs (Table 4.4, Figure 4.2). In skilled jobs (about 250 points), workers in female-dominated jobs earned, on average, 10 percent less than workers in male-dominated jobs at that level. Few structural gender-based inequities were found in professional jobs above 250 points. That is, in this point range there were few female-dominated job classes with lower wage structures than male-dominated classes

Table 4.4
Predicted Monthly Wages of Female-Dominated and Male-Dominated Jobs by Hay Point Scores, State of Oregon, 1984

Equation used	Hay Point Score			
	100	*200*	*300*	*500*
Male actual pay, 0–250 pts.	$1,288	$1,634		
Female actual pay, 0–250	978	1,421		
Male actual pay, 250–500			$2,002	$2,670
Female actual pay, 250–500			1,878	2,622
Recommended pay structure, 4th step	$1,300	$1,600	$1,900	$2,500

Note: Predicted wages from regression equations. See text for explanation of the calculation of these estimates.
Source: Adapted from Final Report and Recommendations of the Task Force on State Compensation and Classification Equity, State of Oregon, March, 1985, p. 24, figure 10.

with similar point scores. However, individual women tended to earn less than men in the professional ranges because they clustered at the bottom of wage ranges. At the 300-point level, the average actual wage for female-dominated classes was 7 percent less than the average actual wage for male-dominated classes (Oregon Task Force, 1985:27). In this point range there were also many mixed-gender job classes below the pay line.

Thus, Oregon analysis, based on individual data, showed the familiar relationship between point scores and wages (Remick, 1984:105). Wages in Oregon were, in general, related to Hay points; variation in Hay scores explained 70 percent of the variation in individual wages, indicating the degree to which Hay scores captured the existing values of the state. However, Hay points predicted male wages better than female wages, explaining 78 percent of the variance for male wages, but only 52 percent of the variance for female wages. Predictably, women clustered in the low-score, low-pay jobs, although the majority of male workers were also in this layer. Seventy-one percent of all state workers were in jobs with 250 or fewer Hay points. "Ninety-two

Figure 4.2
Pay Lines, State of Oregon, 1984: Actual Current Monthly Wages for Individuals in Male- and Female-Dominated Classes and Proposed Pay Policy

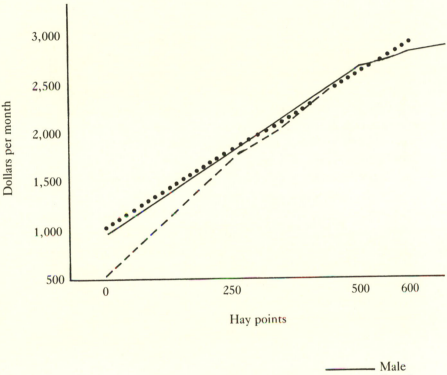

Source: Adapted from Final Report and Recommendations of the Task Force on State Compensation and Classification Equity, State of Oregon, March, 1985, p. 25, fig. 11.

percent of workers in female-dominated jobs are in this point range compared with 53 percent of workers in male-dominated jobs" (Task Force, 1985:27; see Table 4.5).

In social class terms, comparable worth in Oregon based on this analysis would benefit primarily working-class women because of the finding that female-predominant classifications in the middle levels were not systematically underpaid. However, some of the findings for professional jobs may be an artifact of the combination of job classes in the proposed classification system, together with the statistical definition of gender domination. Gender domination was defined as existing when 70 percent of the incumbents in a job class were either female or male. Seventy percent had become the conventional definition of gender domination in comparable worth studies. This cutoff point is arbitrary and may exclude certain types of jobs that have been historically female-dominated. For example, in Oregon, social worker was a job class only 65 percent female at the time of the study, and thus was not female-dominated.

The manner in which the evaluated job groups were regrouped may have further obscured systematic gender-based pay inequities. The evaluated groups were condensed into 593 new

Table 4.5
Distribution of Employees by Hay Point Scores and Gender Composition of Job Classes, For New Proposed Classes, Oregon, 1984

Point Scores	Number Employees			
	Male* Classes	Female* Classes	Mixed Classes	Total
0–250	4,744 (52.7)	10,866 (91.4)	3,029 (50.3)	18,639 (69.2)
251–501	3,339 (37.0)	1,011 (8.4)	2,914 (48.4)	7,264 (27.0)
501+	916 (10.3)	9 (.02)	73 (1.3)	998 (3.8)
Total	8,999 (100)	11,886 (100)	6,016 (100)	26,901 (100)

*Classes are gender-dominated if 70 percent or more of job incumbents are of the same sex.

Note: Numbers in parentheses are percentages.

Source: State of Oregon, Final Report and Recommendations, Task Force on State Compensation and Classification Equity, 1985, appendix 4B.

preliminary classes, as noted above. This new plan, on which analysis was based, had half as many classes as the old class structure it was to replace. This drastic reduction in the numbers of classes resulted in an unintended reduction of observed sex segregation. In the existing system, 75 percent of women workers were in female-dominated job classes, while in the draft of the proposed system, only 59 percent were in such sex-segregated classes (Table 4.6).

This result of collapsing categories is consistent with much research on sex segregation that finds that measured sex segregation rises as the categorization of jobs becomes more detailed (for example, Bielby and Baron, 1987). Thus, we can assume that minimum estimates of gender-based pay inequities would result from an analysis using 600 categories rather than 1,200 categories. The undervalued mixed-sex classes found in the 250- to 500-point range undoubtedly contain some workers from previously female-dominated classes. Since equity adjustments were to go to all undervalued classes, these women might not suffer from the statistical consequences of reducing the number of classes. However, to the extent that the statistic was produced by putting together lower-paid women with higher-paid men, the women would indeed be disadvantaged. Their low pay would appear as a consequence of being at a lower rung in a pay range rather than as

Table 4.6
Distribution of Employees by Sex and Gender Composition of Job Class for Current Actual Classes and Preliminary New Classes, State of Oregon, 1984

| | *Female Employees* | | *Male Employees* | |
| | *Current Class %* | *New Class %* | *Current Class %* | *New Class %* |
Gender Composition				
Female-dominated	75.2	59	8.3	9
Male-dominated	6.3	7	71.2	60
Mixed	18.4	34	19.3	31

Source: Final Report and Recommendations, Task Force on State Compensation and Classification Equity, 1985, p. 17, figure 5, and appendix 2B.

a consequence of the systematic pricing of women's jobs at lower levels than men's jobs. Once again, a technical decision had severe political consequences for women and for this comparable-worth project. The eventual loss of support from middle-level professional workers, many of them women, can be traced to the failure to show wage inequity at this level.

This effect of the reduction of the number of categories points to one of the ways that actual sex segregation of work may be obscured through administrative structuring of job classifications. Baron and Bielby's (1987) work has shown how pervasive is sex segregation when the analysis is done at the firm and position level. Their data precede the period of consciousness about the possibility of comparable-worth initiatives to reduce pay inequities related to sex segregation. Management attuned to risks of comparable-worth claims could restructure at least sections of job classification schemes to obscure this reality.

Task Force feminists thought that the negative consequences of collapsing categories might be reduced as the project continued. There was the expectation that in the final classification plan the number of job classes would be significantly expanded, thus undoing the statistical consequences of reducing the number of categories. Second, as already pointed out, all disadvantaged categories were to be raised. These anticipations were subverted, however, by the structure of the new classification plan, with which I will deal later, and by the location and slope of the trend line the Task Force chose as a basis for the proposed new pay policy.

Analysis of Oregon data showed that the state had several pay policies. In addition to different policies for different bargaining units, the structure of pay for jobs below the professional level was different from the structure for professionals and managers. These differences appear in the regression equations for jobs at various levels. The relationship between points and wages was different for jobs between 0 and 250 points, 250 and 500 points, and above 500 points. In general, the trend lines were steeper for jobs below 250 points than for jobs above 250 points (Oregon Task Force, 1985:20). The slope of the trend line for higher-level managers is much flatter than the slopes for lower-level jobs (see Figure 4.2).

The consultant argued that this reflected a major problem in the public sector, recruiting good managers. Public-sector managers earn less than their private-sector counterparts, and for public-sector managers, more job complexity and responsibility bring lower proportional increases in pay than they bring to subordinates. Consequently, both consultants and state managers felt that the comparable worth study could have an important side effect, raising the salaries of higher-level managers. Task Force feminists did not agree and the pay policy eventually chosen allowed increases for only a few managers. However, the frequent discussions of manager's pay was another way that the feminist intent in doing comparable worth may be deflected to other organizational interests.

A Payline Decision. The policy decision had been made to use the male practice-line, but, as discussed above, there were several male practice-lines for male-dominated jobs in different sections of the hierarchy of Hay points. Thus, deciding on the precise trend line that would be the standard for equity as well as the policy line around which new salary ranges would be constructed was even more complicated. Task Force feminists were most interested in raising the wages of female-dominated jobs below 250 Hay points. Here was most of the wage inequity; here were over 90 percent of the workers in female-dominated jobs. The male practice-line below 250 points seemed to be a good place to start, even though other male practice-lines had different intercepts and slopes. The decision in some sense had to be arbitrary. Whatever line was chosen, there would be different tradeoffs with the market, however defined, and with the dispersion of classes around the line. As the Task Force chair said, "There's so much dispersion around any line, that no matter what we choose, there's going to be a significant number of people above the line." And some of these would be women.

A possible solution, admittedly ad hoc, was proposed by the consultant and supported by the Task Force majority. This line was defined as:

Wages per month = $1,000 + $3.00 × Hay points

The resulting line was close to the actual male pay for jobs below 250 points; from 250 to 500 points it approximated the total average pay; above 500 points it exceeded male practice (see

Figure 4.2). This line appealed to Task Force feminists for a number of reasons. First, it was a single line. Second, it raised the target line at the bottom above the level of male practice, assuring that gender inequity would be erased for the workers in female-dominated classes while minimizing the number of blue-collar male jobs that would be above the line. A final advantage, pointed out by the consultant, was that it was administratively simple, a jewel.

Task Force feminists objected to using the same line for jobs over 500 points on the grounds that increasing the wages of higher-level managers was not the mandate of the Task Force. Therefore, a separate line, closer to male practice, was calculated. This line started at 600 Hay points, rather than 500 which had been the breaking point in data analysis, to make sure that all professional jobs were covered by the first line which had a steeper slope. The equations for the recommended paylines were:

$$0\text{--}600 \text{ points} = \$1,000 + \$3.00 \times \text{Hay points}$$
$$600+ \text{ points} = \$1,450 + \$2.25 \times \text{Hay points}$$

In sum, the location of the payline was guided by more than concerns about raising women's low wages through choosing a target standard free of sex bias. Also entering a rather complicated calculus were consideration of male worker interests, budgetary constraints, the employer's needs to recruit workers, and commitment to a single pay policy. The majority in the Task Force was satisfied with the chosen line. It would maximize salary increases for the lowest paid, mostly women, and deal fairly with both professional and managerial levels, so we thought. Nothing in the resolution of the payline issue indicated problems for women workers or blue-collar men. This appeared to be a reasonable line that would solve the main equity problems.

Dilemmas encountered in selecting a trend line as a standard for equity show how profoundly political is this seemingly very technical question. These dilemmas also reflect the structure of practices and interests that perpetuate low-wage jobs for women. The weight of past practice creates a salary structure that is an accretion of actions and events enacting power differences. Male blue-collar workers have had more organizational power than female service and clerical workers. Professionals have made successful claims to expertise and status that justify higher wages. State budgets are calculated with assumptions about the low wages of large proportions of the female work force. Legislators, accountable to constituencies indifferent to women's low wages, have tried to keep wage costs down and to maintain public salaries at levels below the private market. Implicit questions likely to come from all these sources were part of the deliberations on the payline. The Task Force tried to choose a line that would allow answers to these implicit questions, and thus, a line that could support the legitimacy of the project. This had to be a line that did not too outrageously threaten any of these interests, all manifestations of the underlying class and gender processes.

Implementation Issues

The new salary plan was based on the decisions about a single pay policy and the wage policy line. Also affecting the plan were a series of implementation issues that further elaborated the conflicts between labor unions, between management and labor, and among feminists, labor, and management. Implementation issues were under consideration throughout the project, but were fully faced and voted on in the fall of 1984.

Timing. This was one of the first issues. Should the Task Force try to achieve pay equity all at one time, or should it plan a phase-in over a number of biennia? Although almost all other comparable worth efforts, as in Minnesota or San Jose, had taken place in phases, sentiment favoring an all-at-once approach developed early in Oregon and was reinforced when the governor budgeted $25 million for equity increases. The reasoning behind this approach was both technical and political. A new classification and wage plan could not be easily phased in without creating new, even if only temporary, inequities. For example, if new clerical classes were implemented first, some clerical workers would have higher pay than nonclerical workers in jobs with similar scores. Politically, such new inequities might help to mobilize groups of workers against the plan. In addition, the reasoning went, the political momentum was there and might disappear. Future legislatures were unknown quantities; it was best to complete as much as possible as soon as possible. The decision to attempt a one-time implementation meant simultaneous change in many different parts of the state's compensation and classification systems. An all-at-once approach also became an essential element in arguments over how to implement: through collective bargaining or through legislation.

Legislative Action versus Collective Bargaining. This issue had plagued the project from the start. As concrete decisions for a true comparable worth plan were made in the fall of 1984, dissension became more acute. Decisions to have one pay policy for the state, and to try to implement an entirely new classification and compensation plan at one time, led to the conclusion that legislative intervention was essential. But the arguments for collective bargaining were strong. As one consultant said, "There is no way to say that we will have total comparable worth and we will still have free and independent bargaining. Somewhere along the line, everyone has to say how much we are willing to give up and how much are we willing to give in to allow this to take place" (Task Force meeting, Nov. 15, 1984). Major controversies over giving up and giving in formed around whether implementation of a new wage system should be through legislative fiat or collective bargaining.

The two approaches had different implications for the degree of detail in the Task Force proposal. If the legislature were to enact a new wage plan, the Task Force and the Personnel Division would develop a total plan, linking the new classification structure and the wage structure, and specifying proposed new wages. Legislative implementation would require that the legislature pass a law accepting the Task Force proposals as the state's new compensation and classification plan. Funds to implement, or a pay equity pot, would be included in the bill. The bill would also contain procedures for administrative implementation and a specification of dates for steps in implementation. Legislative implementation of wage rates recommended by the Task Force would require a temporary suspension of collective bargaining.

Implementation through collective bargaining would also require legislative action and an equity pot. But in this alternative, the Legislature would direct management and unions to bargain the new wage rates, distributing the equity pot to bargaining units based on the amount of undervaluation for each unit as determined in the comparable worth study. Bargaining could proceed without constraints—unions and management could bargain the new wages as they wished, limited only by the amounts in the equity fund and in the pre-existing budget. Alternatively, some restraints could be placed on the bargaining parties. The suggestion most discussed was the idea of band bargaining. The Task Force could specify a band around the payline, fifteen percent on either side, for example. Bargained wages would then have to be within that band.

The Task Force did not seriously consider the pay-band proposal for several reasons. Some feminist members were uneasy about leaving equity raises in what they viewed as the untrustworthy hands of male trade unionists. As one said, "The problem had been in the collective bargaining process that the male-dominated units have more clout in that process. So, how do you prevent them from compensating those units at different levels?" Other considerations have already been discussed. The state's largest union, the Oregon Public Employees Union, did not want to bargain the new wage rates. Management, too, in its interest in rationalizing its relations with unions, did not want to have to bargain hundreds of new wage ranges. Finally, the commitment to a single pay plan also ruled out band bargaining as the approach to establishing the new ranges. Nine unions, even if constrained by the limits of a band, could very well bargain many different pay plans.

Although these arguments might have settled the question, serious splits around this issue became more evident as the project progressed. The disagreements had existed from the beginning. Unions took different positions, feminists disagreed, and only management seemed to have a unified stance. Although the Task Force chairperson made strenuous efforts to get agreement, in both formal and informal meetings, these were unsuccessful. The method of implementation was at the core of the recommendations to the legislature, so that the inability to develop an approach backed by everyone was a major fault in the process, a fault that finally contributed heavily to the failure to implement true comparable worth.

The Oregon Public Employees Union favored legislative implementation, accepting a temporary suspension of collective bargaining to achieve it. Initially, many of the smaller unions were inclined to go along with this solution, consistent with their usual pattern of following the across-the-board salary increases negotiated by OPEU. One reason for supporting legislative adoption of a detailed set of wage recommendations was that the union felt it did not have the money or the staff resources to bargain individually for several hundred job classes. As one union staff person said, "If the report does not say anything about how the wages of the new classifications are to be set and it all goes to the table, the system would sink of its own weight overnight." In meetings and informal discussions there were hints that behind this difficulty was fear of the consequences of bargaining an entirely new wage system. The male leadership of the union seemed to be worried that male members in skilled categories would not support proportionately larger raises for women workers. If the legislature made that decision, the union would not have to accept direct responsibility, but if women's special raises were negotiated, the plumbers or electricians, for example, who might feel ill-treated in contrast, would blame the union. Since unions frequently attempted to raid other unions, such dissatisfaction could easily lead to defection. There were even indications that some of top OPEU leadership felt that the union itself would be destroyed if they were forced to bargain a new system in which some of the previously advantaged would be sure to see an erosion of some of their relative advantage.

The American Federation of State, County, and Municipal Employees (AFSCME) was just as adamantly opposed to legislative implementation. AFSCME, with a strong record of using both bargaining and litigation to achieve comparable worth— they were the dominant union in the states of Washington and Minnesota and in the city of San Jose—stood resolutely for implementation of wages through collective bargaining. AFSCME leadership seemed to think that members would be more accepting of adjustments in their relative wages if those adjustments were bargained by their union. AFSCME also represented workers in far fewer job classifications than did OPEU. But most important was that any interference in collective bargaining, no matter how temporary, was an attack on labor's right to representation in AFSCME's view. A particular union should be able to bargain higher wages than other unions for the same jobs, and to work out a fair distribution of the increases in a detailed way for their own members. They should be able to use arguments based on the market, if that were appropriate. Above all, unions should not be bound to a strictly determined set of wage rates that would prevent them from bargaining as they wished. Testifying before the Task Force, an AFSCME official expressed concern that some of their women members had higher salaries than women in other unions in the same jobs. AFSCME did not want these members to be adversely affected.

Task Force plans for a legislative intervention were flatly unacceptable to AFSCME. Such a procedure would leave wage setting to someone not under workers' control. Another problem was the proposed way of facilitating legislative intervention. In order to intervene in collective bargaining, the comparable worth implementation bill would declare that nothing in the bill was an unfair labor practice, suspending for the initial implementation the appeal to binding arbitration. Although the bill provided another appeal process, this was not acceptable to AFSCME.

In the eyes of AFSCME, the Task Force was coming close to attacking collective bargaining, rather than sex discrimination. Testifying on that union's position on implementation, a union representative said, "This is a very interesting discussion. You are shifting the battleground from whether you want to eliminate sex discrimination to whether you want to eliminate collective bargaining. That battle would go on in the legislature and realistically, that would shift your friends to the other side of the issue, because any union that has collective bargaining would be out there to protect it. You cannot presume that unions are not your friends when you are talking about eliminating discrimination. And you don't want to force us into taking the adversary position, which is what you are talking about doing. My union has pretty good experience in combining those two, being able to bargain over comparable worth and not having to eliminate collective bargaining. We say, why don't we continue to bargain. There must be a way to come up with a solution. But it will be a continuing problem. I suspect that you are going to come to the conclusion soon that you'd like to adjust things now and you'd like it to stay perfect forever, but maybe it won't. You need to give us the benefit of the doubt too. Unions have been very successful. That's been part of the reason men have better wages. But men and women are members of unions. It doesn't mean that

we would continue to discriminate against women in the future"
(Task Force meeting, Nov. 14, 1984).

AFSCME thus was a resolute supporter of both comparable
worth and collective bargaining with an impressive record of pay
equity success in other states. Yet, there was some basis for the
apparent OPEU anxiety that AFSCME might gain a competitive
advantage and take away members if new wage rates had to be
bargained. AFSCME was aggressive and successful. While the
comparable worth project was going on, AFSCME was challeng-
ing the Teamsters for representation of workers at one of the big
state institutions. Subsequently AFSCME won an election for
union representation there. AFSCME had also been able to win
higher wages for some of its bargaining units than had OPEU.
For example, a few years earlier, bargaining at the AFSCME-
organized state penitentiary had broken down. State law prescribed that workers there could not strike and that unresolvable disputes would go to binding arbitration. Arbitration in this
case gave prison guards significantly higher increases than those
achieved by OPEU and the other smaller unions that year. Later
AFSCME was able to also get higher raises for secretaries working at the prison, putting them at higher rates than secretaries in
other state agencies. AFSCME had little to lose from standing
firm, even though it had not been so successful for all its members.

OPEU leaders might have been willing to bargain new
wages if they had been able to convince the other unions to come
together in coalition bargaining. Such bargaining would have
protected them against the possibility that workers would defect
to other unions that seemed to offer more success in wage negotiations. Early in the project, several unions had tentatively
agreed to coalition bargaining, but AFSCME never went along.
Management was pushing coalition bargaining and constantly
warning that comparable worth would not work without it. As the
project raced on, previous union support for coalition bargaining
declined. The issue was put succinctly by an OPEU staff person:
"You have a large union that represents a lot of classes, coalition
bargaining is fine. You have a small union that represents one
class and they want to bargain for more, force a strike or arbitration. Coalition bargaining is not going to make that union very
happy."

The rational feminist view was that a single pay policy could not even be projected, given the diversity of unions in the state, without some method of initially installing, as a whole, a comparable worth plan. The consultant supported this view on the grounds that with multiple bargaining units it was difficult to see how equity could be achieved without some initial implementation throughout the state. The fact that the largest union of state employees, OPEU, supported such a plan made it even more acceptable. A one-time intervention in collective bargaining seemed to be reasonable. Bargaining for 1985 wage increases would go on unchanged, followed by implementation of the equity pay structure. After implementation, collective bargaining would resume as before. However, the inability of unions to agree on initial implementation contributed to growing discomfort within the Task Force. Two management-oriented members were joined by one feminist in unwavering support of intervention in bargaining. Other members were increasingly torn—the only way such a massive system change could be implemented, they thought, was through such an intervention. On the other hand, there was probably trouble ahead because there was some validity in AFSCME objections. The Task Force chair was in a particularly difficult position. She publicly advocated the OPEU position—she was their employee—but by the fall of 1984 she was becoming privately more and more convinced that AFSCME was right. Another Task Force member, the feminist senator, had definitely taken a position for implementation through collective bargaining and she voted against the Task Force decision to propose a temporary suspension of bargaining. Thus, before the final report had been written, Task Force feminists split over a class issue, the degree to which collective bargaining should be held inviolate.

Redlining. Redlining was a red flag to most unions. Redlining, also called red circling, is the policy of freezing wages, or denying wage increases for some period of time. To achieve equity, the wages of current male employees might be frozen until female wages caught up. Redlining, by Oregon law, is used on jobs with wages that are above the wage range for that particular job. This is particularly likely to happen if the whole pay and classification system is changed. For example, if the top pay for an electrician is $2,000 per month and management determines, perhaps using evaluated points, that the top pay really ought to be $1,800 per month, workers earning $2,000 would be redlined, would get no increases, until across-the-board increases had raised the maximum electrician wage to $2,000 again. Redlining is preferable to an absolute cut in pay, but workers and unions don't like it. Moreover, redlining tends to create a two-tier wage structure; new employees start at the new lower wage so that workers on the same job may be paid different rates. A union that acquiesces in different pay for the same job may have internal problems with its members.

Consequently, redlining was another implementation issue; what to do with the wages of workers who earned more than the new wage plan specified. The Task Force had tried to minimize the problem through the choice of a line close to male actual pay. However, a line is only a central tendency, and there would be employees above any line except one defined by the very highest wages. People with different positions on this issue used different terminology. For Personnel and some management Task Force members, these people were overpaid. For those with allegiance to organized labor, they were out of range. The Personnel Division's preferred solution was to lower the wages that were overpaid, and personnel staff had argued that "if employees are told that wages won't be cut, people will have false expectations."

Most Task Force members were against reducing wages, but supported freezing those above the line until the new wage structure caught up to their salaries. This was reasonable, for wage equity could never be achieved if the higher paid continued to get proportional increases that equalled those going to the lower paid. However, unions objected to redlining. In the interests of union support, and fairness to the male workers whose wages were not high even though they earned more than many women, the Task Force recommended modification of the state's redlining law to allow all workers with wages above the new salary ranges to receive one-half of any general salary raises.

This solution was not acceptable to at least one management representative on the Task Force who favored wage reduction and, at the very least, total redlining. One feminist also took this position. She had, she said, no sympathy for people with wages over the line who, it seemed to her, had been overpaid for a long time. She argued that if they continued to get one-half of general increases, the state would continue to be vulnerable to sex discrimination charges. According to her, the only way to save the state was to be hard-nosed, draw a line, and let people catch up. The support for partial redlining came from other management people and other feminists on the Task Force. The feminist position was breaking up, but management, also, had a variety of perspectives.

The redlining issue had an ironic twist. The issue would not have arisen if true comparable worth had not been the goal. The strong argument underlying the pure approach was that all wages should be related to points. One reason for using that argument lay in the strategy for getting male support for comparable worth by raising all "underpaid" jobs regardless of the reason for underpayment. But if the general argument for payment by points is made, it applies just as well to wages over the line as under the line, leading to the charge that some jobs are overpaid. Thus, a strategy for legitimizing the project with certain groups of male workers undermined its legitimacy with other groups.

Maintenance Issues

How to keep pay equity from eroding after once established was related to implementation questions. The large number of unions bargaining with the state made some erosion inevitable. The issue was how to maintain some integrity of the system after the work of the Task Force was over. One feminist was in favor of legislation to hold unions liable for sex discrimination if they did not bargain equally well for women and men, saying, "I fail to see what rationale there is, other than impinging on a perogative, for saying that unions should be able to bargain however they want, disrupting the comparable worth system." The most extreme proposal for controlling the possible propensity of unions to recreate old inequities through bargaining up the wages of their male members was to force unions into coalition bargaining and not allow any bargaining for individual job classifications. A less constraining version of this would be to establish a bargaining band, as described above, and hope that over time, a more or less equitable pay practice would emerge. The difficulty with this approach was in determining how the level of the band would be established. If it were not done through coalition bargaining, inequities would reappear quickly. The opposition to coalition bargaining made this almost certain.

One proposed restriction on bargaining would help to assure maintenance of wage equity in the future. Parties in collective bargaining, arbitration, and administrative decision-making were to be bound by legal language requiring that the primary consideration in setting salaries for state employees shall be the comparability of the value of the work. But unions objected to the wording "*the* primary consideration" on the grounds that down-the-line management could refer back to the law and, because they controlled job evaluation, take over wage determination totally. Moreover, requiring comparability as *the* primary consideration would reduce the possibility of introducing market and recruiting differentials into the bargaining process. This would put particular burdens on unions bargaining for only one occupation. The Task Force, convinced by the arguments and wishing to be responsive to organized labor, voted to change "the" to "a". The Personnel Director's reaction suggested that such wording might have figured in Executive Department plans for the future. She was furious: "Don't bother me with this stupid system of job evaluation unless you're going to live with it," was her comment (Task Force meeting, Feb. 13, 1985). This was only one indication that she favored as many controls as possible to keep evaluated points as the basis of wages.

Other maintenance issues also had implications for bureaucratic power, labor management relations, and pay equity. These dealt with appeals of classification decisions, allowable deviations from the wage policy, and the authority to allocate positions to job classes.

Appeals of classification decisions were to go to the Employment Relations Board, an already existing agency, with final appeal to the state Court of Appeals. Absent from this procedure was arbitration, an absence that brought objections from unions with the right to arbitration of certain questions. The Task Force, intent upon developing methods of protecting pay equity, was of the opinion that arbitration by a number of different arbitrators would soon create out-of-line wages and undermine equity.

Allowable deviations from the wage plan were to be for recruitment difficulties and for bargained differentials, such as those for night shifts and difficult or dangerous working conditions. Such differentials might also be a way of diluting pay equity. Some managers on the Task Force wanted to be sure that market differentials would be reviewed regularly and removed if the recruitment difficulties had disappeared. Such problems were far in the future, and this issue, at least, raised no strong divisions.

The power to allocate positions to job classifications had to do with the power of agencies versus the power of the Executive Department and its Personnel Division. Previously, agencies allocated positions to job classes. In the creation of the new classification plan, The Personnel Division was taking over that task. Personnel wanted to retain this control after implementation, but to delegate it back to agencies whose personnel would be trained in job evaluation. Such central control was necessary, Personnel argued, if pay equity was to be maintained. Many agencies were not convinced; this move seemed to confirm fears that the central administration was trying to increase its power at the expense of state agencies.

The long-term maintenance plan finally worked out included the requirement that comparable worth be *a* consideration in wage setting and that the Personnel Division report progress to the Legislature every two years. With this maintenance plan the Task Force recognized that, in the future, the ideal of a single pay plan for the state of Oregon could not be attained. The reality was that there would be multiple pay plans in the future, with equity within bargaining units.

Task Force Recommendations: True Comparable Worth

Balancing all these conflicting pressures and still without a completed classification plan, the Task Force formulated a set of recommendations that approximated a true comparable worth plan. Implicit but necessary assumptions upon which the plan was built were that the forthcoming classification plan would be acceptable and that the $25 million in the governor's budget would be available. The plan included the Legislative and Judicial branches of state government as well as the Executive Division. Most of the money would go to women workers (see Table 4.7).

The Legislature was asked to adopt the classification and

Table 4.7
Recommended Pay Policy
Distribution of Annual Wage Increases in Millions of Dollars,
by Gender and Hay Points, State of Oregon, 1985

Hay Point Score	Women		Men		Total	
	N	*Amount*	*N*	*Amount*	*N*	*Amount*
0–250	6,619	$14.3	1,394	$ 2.4	8,013	$16.7
251–500	646	1.7	468	0.7	1,114	2.4
501+	62	0.2	123	0.7	185	0.9
Total	7,327	$16.2	1,985	$ 3.8	9,312	$20.0

Note: Pay Policy not implemented. For Executive Branch only, excluding other payroll costs, such as medical benefits, Social Security, etc.
Source: Final Report and Recommendations, Task Force on State Compensation and Classification Equity, 1985, p. 43, figure 20.

compensation plan contained in the Task Force report. The pay plan was built around the policy line with the fourth step of each range located on the line. Each wage range would contain six steps at 5 percent intervals. The first step of each range would be 15 percent below the line. There would be 30 wage ranges defined by an 11 percent difference in Hay points between the mid-points of the ranges (see Table 4.3). Employees with wages more than 15 percent below the pay line would move up to the first step of the new salary range. This meant that many employees would move from a higher step in their current range to the first step of their new range. For them, equity would be achieved only after a series of annual merit raises. The Task Force preferred a step-to-step plan that, for example, would have moved a worker at step six in her old salary range to step six in the new salary range. However, this would have cost far more than $25 million and there was no hope of getting any additional funds. A least-cost implementation seemed dictated by political necessity, one more technical choice with class/gender implications. In effect, some women workers would lose the benefits of seniority, finding themselves in the same salary step as new and inexperienced colleagues.

The Task Force recommended:

Pay Policy. ". . . that the State of Oregon should attempt to achieve a consistent relationship between compensation and evaluated worth within each branch of government and that comparable worth become a primary consideration in wage setting decisions."

Implementation. "A one-time intervention in collective bargaining in 1986 to implement comparable worth pay policy. Beginning in 1987 collective bargaining would be unaffected except that comparable worth would become a primary consideration in setting wage rates within each bargaining unit."

". . . that this pay plan be adopted on July 1, 1986, adjusted for the average cost-of-living wage increase received by state employes for the 1985–87 biennium."

". . . that wages of individual employes which are below the first step of the appropriate new salary range be increased to the first step."

". . . that current employes be partially exempt from the "red-circling" statute. The Task Force recommends that an employe with wages above the new salary range receive one-half of across-the-board wage increases bargained or granted to other employes."

". . . that the proposed classification system be reviewed by agencies and employes during 1985 and that it be reviewed and accepted by the Task Force and the Emergency Board before implementation on July 1, 1986."

Maintenance. ". . . that the evaluation system be kept current and that evaluation scores become a primary consideration in wage rates. Each Branch of state government would report to the Legislature each biennium on its progress on implementing and maintaining an equitable relationship between evaluated worth and wages. Exceptions to the pay plan would be allowed for market recruiting difficulties and other criteria not related to gender or race. Agencies would continue to be responsible for allocating positions to classes with Executive Department review. To provide flexibility the Task Force recommends that Legislative review of reclassifications is eliminated."

". . . that the dispute resolution process for classification grievances culminate at the Employment Relations Board so that decisions on point scores are made in a consistent manner."

(Task Force on State Compensation and Classification
Equity, Final Report, March, 1985)

The Task Force report presented alternatives to the proposals and spelled out the effects on collective bargaining. The report was delayed because of delays in the completion of the classification plan, and by the time it was released in March of 1985, the downfall of true comparable worth was well underway.

Discussion: The Politics of a Compensation and Classification System

Political conflicts with implications for class and gender were endemic in the technical processes of attempting to construct a new compensation and classification system. For example, technical work on the classification system was closely guarded management territory. Representatives of feminist and labor interests could get only limited access to it, but had to take some responsibility for the resulting structure. The technical work, which initially produced half as many job categories as had previously existed, had statistical consequences with political implications. With the reduction in the number of categories, the observed gender inequalities were reduced. This meant that the project resulted in a minimum estimate of wage inequity, but also that, for most middle-level female-dominated jobs, there was no measurable structural inequity. This, as we shall see, had grave political consequences for the project.

Another technical problem with political implications was the choice of the pay policy line. It seemed to some that the feminist point had been won when the Task Force decided to use the trend line calculated on wages in male-dominated jobs, the line without gender bias, as the standard for equity. However, the problem was more complicated than that because there may be many male trend lines, depending on which jobs are used in the calculation. If only one line is used, based on all male-dominated jobs, workers at different levels of the point hierarchy will be affected differently. For example, such a line would indicate that managers and professionals over 600 points are quite underpaid. In addition, how much dispersion exists around a line is an important political question if evaluated points are to be used in setting a wage system into place. There seemed to be no technical solution without political costs in terms of threats to the interests of one group or another.

In an adversarial situation, management and labor can openly fight over those costs. In the comparable worth project, however, some compromise had to be sought within the process, which was supposed to be a cooperative venture between feminists, unions, and management. As I have discussed above, this raises the complicated question, which is both theoretical and practical, about collaboration of adversarial groups on grounds controlled by only one of the groups. Conscious organization as an adversarial group begins to alter the bureaucratic power balance, but the control of bureaucratic processes remains within the bureaucracy. Outsiders who are placed, or place themselves, in a situation in which they have to take responsibility for the results of these processes, take many risks.

The controversy over implementation reveals contradictions of class and gender that are more complicated than management interests versus those of labor or men's interests versus those of women. This example can be examined within the broader theoretical questions of under what conditions the class situation of women and men produces divergent interests and whether, how, and when working class men, in pursuit of their own advantage, act to reinforce the subordination of women. The conflict over implementation is an instant in the interweaving of gender and class in the continuing reproduction of the wider social structure. In this case, interunion competition, even hostility between the male leaders of the strongest unions, contributed to a divisiveness that undercut the effort to raise women's wages. It was this, perhaps more than male workers protecting their own territory, that kept disagreement alive. However, the interests of male workers were also involved.

Leaders of both unions were sensitive to demands of male

workers, yet also willing to support measures to improve the relative situation of women workers. How to do that within the limited amount of money available and without undermining the male sense of status and male income was the question. Both unions intimated that male members were more vocal, pushing harder for increases than women. On the other hand, both unions on the national level were using comparable worth as a major organizing tool, and particularly AFSCME had considerable success. Within state employment in Oregon, both unions had a majority of women members, but, with the exception of a few women on union staffs and a few women activists, the voices of women workers were silent. In this silence, the unions' perceived need to protect themselves from the claims of injured male status were paramount. For AFSCME, the suspension of collective bargaining would make such protection impossible. AFSCME wanted the freedom to adjust relationships between jobs at the bargaining table, so as not to disadvantage any member. In adopting this strategy, AFSCME also avoided undercutting a basic right of organized labor in Oregon, the right to bargain wages with the state. Union leaders also had concerns about the status claims of women workers and wanted a free hand, for example, to try to raise a woman as well as a man more than any plan allowed. For OPEU, protection from the claims of male members was, in complete contrast, through the suspension of bargaining. OPEU top male leaders wanted to shrug off responsibility for any wage decisions that would sit badly with their male members. Oregon labor could not get together. AFSCME's stand maximized its competitive position in relation to other unions, an indication of a lack of working-class solidarity. However, OPEU policy can also be seen as framed to maintain its competitive edge. The resulting failure to achieve a united approach by labor created difficulties for the Oregon project and marginalized the interests of women workers.

If the state had had sufficient money to bring all workers' wages up to the AFSCME male level, there might have been no conflict. However, given the budget constraints, the limits to gains that low-paid women workers could expect were set by the unions' obligations to male members and union leaders' sense that they must tread carefully lest they be seen as favoring women at the relative expense of men. Gender differences operating within union structures tended to preserve the conditions of male advantage.

But the situation was contradictory for women workers. OPEU had committed substantial resources to the project, assigning its research director to almost full-time work as Chairperson of the Task Force and allocating considerable time of other staff to project work. Without this contribution, the project might not have been accomplished at all. Moreover, without strong unions that can bargain wages, women would have no possibility of guaranteeing the continuance of pay equity. The AFSCME position—strong on union autonomy and collective bargaining—may have been more in the interests of women workers than the OPEU position. However, AFSCME's refusal to entertain the possibility of coalition bargaining, and its insistence on the right to bargain outside the boundaries of any pay equity plan, indicated its commitment to its own members at the expense, possibly, of disadvantaged women belonging to other unions or to no union. Thus, there were some real, if potential, contradictions between a feminist strategy to try to achieve general wage increases for low-wage women within an employing organization and the AFSCME strategy.

Theoretical formulations in which patriarchal male workers and unions in league with capitalists produce the subordination of women in paid work are clearly too simple for this case. The interests of women workers were, at the same time, supported and undermined by actions of the trade unions, all male-dominated even though women constituted a majority of members of the larger unions. The wider structure of union competition and the varying problems of different unions within that structure were real. The absence of organized strength of women workers was also real.

Management, too, pursued its aims for a new classification system without regard to what this might mean for the pay equity goal, insisting on a maximum restructuring of job classifications. Women's interests were undermined in the statistical reduction of measured inequities and in the massive nature of the changes. In sum, imbedded in the technical processes were class- and gender-based conflicts detrimental to the interests of women workers.

Of most theoretical interest is that processes that on the

surface seem to have little to do with gender, such as technical decisions about how to construct a new job classification and compensation system and business-as-usual interunion competition, contributed to a complex process of maintaining women's low wages through marginalizing women's interests and creating barriers to the success of this change process.

CHAPTER FIVE

From True Comparable Worth to Poverty Relief

Traditional class politics—management versus labor—and bureaucratic wrangles, evident in early Task Force meetings and still troubling as the implementation plan was developed, emerged even more forcefully as the plan went to the 1985 legislature. The outcome was the destruction of "true" comparable worth. However, women active in the Oregon Public Employees Union and the legislature would not let comparable worth die. After a substitute plan failed, two more years of work led to a more politically pragmatic approach and a partial success. A shift from a focus on technical questions to a focus on political organizing marks the transition from failure to a beginning of pay equity.

In the process, true comparable worth was redefined, first as equity for the most undervalued and then as poverty relief. The pay plan passed in 1987 had little resemblance to the true comparable worth of 1985. In 1987, several thousand low-paid workers received wage increases as a result of a compromise that removed everything upsetting to either management or the unions from the comparable worth plan. The compromise, although alleviating poverty, left largely unfulfilled the goals of the women's movement for attaining equity based on the evaluation of the worth of jobs.

151

The Fall of True Comparable Worth

"True" comparable worth was the victim of class, status, and bureaucratic politics, but it may also have been a victim of its own limitations, its focus on a technical solution insensitive to the realities of those politics. The history of the fall calls into question the viability of true comparable worth as a policy approach to pay equity, while showing how the interests of low-wage women workers were marginalized as the contradictions of their positions within class politics became clear.

The conditions for failure were there from the start. Early project issues expressing conflicting interests and goals had not been resolved, although the Task Force had made many policy decisions. As the legislative process began its inexorable course in January, 1985, backstage worries and fights erupted as public issues. The legislative process began with the prefiling of a bill to implement the plan that was still in the process of completion. Next came hearings before the Senate Labor Committee. Then the bill would go to the House committee, to Ways and Means, and finally to the Senate and the House. The committee process had to be completed by the beginning of May and the legislation had to be passed by the end of June, the scheduled date of adjournment of the legislature. Thus, work on the Task Force comparable worth plan was still underway as the legislature began its deliberations. A complicated process can be captured by looking at the ways that earlier issues, discussed in Chapter 2 and Chapter 4, were played out. These were (1) the operational definition of comparable worth, (2) problems of control, scope, and timing of the project, (3) the relative emphasis on pay equity and classification, (4) the maintenance of legitimacy for the project, and (5) the problem of combining comparable worth and collective bargaining.

The Dynamics of the Fall of True Comparable Worth

The Operational Definition of Comparable Worth. The operational definition of true comparable worth as a comprehensive wage determination system with sex-neutral, unbiased job evaluation scores as central criteria for both wages and job classifications had been adopted early in the project. This was, perhaps, the most fateful decision because it implied certain other decisions regarding the project's scope and the necessity of intervention in collective bargaining, as I indicated in Chapter 4. Conflicts around these issues fragmented the feminist-labor coalition and undermined the legitimacy of pay equity. The definition of true comparable worth also meant a large project that could be done only with a full-time staff, and that staff belonged to management. Thus management had complete control of the technical work, allowing them to pursue the goals most important to them. The far-reaching implications of the definition of true comparable worth became completely clear only as the political process went forward.

Control, Scope, and Timing. Delay in the construction of the new classification system, and the Task Force's lack of knowledge about the exact status of the work, became an issue months before the legislature began to consider the plan. With the beginning of the legislative process, this delay became a primary obstacle to comparable worth (see Figure 1.1). The Task Force had planned a thorough review by management and workers of the new classification system prior to sending the plan to the legislature. However, that review never took place because of project delays.

In September, the Personnel Division anticipated the release of initial classification information to agencies in early November. In early November, the release date was December 15. By mid-November, December 15 had become an impossible deadline, but early January seemed feasible. In early January, an initial structure had been created and this was used for part of the statistical analysis. However, the material for agency review would not be ready until late January. Finally, on February 13, Personnel told the Task Force that the new class concepts would be sent out the following week and the review process would start. However, by that time Personnel had created only 716 job classes, contrary to the urging of Task Force members, who were convinced that broad classifications would not serve the interests of either women or unions. Personnel agreed to increase the number of job classes. No information had been sent out by February 25, and the first legislative hearing was to be on that day. Personnel thought that information for the first agency review would be ready by mid-March and that the full classification structure could be presented to the legislature, agencies, and employees by mid-April.

The reasons for this delay were rooted in the early, politically motivated, decision to do a complete classification study in one year. A year was not long enough to accomplish this complicated project. In addition, Personnel, in pursuit of its own goals as I have described earlier, created a process that completely tore apart the old classification structure and then had difficulties putting a new one together. All of this greatly increased the time required.

Delays in completing the classification plan slowed down the issuing of the final report. As a result, the legislative process could not go forward. A bill to implement the new plan had been prefiled in December. The legislature started its session at the beginning of January and legislative committees planned to finish their work by May 1. At the end of February, the delay became a crisis. There was no possibility of completing a first review of the classification plan before the middle of April, and the Task Force had not seen the plan they were recommending. By this time, the early management-labor/feminist conflict over project control had become so severe that cooperative work was exceedingly difficult. Suspicions escalated among Task Force members that the Personnel Division never would produce an acceptable plan.

Among the most skeptical was the feminist legislator who had initiated the original 1983 bill. Because of her concerns over the collective bargaining issue, she had as early as December 1984 started to formulate a substitute comparable worth bill that would implement pay equity through collective bargaining. Not only was she a member of the Task Force, she was also the chairperson of the Senate Labor Committee to which the comparable worth bill was assigned. She began hearings on comparable worth on February 25, in the absence of a report and a completed plan. Earlier she had warned Personnel and the Task Force that she would see that a plan went through. "I want to tell you, everybody in this room, that we're going to make sure an appropriation bill goes through this session and it's going to be worked out somehow this session if they have to do it on the old classes because I am totally outraged if I'm being told that we have to put this whole thing off into some indefinite future. That was my big reservation in the beginning. I simply will not tolerate that. That's not what all the energy was put in on this bill and the Task Force for, as far as I'm concerned" (Task Force minutes, Feb. 13, 1985).

Her determination was reinforced by reactions of Senate Labor Committee members who wanted to see the classification system. Comparable worth opponents were using the lack of information as grounds for opposition. Senators who favored comparable worth were under pressure from labor unions for release of the proposal. Labor-backed senators were also hearing from national unions about the plan, particularly its implications for bargaining. One senator started legal proceedings against the Personnel Division to force them to give classification information to AFSCME. There was no way to get the bill out of committee without public scrutiny of the new plan. "When you've got a log jam, you have to dynamite," the feminist senator said later. The senator forced the issue in the Task Force, which on March 14 made the decision to release, without review, all information, including job class titles, evaluated scores, salary ranges, and individual employees' placement in the structure. Recognizing that a plan to reclassify 32,000 jobs would have many errors, Task Force members knew that this move was supremely risky, but they saw it as inevitable given the political realities.

The feminist senator's decision to force the release can be interpreted as a move to kill both the classification plan and the Task Force implementation plan in order to facilitate a substitute bill more acceptable to labor and more likely to pass. An additional reason for this decision was that in the rapid march of legislative events, comparable worth money had not been protected, and all but $5 million of the budgeted $25 million had been allocated to other uses. This made a one-time implementation impossible, implying that intervention in collective bargaining might have to be repeated several times in a phased-in implementation. Although the senator might have, finally, accepted a one-time intervention, it was unacceptable if it were to be more than a one-time thing. As the senator said, "Personnel would get complete control over the system, assigning points, allocating jobs, etc. Maybe it wasn't the right decision, but something had to be done." Thus, in her view, the implementation approach had to be changed and the classification plan, now discredited by excessive delays and altercations over narrow versus broad classes, had to be scrapped. Struggles over project control, rooted in class antagonistic relations as well as union opposition to the means necessary to accomplish true comparable worth, had led to a political act to save pay equity through sacrificing "true" comparable worth.

The Relative Importance of Pay Equity and Classification.

Behind the problem of time, delays frustrating the determination to get some sort of bill through a short legislative session, lay the unresolved issue of the primary goal, pay equity or classification. Management wanted a new classification plan and, it was now clear, that would take longer than the time allotted to the project. Legislative supporters and some Task Force feminists wanted pay equity in 1985, not at some future time when management's new classification had been completed. Management control over the technical work, supported by Task Force belief that pay equity depended on classification, resulted in the displacement of the project goal from comparable worth to job classification, a danger one of the consultants had warned against in early project stages, discussed in greater detail in Chapter 4.

Some Task Force members knew this was happening. They began to ask whether it would be possible to decouple or take apart the classification and compensation parts of the plan, so that pay equity could be achieved before the completion of the revised classification scheme. Arguments against doing this were persuasive. First, unions and management still had an interest in both classification and pay. Classification as well as pay was contested terrain (Edwards, 1979; Crompton and Jones, 1984) for labor and management. Although the establishment of the classification system as a whole and the definition of duties and responsibilities of specific job classes and positions was a management prerogative, the assignment of wages to a class was bargained and other classification issues were permissible bargaining areas. Many union grievances had to do with classification problems. This is one reason that OPEU so strongly supported a new classification system. Since wages and status were tied to classifications, a rational and reasonable classification structure was essential for a wage structure that union members could see as legitimate. Consequently, aside from any consideration of pay equity for their lower-wage members, an understandable, just, and fair classification plan was important to some unions.

A second argument against decoupling was that it was very difficult because of previous technical decisions; to go back and make those decisions differently was impossible within any reasonable time limits. The critical technical decision, discussed in Chapter 4, was to regroup all positions and to evaluate these groups, which would then be recombined in new classes. The old classes, still in use, had no point-factor scores because of their extensive decomposition in the original questionnaire grouping process. Therefore, if old classes were the basis for equity raises, synthetic scores, constructed by averaging the scores of the positions in the old classes, would have to be assigned to them. These scores could represent averages of positions that differed widely in complexity and skill level; pay raises established on the basis of such scores would be difficult to defend. New inequities would almost certainly be created. Thus, decoupling would not create a reasonable, equitable, and legitimate pay system. As long as the possibility existed of achieving the single, equitable pay plan goal, the Task Force went along with Personnel's promises that a satisfactory classification plan would appear.

The displacement of the project goal was a consequence of the underlying class/gender conflicts of interest and the relative powerlessness of feminist and labor identified Task Force members. Management, as previously discussed, was most interested in classification. OPEU male leadership, in conflict with leaders of other unions, also focussed on a new classification system. Task Force members could not stop Personnel's determination to completely overhaul the classification system, nor could they get competing labor unions to coalesce around an alternate strategy. The result was the marginalization of women's interests.

Maintenance of Project Legitimacy. Legitimacy, a primary concern in many project decisions, was, in the main, an issue internal to the state as an employing organization. A scattering of conservatives testified against the bill and a small right-wing letter-writing campaign produced a few letters in opposition. However, the main constituencies in touch with politicians were state managers and workers and their unions and associations.

Suspicions aroused by delays in release of the comparable worth plan and the apparently extensive classification changes it would contain endangered the legitimacy of the project, contributing to the feminist senator's decision to force the premature release of the plan. Anxieties about the forthcoming new classification plan spread through the bureaucratic structure in late 1984, as Personnel began to discuss parts of it with agency managers. The creation of the new system centralized, at least on a one-time basis, a primary part of the personnel function. The Personnel Division was not only creating new classes, but allocating positions to those classes. Allocation, as noted above, had previously been located in the agencies and their personnel departments. As Kanter (1977) notes, territoriality is an organizational issue, particularly for relatively powerless departments with staff functions, such as personnel. Oregon was no exception, and there were those in the agencies who feared that Personnel was out to grab as much control as possible.

There was some basis for the fear, for Personnel argued that it must have greater continuing control over the classification system if comparable worth were to be maintained. Its first-choice strategy, as outlined in a memo to the Task Force, was to locate all classification functions in its own hands, but it agreed to accept less control in a plan that would delegate its power to allocate to the agencies. Personnel was also intent on establishing many more job classes that cut across agency boundaries, reducing significantly the perhaps two-thirds of all job classes that were specific to particular agencies. This move would increase the Personnel Division's control over the personnel function generally because job classes that cut across agency boundaries would have to be centrally monitored to see that there was consistency in the positions and tasks included in the categories. Some organizational power was vested in allocation of positions to job classes because allocations could affect relative status and wages of employees. Control over their own personnel functions was important to individual agencies. Consequently, out in the periphery of state agencies there was a wait and see attitude toward these maneuvers.

Among individual workers anxiety was widespread. Rumors circulated that the plan would result in demotions, even dismissals. Workers were concerned about security and level of pay, but also about relative pay and status. Such status concerns are, perhaps, integral to any finely graded hierarchy, such as the state of Oregon. Sociologists (for example, Thompson, 1983:173) argue that position in the organizational hierarchy becomes a badge of self-esteem, compensating for actual powerlessness and obscuring the class realities of the workplace. Individual success through promotion may provide small increments in pay but also symbolically larger increments of respect. Thus, feared reductions in pay may have serious status implications. One of the categories determined to resist any assault on their relative pay, the gossip networks indicated, were recently promoted women managers.

Blue-collar men were another category who were suspicious. Considerable research now exists suggesting that masculinity may be threatened by processes of deskilling male-defined jobs (Phillips and Taylor, 1986; Cockburn, 1983) because to become deskilled is to become feminized. Similarly, job evaluation that finds that male jobs are really not more valuable than female jobs may imply an attack on masculinity. And an attack on masculinity is an attack on fundamental status. Thus, internal stratification along lines of gender as well as occupation created interests that might be jeopardized by any change, and this could undermine project legitimacy.

The release of the Personnel Division plan confirmed the worst fears of the Task Force, agency managers, state employees, and their union leaders. The problems were detailed in letters, memos, telephone calls, and conversations. The agency review of the structure had been eliminated with the early release of all information, but the review procedure allowing for appeals from individual employees was still in place and such appeals began to arrive.

Employees at different levels and in various agencies looked at their own positions in the new plan and saw what they interpreted as callous assaults on their dignity and their status. Although almost 10,000 workers were to receive pay increases, 3,962 employees had salaries more than 5 percent above the new ranges, making them subject to partial redlining (Table 5.1). They would suffer no actual cut in wages, but their wages would rise more slowly than those of others until they were again within range. The significance of a lower salary range was in its implica-

Table 5.1
Number of Employees More than 5 Percent Above Proposed New Salary Ranges By Gender and Hay Points (Executive Branch only), State of Oregon, 1985

Hay Points	*Women*	*Men*	*Total*
0–250	918	1,747	2,665
251–500	257	973	1,230
501+	4	63	67
Total	1,179	2,783	3,962

Source: Final Report and Recommendations, Task Force on State Compensation and Classification Equity, 1985, p. 43, figure 20.

tions about the relative value of the person and the work. The most concerned were professionals and technical workers in the 250 to 500 Hay point range. As Larson has observed in discussing professionalization, "Income and other indicators of status are important not only in themselves but also in comparison to the status indicators possessed by other social groups and individuals" (1977:157). Mere inclusion of one's job in the comparable worth study had been perceived as a status threat to some professional workers who compared themselves with others not included in the study. For example, university middle-level administrators without academic rank objected to inclusion in the study, obviously comparing themselves with faculty who were not included.

Another aggrieved group were psychiatric social workers at the state mental hospital whose relative status was in jeopardy as a consequence of study results. This job was not a benchmark job, and the evaluation was probably one of the errors that could be expected and that would be rectified in a review of the system. I use it here only as an example of reactions to a plan full of problems and not yet ready for release. As members of treatment teams, psychiatric social workers worked as colleagues with psychologists and psychiatrists. Their jobs, they pointed out, required professional graduate degrees and supervised clinical training. Currently they were earning less than nurses with bachelors degrees. In their view, their work should have been compared with that of psychologists and psychiatrists, not with other social workers. However, psychiatrists were not even in the study, which had exempted all doctors. Instead of recognizing the clinical social workers' skills and upgrading their classification, the study results proposed placing them in a new broad classification of social workers and counselors. This was tantamount to declassing.

Another affected group were pharmacists, who had been allocated to a lower pay range than they currently occupied, although, as their testimony showed, they were already earning less than other pharmacists in the area. This was an example of an inevitable problem when wages are to be set on the basis of internal equity: there is always potential conflict between internal and external equity. Some male blue-collar workers were also upset; they were the largest category with present wages more than 5 percent above the new ranges, and thus accounted for the largest group who would be redlined. Equally upset were some supervisors who found that they would be hardly making more than the people they supervised.

Thus the pay line contributed to the failure of legitimacy and the downfall of the true comparable worth plan. Even though it was very close to the male line, the chosen payline was under market wages for many professional jobs in the range between 250 and 600 points. The plan failed to raise their wages and, in some cases, their wages would even be frozen for a period of time. In addition, the reduction of the number of job classifications, discussed in Chapter 4, involved the combination of previously female-dominated classifications with mixed or male-dominated classifications, obscuring some gender-based inequities. All of this alienated many middle-level employees from the plan. The legitimacy of the project was shaky, and anything that further shook it, such as a trend line that failed to raise wages for workers who thought they deserved a raise, was dangerous for the whole project.

Although these anomalies caused serious morale problems, some were simply mistakes, and others could be corrected by taking market differentials into consideration. More serious were pervasive structural problems in the proposed system. These structural problems also produced status indignities, leading administrators in one agency to call the plan "unworkable, demoralizing, insulting" (Task Force minutes, March 27, 1987). Administrators' criticisms were that the plan failed to reflect professional and technical capabilities, making recruitment and retention difficult and putting limits on career prospects. The Task Force member who headed one of the state's largest agencies took the lead in criticizing the classification plan. "Some of the strongest reactions I have received are from women in those areas who have changed from traditional jobs to nontraditional jobs and now see some limits on their careers," he said.

The plan fragmented functional job hierarchies and destroyed long-standing career ladders. The engineering series was the most serious example. Highway Engineer 1 was split into 20 new classifications with eight proposed pay ranges, raising some salaries and lowering others for a group that had been in the same salary range. Highway Engineer 3 was distributed into 22 new classes. There may have been such diversity in the work of highway engineers, but dividing them in this way fractured their work solidarity and, in their view, undermined their career prospects. On the other hand, some long-existing job hierarchies had been collapsed into one class. This also distorted expected career progression.

Some formerly broad classes had been minutely subdivided. For example, clerical workers had been put into 10 new classes in an Administrative Specialist series. These classes were so general that they could not be easily distinguished one from another. In some cases, as a Teamsters staff person pointed out, secretaries who had been working together and were in the same job class doing the same things had been distributed throughout five or six Administrative Specialist levels. This could also have been an error, easily corrected. Although many clerical workers would get raises, they found it difficult to see how and why they had been assigned to one class rather than another, and how the value of their work had been determined. While happy about their pay, they were mystified and skeptical.

In sum, support for the project was severely undermined by the problems with the proposed classification plan, which was perceived by many workers as an attack on their status, although the changes in no way altered the fundamental hierarchy. The rush of legislative events allowed no time for review and correction. Animosities based on both class and gender interests between some of the primary participants had grown so strong that there was little sentiment in favor of seeking delaying legislation that would allow the plan to be revised. Technical errors, in this context of conflict and time and money pressures, undermined legitimacy with severe consequences for the interests of women workers.

Collective Bargaining versus True Comparable Worth. The continuing disagreement over whether the plan for true comparable worth would undermine collective bargaining had never been resolved. This conflict also contributed to the abandonment of the plan. By the time the legislative session began, among the unions, only the Oregon Public Employees Union was supporting true comparable worth. Intervention in collective bargaining and partial redlining, discussed in Chapter 4, were the main grounds for union distrust of the plan. However, there were other issues.

Although the Oregon Public Employees Union had a stake in a new classification scheme, this was not equally true for all unions. Some unions were anxious about what the new plan portended because a completely new classification system might be a wedge to force the unions into coalition bargaining, which might, over time, reduce the power of certain unions. The reasoning on this point requires some amplification, for one could argue as well that unions would enhance their power through coalition bargaining. This was probably true for the Oregon Public Employees Union, which was already a coalition of many different types of workers. But smaller unions, if swallowed up in a coalition, would have less power to work for the interests of their own members, particularly if the only wage issues they could bargain were across-the-board increases. Thus, coalition bargaining could weaken the claim to members that their particular union could get the most for them, opening the possibility of raiding by other unions. Competition between unions for members, part of the reality of this situation, made coalition bargaining risky for some unions and their members. At the same time, in statements in Task Force meetings and in legislative hearings, representatives of the Executive Department provided ample evidence of their intention to force coalition bargaining if at all possible. For them, coalition bargaining was essential to implement a new classification scheme, and a way to gain more control over the wage system.

The cohesion of the Task Force around the plan for true comparable worth was badly shaken by collective bargaining issues long before the classification proposal was revealed as inadequate. The feminist senator publicly, and the Task Force chairperson privately, opposed the suspension of collective bargaining in the initial implementation of the plan. AFSCME, as discussed in Chapter 4, energetically opposed such intervention in bargaining. Some union representatives saw any limitations on bargaining for the purpose of maintaining pay equity as anti-union. National AFSCME staff testified before the Oregon legislature in favor of comparable worth, but against implementation through any restraints on bargaining. Rumors suggested that the state AFL-CIO was worried, and that the Service Employees International Union, to which OPEU was affiliated, was asking urgent questions about what was going on in Oregon. In addition, pressures on OPEU were building internally as members became anxious about the plan. Support for the Task Force plan within the OPEU now came only from its top executive, a man who was the prime advocate of intervention in collective bargaining. Losing support among his staff and members, he resigned on the day after the classification system was released. With his departure, OPEU and the Task Force chair withdrew support for the Task Force plan. With the loss of this support, true comparable worth was dead.

True Comparable Worth Abandoned

The Task Force, meeting immediately after the release of the plan and the resignation of the union leader, considered what to do. The structural problems seemed so severe that "fine tuning," the term usually used for the projected employee-by-employee review process, would not fix the system. One Task Force member summed it up: "I wonder why do we have a personnel system to begin with? Obviously, it's to make our agencies work better, serve the public better. This doesn't help me get there. I step back and wonder how the Task Force was created. There was a focus on gender-based inequities. This seems to be all aside from that and drawing attention from that.

I'm not sure what that fix is going to be. I'm concerned that the review process is weighing us down. I don't think that what's going to come out is something we can live with" (Task Force minutes, March 27, 1985).

With no support from any union for the Task Force implementation plan and faced with a classification plan that could not be implemented, the Task Force decided to stop the individual review process and modify its proposals along the lines it had recently rejected. Instead of a comprehensive comparable worth plan, they decided to (1) decouple compensation and classification, (2) use the job evaluation data to identify individual workers with the largest wage inequities, (3) propose that the remaining $5 million for comparable worth in the state budget be used to begin to rectify those inequities. Thus, "true" comparable worth was abandoned as a feasible goal. Some continued to see it as desirable, but for others it was no longer even a desirable goal.

After the Fall

The decision to separate classification and compensation in the proposal marked the final collapse of the coalition between, on the one side, the governor's office and his Personnel Division, and on the other, OPEU and feminists. Interunion conflict ended and a new coalition of feminists and labor rallied around an amended bill introduced by the feminist senator. With no functions left, the Task Force stopped meeting.

The amended bill followed the Task Force substitute plan to separate classification and compensation and to provide equity adjustments based on calculations for existing job classes using weighted average point scores from the Task Force study. Comparable worth was now implicitly defined as pay equity for the most undervalued, rather than a new equitable wage system. The bill stated that the first priority shall be "equity for the most undervalued classes in the lowest salary ranges," and $5 million were provided to begin equity adjustments for the most undervalued jobs in the lowest salary ranges. Management and the unions would have to agree before money could be distributed. The process would be supervised by a legislative committee. Finally, the bill provided $500,000 for the completion of the classification plan by the Personnel Division.

This amended bill drew much support. Women's groups, state workers, and union representatives spoke in its favor. At the same time, the governor's office and his Personnel Division were opposed to the new bill. Conflict between labor and management became even more open. State Executive Department representatives testified that pay equity could not work without coalition bargaining. But coalition bargaining was still rejected by all labor unions. Efforts to forge a compromise to avoid a veto by the governor were unsuccessful. Now the governor's office wanted wage freezes and downward classification of jobs in return for support for a bill. These demands were unacceptable to labor. Nevertheless, comparable worth maintained its support in the legislature. Women lawmakers, in particular, were determined to pass the compromise bill. The state Senate passed it with a two-thirds majority. When it was stalled in the House, many Senate Republicans, breaking with the governor, lobbied their House colleagues to put the bill to a vote. On the last day of the legislature, this amended bill was passed by the state House of Representatives. The governor, true to his word, vetoed the bill.

The governor's veto message clearly outlined the goals of the state executive department in their support for comparable worth. The reasons for the veto were: The review procedures specified in the bill would delay the creation of a new classification system; the Executive Department of the state was not given adequate control over the continuing development of a compensation and classification plan; the bill forbade any wage freezes or downward classifications of positions and this "would have ruinous consequences for the personnel classification system" (Atiyeh, July 15, 1985: 2); and the bill set up a system in which both job evaluation and collective bargaining are used in setting wages and this fails "to come to grips with the conflict between collective bargaining concepts and the declared public policy of Senate Bill 484 (1983) that rates of pay should be set according to a system of comparable worth job classification" (Atiyeh, p. 3).

In sum, when Executive got neither its classification plan nor its controls on collective bargaining from the legislature, the governor vetoed the comparable worth bill. Thus, a class issue, the fundamental ground rules for the collective bargaining of wages, was fought out in the political battle over comparable worth. Neither management nor the unions would give way and comparable worth was lost in 1985.

Summary: Gender and Class in the Fall of True Comparable
Worth

Oregon's true comparable worth plan could not gain political
support, and thus its downfall was assured. Two problems were
primary: First, the goal of a new classification system gained
precedence over pay equity and the resulting classification plan
had serious defects; second, true comparable worth included
implementation and maintenance procedures that organized labor perceived as contrary to its interests, but that management
welcomed. Conflicts over these issues divided one union from
another and one feminist from another, while management attempted to use the conflicts for its own advantage.

While for feminists and working women the primary goal
was pay equity, for the Executive Department and the male
leadership of OPEU a new classification system seemed to be in
first place. In the process of maintaining the coalition between
the state administration and the OPEU, the feminist goal of pay
equity was displaced by the goal of a new classification system,
which was to have been only a means to the end of comparable
worth. The achievement of pay equity became contingent upon
the implementation of new classifications.

However, the proposed classification plan had serious technical problems. Pay equity had been welded to a mammoth
system change that reverberated through every office, kitchen,
and workshop. Far too much was attempted within a limited time
frame. In addition, political pressures forced the too-early exposure of the plan. The underlying technical work of job evaluation was good, but the recombination of evaluated job groups into
job classes and the payline used to construct the new salary plan
left more people upset than satisfied. The change was perceived
as hasty and ill-considered. Too many saw the plan as threatening
their status and pay. The legitimacy of the project was destroyed
and support for the classification plan disappeared.

The goal of a new classification system, and its accompany-
ing true comparable-worth wage system, required implementation policies that ran counter to some goals of labor unions other
than the OPEU, and finally to some goals of that union as well.
The unions faced competing aims—achieving higher pay for
women, but defending other interests. The unions were supportive of pay equity so long as it did not threaten the relative

advantages of any members or threaten collective bargaining rights. However, true comparable worth implied both these threats because it allowed partial redlining or holding high wages constant, while low wages were being raised, and it provided for intervention in collective bargaining. In addition, the policy of establishing wages by job evaluation points opens the possibility that some jobs may be defined as "overvalued" and subject to wage reductions. Job evaluation as the primary tool in wage setting also reduces the centrality of collective bargaining in the wage process. Management support of measures to rationalize and extend its control over collective bargaining, using true comparable worth as a tool, increased labor's anxiety. Thus, even if the new classification plan had been perfect, organized labor might have opposed true comparable worth as formulated by the Oregon Task Force.

A difficult contradiction faced Task Force feminists and the women they intended to represent: The class interests and the gender interests of low-paid women workers appeared to be at odds with each other. Unity with men in the union on a class issue, to defend the right to bargain collectively, was important for the women. But unity with union men was linked to labor opposition to any redlining. At least partial redlining for a limited period of time seems essential to achieving equity, for if higher wages were never held constant, the wage gap would never be reduced. Opposition to all redlining implied such an outcome. The union opposition to redlining is an example of the ways in which the subordination of women's interests within a gender-divided class structure has meant that men's interests become identified as class interests. A different view of class interests might emerge if women were seen to represent the working class. For example, redlining in the interests of equity might be interpreted as essential to union solidarity and strength.

Class conflicts between unions and management were played out over the terms of comparable worth, pushing to the side the interests of low-paid women workers. Conflicts between unions that prevented a coalition around comparable worth goals also had the consequence of marginalizing women's interests, as did management's insistence on a complete classification system transformation even at the expense of pay equity. The perpetuation of the gender-based wage gap for state workers in Oregon was "caused" by these events and by the governor's veto of a substitute bill that met labor's objections to true comparable worth.

A More Pragmatic Pay Equity

Comparable worth did not die with the governor's veto. Instead, he issued an executive order directing the completion of the new classification plan, this time to be implemented in 1987, requesting money to continue the study and $5 million to begin pay equity[1] payments. Work on pay equity continued within a new configuration of actors. Some of the conflicts of the first attempt were dampened, but many of the old issues of class and gender emerged again. In a process of bargaining and compromise involving management, the Oregon Public Employees Union, and feminists in and out of the legislature, true comparable worth was redefined to mean a system for raising the wages of the undervalued rather than a pay system for all employees constructed on standards of equity. In this guise, comparable worth was enacted by the 1987 legislature and, after a strike and a settlement that further redefined pay equity as poverty relief, wage increases totaling over $22 million went to nearly 6,000 workers. The legislative process, involving informal bargaining over what the terms of the bill would be, and the labor-management negotiation process, involving formal bargaining over the implementation of pay equity, went on simultaneously, each process influencing the other.

A New Political Context for Comparable Worth

The primary participants in the new pay equity efforts worked in an altered arrangement of power that did not disturb business as usual as had the previous Task Force arrangement. Management and unions agreed that any wage changes would be bargained. Personnel also returned to its traditional methods of working with classification problems. At the same time, in this phase, there was more conventional political mobilization than there had been the first time around. Each of these differences probably contributed to an altered outcome.

New Power Relations, New Participants. The most strik-
ing organizational difference between the 1983–85 comparable
worth effort and the 1985–87 effort was that in the second phase
the original Task Force was gone. Hay Associates had finished
their consulting contract and they also were gone. Thus, there
were no longer extra-bureaucratic bodies carrying out a study of
administrative processes of the state. A new task force appointed
by the legislature's Emergency Board to evaluate the Executive
Department's request for funds, and to provide ongoing legislative oversight, had a very different function. Rather than directing a study, this task force, composed only of legislators, was to
set the broad guidelines and to approve any resulting plan or
proposal put forward by the Personnel Division, which was now
in control of all the technical work, unhampered by a feminist-
dominated Task Force that wanted to interfere at every step.

Management did not have complete control, for the co-
chairs of this new Task Force were experienced legislators who
favored comparable worth, as were other members, including
both the feminist senator who had initiated comparable worth
efforts in the state and a powerful labor-backed senator, who was a
leader of the Teamsters union and the man who had threatened to
sue Personnel on behalf of ASCME. These were seasoned fight-
ers who had just been through the emotionally charged and
distressing process that ended in the veto of the comparable
worth bill, and they were wary. They wanted oversight and some
guarantees. They were unwilling to let the governor's staff have
complete control over the still contested territory of job evaluation, classification, and wage setting. By October, 1985, the Task
Force and top management reached an agreement. The Executive Department would get approximately $500,000 to finish its
classification work, but would not receive the money until the
Task Force approved their work plan. There were other conditions: any pay equity funds available in the 1985–1987 period
would go to the most undervalued; a new system for the most
undervalued classes would be ready for implementation on July
1, 1987; an appeals process for new classifications should include
representatives of employees as well as management; unions
should be informed and allowed to comment on any proposed
changes; and the Task Force should oversee the entire ongoing
process of developing the new compensation and classification
plan.

The role of unions had also changed dramatically. The suspension of collective bargaining was no longer an issue; everybody expected that any changes in wages would be bargained. As a result, the idea that the state could have one wage system had also been abandoned. In the absence of these issues, a consensus between all the unions bargaining with the state was no longer necessary. The Oregon Public Employees Union, continuing its involvement with comparable worth, was now the only union working intensively on the issue. After the resignation of the OPEU director who had supported legislative intervention, a new director, a woman lawyer, was appointed. OPEU decided to make comparable worth its primary organizing focus, headed by the union's research director, the former chairperson of the original Task Force on State Compensation and Classification Equity. She, all agreed, knew more about comparable worth than anyone else in the state. She was an instrumental participant in every step of the work for the next two years, as she had been in the last two years, but now always in the role of union representative, who could comment on phases of the work and bargain over implementation, rather than as leader of a technical study.

The election in 1986 of a new Democratic governor also changed the political context for comparable worth. The governor had committed himself to pay equity in his campaign and had promised that money for pay equity would be in his new budget. He appointed as his chief executive officer the former head of the state's Department of Transportation and former member of the 1983–85 comparable worth Task Force. Energetic and articulate, the new governor came into office committed to reversing the state's miserable economic situation, and he appointed people like himself to help. The atmosphere in the capitol building had changed. As one observer of the scene said, "The world began with this administration. Everything is going to be different. History doesn't exist." The active, aggressive, and confident approach to getting things done was accompanied by an effort to remain free from hampering controls, such as legislative directives about how money could be spent. "Give us the money and we'll do right with it. Why do we have to have all these restrictions," seemed to be the sentiment of the new administration. Another aspect of the new approach was an emphasis on participatory management, bringing people from the agencies into the decision-making process, de-emphasizing control, encouraging and supporting innovation in the interests of better service. All of these changes had implications for the politics of comparable worth as they developed in the new legislative session beginning in January, 1987.

New (or Old) Technical Approaches. The new round of technical work began under the old administration in 1985. Although Personnel and OPEU disagreed about how quickly a new classification plan could be implemented, they were again in accord on the necessity of such a plan. The leading feminist protagonists, the research director of OPEU and the feminist senator, had given up the efforts to decouple compensation and classification, the rather desperate strategy they had pursued in the attempt to save pay equity from an unworkable classification and implementation plan at the end of the last legislative session. OPEU still wanted job classification reform, and they both believed that in the long run comparable worth had to be based on an accurate description and evaluation of women's jobs, and that meant a new classification system. Thus, in this new effort, comparable worth was still linked to a new classification system, in effect continuing the approach of the old Task Force, but without the insistence on a single pay policy for all agencies and with implementation through collective bargaining.

Personnel returned to its old approach to classification change, working much more slowly, agency by agency, in close cooperation with agency management. With a staff of 13 analysts, they started over again, focussing on undervalued series such as clerical and food service work. Using the data from the 1983–85 questionnaires, staff selected certain jobs to audit, interviewing workers and rewriting the classifications. The union had the role only of review and comment: "We put our nose into it when we could. Where we had activists, they tried to get audited. Or we worked with management at an agency level."

Although management was fully in control of technical work, now there was actually broader worker participation in rebuilding the classification structure as the union used already existing rights to review and comment as a way of involving their women members in the comparable worth process. "We worked really hard on the psychiatric aid series, the clerical series," said the union leader. "Some were quite easy, with specific duties.

You get into a lot more trouble when you try to restructure the general clerical series. And there were some controversial things, such as merging the groundskeepers and the laborers, that would be punitive to the groundskeepers." The union reviewed thousands of pages of job descriptions and allocation of positions to benchmark classifications. Active members were involved in the detail of the review at every step, reading and commenting. These comments went back to Personnel and, on the whole, union leadership was satisfied with the process and the results.

Personnel used the validated job descriptions as the basis for new job evaluations done by Personnel staff using the Hay method in which they had been trained during the first project. The old benchmark scores were still used as a guide for the overall structure. This way of working was slow, however, and a year later in the summer of 1986, it was clear to both the union and to the members of the Legislative Task Force that the complete new classification system would not be ready for implementation as a package in the summer of 1987, nor would it be ready as a whole to constitute the basis for a new comparable worth bill for the 1987 legislature.

To solve this problem, the Oregon Public Employees Union and the state Executive Department negotiated a more modest plan to implement some new classifications and provide wage increases to the most undervalued, defined as those 15 percent or more below the male payline as determined in the 1985 study and at salary range 19 or below; all the large female-dominated clerical jobs met these criteria. One hundred and ten of the most undervalued classifications would be in the plan along with related classes for a total of 280, covering about 17,000 workers statewide. Both sides agreed that related classes must be changed along with the undervalued. For example, if the secretary gets a new classification and a salary increase, the administrative assistant who is almost always the secretary's supervisor may also have to have a raise to maintain some salary difference that recognizes the greater responsibility of the administrative assistant job.

No serious disagreements arose over the technical work. Cooperation seems to have been a primary consideration in Personnel's work with agencies. The union was also satisfied with the plan. The number of classifications that would be implemented was small enough for the union to effectively bargain the wages. Moreover, as discussed above, some of the bases for union-management conflict had been removed by eliminating the ideas of legislative implementation and one pay plan for the entire state.

New Political Mobilization. Other things had changed since the 1985 legislative battle over comparable worth: There was new political mobilization, both in support and in opposition. The prime mover in the mobilization for pay equity was the Oregon Public Employees Union and its research director. "She probably did more, and kept it alive this session with the union and with the organizing of the public employees, . . . it became important to the workers," according to one legislator. Organizing women union members to analyze and respond to management's proposed classification changes, as described above, gave these members a detailed understanding of the process and a stake in its outcome. Some became members of a pay equity bargaining team. The union also organized a series of testimonial meetings on the campuses of universities throughout the state. To these meetings they invited their local representatives to the state legislature. The speakers were classified workers who talked about what they did on their jobs, and how much they got paid. "It was a real eye-opener to the legislators. Sometimes they were preaching to the believers, but even the most supportive legislators who had always been for comparable worth were a little shocked and surprised," said one such long-time supporter.

Most shocking was that full-time state employees could earn so little that they would qualify for welfare benefits: "I've been a clerical assistant at Oregon State University for more than a year. I gross $870 per month. I have $650 to spend for rent, food, transportation, school supplies. I have to get a child care supplement, Section 8 housing subsidy, the free lunch program and food stamps. My resources have run out for (November), so I'll be getting donated food for the holiday. I'm an OSU graduate" (Hallock, 1987).

These meetings were buttressed with letter and postcard writing campaigns. For example, the union presented to the Joint Interim Legislative Task Force 2,000 cards from workers in 43 state agencies expressing support for pay equity legislation. The union's political mobilization efforts included a large rally in January, 1987, kicking off the new legislative campaign.

This rally was not only an outpouring of pro-sentiment, but also a sign of the opposition to pay equity that served to sharpen, for its proponents, the necessity for concerted political vigilance. The theme was "It's Time for Pay Equity." It was to be an old-fashioned rally with banners, music, celebrities, held on a Saturday morning on the steps of the state capitol building for public employees to make sure that comparable worth didn't disappear again. It was well planned and publicized months ahead. At the very last minute, someone, identity unknown, telephoned the scheduling office in the state capitol and cancelled the union rally. Immediately, another group related to the Eagle Forum, the far-right women's organization headed by Phyllis Schlafley, scheduled a rally for the same time, same day, same place. The union was not informed until the day before. Outraged late-night telephone calls resulted in a decision that neither group would have the front steps of the capitol, and that they would be moved to steps at either side of the building. It was a rainy morning, but 500 people showed up for the union rally, while 20 came out to the Eagle Forum side of the building. That night on television news, the pictures and commentary made it appear that both rallies were of similar size and importance.

There were other reasons to be nervous. As one legislator said, "I saw organized opposition for the first time. . . . There was the Portland Chamber of Commerce that had come out in opposition to it. They hadn't done that before. The importance and the clout of business groups had become much greater since '81, partly because of our economy. I was nervous that first it would be the Chamber, and then they would tie up with Oregon Industries, and then it would be the utilities and timber. . . . A combination of some of those business groups could have done it in." Partly in response to these concerns, the women legislators began to get together to try to figure out what they could do.

Also alerted were women's advocacy groups, which had assumed that the comparable worth bill would pass easily and had not put it at the top of their lobbying agendas. The full-time lobbyist hired by the Women's Rights Coalition, a group of some 50 women's organizations in the state, began to take an active role in the legislative process. Unions together with the Women's Rights Coalition formed a Pay Equity Action Coalition that could rally critical support. Thus, the new legislative period opened with broader political participation, grass roots activity by women workers, and a more conscious alliance between feminists and organized labor in support of pay equity. Working with them was a new administration, committed to a participatory approach, that had shown its dedication to comparable worth by allocating $22.6 million to that purpose in its first budget. With these new politics, the class and gender conflicts that had wracked the previous pay equity attempt seemed to be resolved.

Class and Gender Conflicts Return

The 1987 legislative process began in an atmosphere of agreement with the introduction of a new bill, accepted by management, OPEU, and the Joint Task Force on Comparable Worth. Old conflicts of class and gender still existed behind the new spirit of consensus, but were temporarily quiescent. Senate Bill 288 established a pay equity fund to raise the wages of the most undervalued and the use of a point-factor job evaluation system in an ongoing process of identifying undervalued jobs. Implementation was to be through collective bargaining. In addition, the bill provided for negotiation of appeals procedures, protected workers from any salary reductions or loss of increases, and required that no job classification could be reduced in grade. This was the union's ideal bill—no one would get hurt.

Feminists speaking through the Women's Rights Coalition were also satisfied with the bill. Amendments had weakened the policy statement by changing comparable worth from "a primary" to "an important" consideration in wage setting. The lobbyist for the Women's Rights Coalition had some reservations about this and about the Executive Department's insistence on certain wording that seemed to weaken pay equity by allowing more weight in wage setting to market factors, to alleviating the compression of middle-level salaries for managers and professionals, and to considerations of the state's ability to pay. However, the bottom lines established by the Women's Rights Coalition had survived substantially intact. These were the continued use of a point-factor job evaluation system, the continued targeting of the money to the most underpaid, and use of the male pay line as the standard, as opposed to the average, pay line that the Executive Department favored.

The proposed bill was apparently acceptable to the new

management also. In legislative hearings, the head of the Executive Department and the new Director of the Personnel Division and Labor Relations both testified in favor, and the bill moved successfully through the legislative process. Legislators, OPEU leadership, the head of the Executive Department, and the Women's Rights Coalition lobbyist all agreed on amendments. The Senate Labor Committee voted out S.B. 288, and the senate approved it 22 to 8 on May 4, 1987.

Much of the substance of the plan, including the exact classifications that would be changed and most of the implementation rules, was not in the legislation and had to be negotiated between management and labor. In these negotiations union-management conflicts re-emerged, often in new form, and the demands of the women's lobby and the interests of women workers were once again pushed to the periphery of the political process. Conflicts centered around the need for a new classification system, implementation issues such as grievance procedures and redlining, and broader union-management issues in which pay equity became a resource in other battles.

The Need for a New Classification Plan. Early in its administration, the new executive questioned the need for a completely revised classification plan. The union, having invested heavily in organizing its members to work on new classifications, could not agree. As the union leader told the story, "The legislative Task Force thinks it has a plan to implement new classifications. We [the union] think we have an agreement on a grievance procedure and a classification system. We have a new administration, a new boss who is reorganizing the Executive Department, new people and they start saying things like, 'Why do we need a new classification system?' He [the new Director of the Executive Department] said, 'I think we just ought to dump this whole thing. Forget about it, spend this money, this 22.6 million and forget it.' I [the union leader] said, 'Two years ago I would have agreed with you, but unfortunately now we are vested in this project. We had people out there writing responses to the proposed classes, and winning. We won a new classification for Library Technician. We have a classification series for the Psychiatric Aides and the Psychiatric Security Aides that gets rid of a 25 percent salary differential for those jobs which should not exist.

We think that's positive. So, he says, 'That's more complicated than I thought.' "

After another round of meetings, the decision was made to go ahead with a partial implementation of new classifications. However, as we shall see, the Executive Department's commitment to a new classification system was not strong enough to lead them to any concessions on questions of grievance procedures and redlining. Ultimately, they were willing to postpone classification revisions until they could implement them as they wished.

Implementation Issues: Grievance Procedures. Broader class-based disagreements emerged as management and the union discussed the practical implementation of new classifications. The new management began to question the rights of workers to certain kinds of job security that had long been in place. This was evident in their reaction to an agreement on appeals and grievances that had been reached between the union, the previous executive, and the Interim Task Force. The new management refused to ratify it, arguing that the old Executive Department had sold out just to secure the classification system. The new top administrators said that there really never was an agreement, because it was never signed. They wanted to start over on implementation procedures.

Job security issues disrupted the first negotiation session as labor and management discussed the ground rules on which there had been prior agreement, in the understanding of union staff.[2] As the union negotiator said, "These were to negotiate procedures on grievances, what happens to bumping rights and layoff and transfer rights when you change classifications, because all of your seniority is built up by classification and when that classification disappears and you get laid off, where can you bump? . . . In the first five minutes we were in a fight on these ground rules and she refused to agree that the state would negotiate transfer and layoff provisions because it was permissive." The law specifies mandatory bargaining on wages, hours, and terms and conditions of employment. Other issues are permissive and may be negotiated. Seniority rules, including the rights of displaced workers to "bump" or move into jobs of other workers with less seniority, have been negotiated by unions and management for years. Refusal to bargain on these issues upset the clear trajectory toward success of the comparable worth effort based on a new and better classification plan. In addition, refusal to bargain on permissible issues suggested that management had a new agenda for labor that went further than problems around the implementation of comparable worth.

A number of management concerns underlay their refusal to bargain on these permissible questions. According to the Director of the Executive Department, "I'm not anxious to set up a huge bureaucracy on reviewing those things [grievances and appeals on classification issues]. We'll negotiate some and we'll do a good job setting the points and the market-organization relationships, and I don't know that we need a huge structure to review all that. That can be done right now with the existing machinery we have. At one time, maybe it made some sense, a lot of new things were being done and people didn't understand the system. I like to think we're bringing people more into participation and there will be less controversy" (Interview, July, 1987).

The Personnel Director was more concerned about the union's demand for promotion preference rights for workers who might be downgraded in the new classification plan. She had never liked this provision. "It goes back to management's right to fill vacancies, that we select the most qualified, not necessarily the fact that they were in an old class and may qualify. They may be qualified, but are not the best choice. We don't mind promotion consideration in interviewing, but to dictate that they have promotion rights to a higher class, maybe a class that they have little or no background in, we could not agree to" (Interview, July 1987).

Reservations about collective bargaining itself may also have been a factor in the refusal to bargain on permissive items. As the Personnel Director said, "I don't think you get the best unless you get all the parties talking and in-putting their ideas. Where we get in trouble is when you're locked into a strict contract renegotiation process, sometimes that acts as a barrier to an agreement as much as anything. It's that contractual process. . . . I don't mean to imply that legally set collective bargaining is wrong. But the informal working relationship you might get might be easier. The contractual relationship bogs things down" (Interview, July, 1987).

The state continued to take an adamant stand on the question of bargaining on permissive issues. State negotiators told the union that they were removing from the contract all seniority provisions as well as all other language on permissive items. And, in the future, they would decline to bargain about any such issues. In the eyes of the union, this was hardball, an unusually antiunion position. From management's point of view, "That's a union issue right now, to get people interested . . . basically, permissive items we don't have to negotiate on unless we chose to, mandatory we do. If we choose to say one is permissive, because we think it is, and the union adds money to it and says now it's mandatory—there are games played there. They seem to have the ability to turn something we think is permissive to mandatory" (Interview with Director of Executive Department, July, 1987). These issues were only resolved, in the union's favor, after a strike in the fall of 1987. Comparable worth implementation, it seems clear, was embroiled in a complex set of maneuvers over questions of power and control between management and labor.

Implementation Issues: Redlining. The old question of whether the wages of any classifications could be held constant or reduced in the process of attaining equity emerged again to plague the 1987 pay equity efforts as it had the 1985 project. A Women's Rights Coalition legislative alert said, "The Executive Department wants all protections against lowering or freezing wage classifications removed from the bill. They argue that if they are required to use a point system to assess undervaluation of certain jobs they want also to have the ability to use that system to find *over*valuations." This was a crisis for the women's movement and the union because it was already the middle of May and the legislative session would close by the end of June.

The Executive's stance on redlining seems to have resulted from the new Personnel Division's growing recognition of the complexities in constructing a new classification system as well as from their reconsideration of the implications of the wording of the pay-equity bill. As the Personnel Director put it, "When we looked at some of those new classes, even though they were largely replacement classes, some people were going to be put into a lower class than they are currently in. . . . We were going to begin a two-tier system. Senate Bill 288 at that time had the words that we could not redline nor lower an existing class in grade. In other words, it was all written so that if you were implementing a new class system, everything had to go up" (Interview, July, 1987).

The new management team, according to their account, had not initially recognized the far-reaching implications of the wording of the bill. With a new legal interpretation, in consultation with the governor, they decided that "if the bill passed that would mean we would never get a reasonable classification system" (Interview with Director of Executive Department, July, 1987). "We didn't want to embark on a new system that inhibited us from taking care of overevaluation in a reasonable or rational way in our view" (Interview with Director of Personnel and Labor Relations, July, 1987). "So, the issue never was should we ever make pay equity payments, the issue was can we ever have a reasonable classification system. I wasn't willing to give that away" (Director of Executive Department).

Thus, once again, conflict centered on control of the classification system and the wage implications of that system, and, in particular, whether pay equity means lowering as well as raising salaries. To solve their immediate problem, the Executive Department decided to withdraw all recommendations for new classes, delay a new classification system until 1989, and implement pay equity increases for the current classes in 1987. A second part of the solution was to amend the comparable worth bill to remove all prohibitions against redlining—or withholding pay increases to "overvalued" jobs—and against lowering the salary grade of any job classification. They needed, they argued, the flexibility to readjust wages and classifications when they implemented an entire new classification system in two years' time.

Management insistence that all protections against wage reductions be removed from the bill was, of course, opposed by labor. "Our bottom line was the red circling issue," said OPEU's representative. "And as soon as we lose that, all of this delicate balance falls apart. . . . I don't want anybody to feel statutorially obligated to create a strict relationship (between points and dollars), when there's no prohibition against freezing wages." Thus, a bill that specified that the state should use a point-factor system to evaluate jobs and set wages was unacceptable unless it also stated that the system could not be used to undercut male wages.

Consequently, the Oregon Public Employees Union wanted references to a point-factor system removed from the legislation. The Women's Rights Coalition, on the other hand, had a strong commitment to the use of a point-factor system as a test for the undervaluation of jobs. At the same time, they opposed red circling and understood the union's argument against punishing men while achieving gains for women. Management's new demands threatened to drive a wedge between the women's movement and organized labor. As the Coalition's Legislative Alert on the new crisis pointed out, *"It is distressing and frustrating to be pushed into this corner so late in the session and after making significant compromises in order to gain the support of the Executive Department"* (emphasis in original).

Women's groups in the coalition responded with letters to the governor criticizing the sudden opposition to the bill when it was three-quarters through the legislative process. Women legislators also began to put pressure on state management, which responded that it was not their problem. As the Women's Rights Coalition lobbyist said, "Their [Executive Department's] position at that time was, well, this is really a problem between you two [women's groups and unions]. We can live with the bill either way [with or without a point-factor evaluation system]. What can we do to facilitate the problem between you?" Women's groups held the Executive Department responsible for actions that led to union demands to take the requirement of a point-factor job evaluation system out of the bill; nevertheless, the issue of red-lining and the acceptability of wage setting through job evaluation threatened to undermine the coalition between women's movement groups and women in the labor unions.

As in the 1983–85 comparable worth effort, the question was, are the interests of working women best served by maintaining solidarity with working men within trade unions or by establishing some controls that will prevent both unions and management from continuing to set women's wages below their "value"? Women's movement groups took the latter position. The middle-class feminist stand on labor unions is ambivalent and this affected some feminist approaches. Evidence exists that working-class men and their unions have played a part in keeping women out of many jobs and at the bottom of pay scales in the jobs they do hold (Hartmann, 1976; Cockburn, 1983). Given this evidence, some controls to diminish the male power advantages seemed perfectly logical. On the other hand, the Women's Rights Coalition lobbyist and the women in the legislature recognized that without the persistent leadership of the OPEU research director there would have been no comparable worth bill to discuss. Moreover, they could understand, while disagreeing with, her insistence that point-factor job evaluation should not be required for wage setting if there were no prohibition on redlining. Ultimately her position, that working women have no chance of improving their conditions without union solidarity, won in new rounds of negotiation with management, removing the requirement of point-factor job evaluation and producing a new version of comparable worth.

Pay Equity As A Resource In Union-Management Conflict

Pay equity was an apple-pie issue by the end of the second legislative process. No one would openly oppose it, but they would try to define it so that no other interests would be undermined. In contrast to the first project in which the Executive Department seemed willing to sacrifice comparable worth if it did not achieve greater control over the bureaucracy and over unions, the new Executive, with its more participative, employee-friendly, and flexible-management approach, maintained a positive view on pay equity while at the same time implicitly using it as a resource in a battle with organized labor.

Although the new governor had been enthusiastically supported by organized labor, and union people, including the OPEU comparable worth leader, had worked on committees facilitating the transition to the new administration, management-labor conflict persisted. The new management seemed to take an even tougher line toward labor than the previous management. Pay equity was one of the negotiating issues in which this was evident. They were more adamant than the old executive in opposing restrictions on redlining, insisting that if undervalued were to be raised, overvalued should be lowered. They were less willing than the old administration to let unions participate in management processes, as was evident in their opposition to bargaining grievance and appeals procedures for the implementation of a new classification system. Finally, they were pushing to eliminate from the contract issues that several previous administrations had seen as legitimate. Pay equity for women was caught once again in the interstices of a battle between management and the unions.

Pay equity was also a major resource for the Oregon Public Employees Union, which had made comparable worth its prime organizing issue, as discussed above. Bargaining on other issues, as well as on pay equity, went slowly; after six months of negotiation, as the legislature finished its session, no agreement had been reached. The union made a decision not to settle on the distribution of the pay equity funds until settlement was reached on other items. These included a general pay increase as well as the permissive items such as seniority.

Management and OPEU had each brought a proposal to the table. The state had offered a two-percent wage increase, but also proposed an increase in employee contributions to health benefits that almost cancelled the wage increase. Therefore, the union was holding out for more. The governor had asked the unions to trust him and to wait, to take the two percent with his promise that in another two years more substantial increases would be there. The union could not accept that solution.[3] By the time that the comparable worth bill was signed, an impasse had been reached in bargaining, some 35 contested issues had gone to fact-finding, and management was making vague allusions to a strike.[4] Thus, although the legislature had approved the use of $22.6 million for the raising of wages of the most undervalued, the exact way this was to be done was before a fact-finder.[5]

The fact-finder upheld management's proposal, discussed below, for pay equity implementation, while finding for the union position on other questions. Neither management nor the union accepted the fact-finders' recommendations and, failing to get agreement with further bargaining, the union decided to strike. Morale among state workers was high. They were angry that the state wanted to take back such a small wage increase and that guarantees such as seniority rights were under attack. According to the union, 70 to 80 percent of workers walked off the job in agency after agency. Nine days later the strike was settled. The union won back full medical benefits, achieved a small bonus for all workers and selective raises for some, including pay for workers doing union negotiation. They also retained all permissible items, including seniority, in the contract. The wage settlement included the 2 percent management had offered and management's comparable worth proposal. Pay equity meant $22.6 million distributed to 63 classes, representing 5,839 workers, 79 percent of the most undervalued jobs represented by OPEU. These workers had an average increase of 10 percent; almost all of them had been earning $1,100 or less per month. The years of organizing around comparable worth contributed to an outcome that injected new energy into the union, making "this union feel like a union again," as one union activist said.

Because the union had made comparable worth part of a list of issues that had to be settled as a package, the strike and the resulting delay in pay equity payments might be seen as a temporary setback for women's interests for the sake of the union's interests in its conflicts with management. This raises again the issue of when women's class interests are the same or different from those of men, as well as the question of whether we can speak of general working-class interests instead of gender-specific class interests. In this case, women workers had an interest in the other issues and in keeping a strong union in the face of management's moves to weaken its power, not least because the union had carried the two-year effort for comparable worth to a conclusion that gave raises to thousands of workers. Women's issues had become an integral part of union issues.

Poverty Relief or Pay Equity? The Redefinition of Comparable Worth

The final compromise bill was passed, as in 1985, at the end of June on the last day of the legislative session. The governor signed it on July 17, 1987, in a ceremony full of good will and reconciliation, publicly recognizing the contributions of women legislators and paying tribute to the woman who had carried the fight for the Oregon Public Employees Union. Delighted that pay equity had survived so many crises, comparable worth supporters felt that they had won. However, they had won something quite different from "true" comparable worth, and before equity money appeared in the paychecks of women workers, the meaning of comparable worth was to be still further modified. Thus the operational redefinition of comparable worth took place in two stages: in the compromise bill that resulted from the legislative process and in union-management conflict over implementation of that bill, finally settled with the strike.

The framers of the compromise bill had altered the focus from a system to set all wages to a system for raising the wages of the undervalued. The policy statement retained broader implications: The State of Oregon would attempt to achieve an equitable relationship between the comparability of the value of work and the compensation and classification structure of the state. However, the rest of the bill made clear that this referred only to undervalued jobs and job classifications. The first priority was to be compensation equity for the most undervalued in the lowest salary ranges. Equity was to be an important consideration in wage setting in the future. The state was instructed to use a neutral and objective method of determining the comparability of the value of work, and reference to a point-factor job evaluation was eliminated.

The bill further required that there be no wage decreases to achieve the policy. The possibility of withholding general salary adjustments to achieve the policy or of reducing the grade of a job classification was not mentioned, in principle leaving management free to take such measures. A Pay Equity Fund was established, with funds to go first to the most undervalued jobs and the distribution of the funds within each bargaining unit to be determined through collective bargaining. A Joint Legislative Compensation and Classification Committee would provide continuing oversight. Finally, the branches of state government were required to report every two years on progress in implementing pay equity, with proposals for upgrading undervalued classes.

The methods for determining which job classifications are undervalued were unspecified: The legislation contained neither point-factor job evaluation nor mention of a target wage line. Gone also were any restraints on wage setting in the form of amendments to legislation on the merit system, collective bargaining, and arbitration. Such amendments had been in the original legislation to ensure the future maintenance of pay equity. Feminists, in particular, had been worried that after a one-time adjustment of women's wages, both unions and management would go back to old ways that gave more attention to male than to female wages. AFSCME, as previously discussed, had always opposed any restraints on bargaining and this was the one issue on which they were emphatic this time around. In addition, in the view of the Oregon Public Employees Union, "Once we got women up to a certain level, the only effect of that statute (restraints on bargaining) could be to punish the men. I felt confident that through the power of organizing, we could push women just as far as we could go. After that, I want this thing to disappear. I don't want points to determine the wages for groundskeepers and painters."

In sum, the compromise bill called for an effort to achieve wage equity for undervalued job classifications within a general framework of intent to continue this effort in subsequent years. Concrete specification of methods were left to management and to the bargaining process. The implicit definition of comparable worth was a process of pay equalization that works toward similar pay levels for jobs of similar value, rather than a comprehensive wage system.

In the final negotiations between management and OPEU another implicit definition emerged: comparable worth as poverty relief. Proponents of comparable worth would say that it means both poverty relief and equal pay. However, it would be possible to reduce poverty without achieving comparable pay. This, the union charged, is what management's proposals would do. Management, on the other hand, cast the differences between the two proposals as an issue of what is sensible and feasible. In their eyes the union's specific proposals for wage increases were unrealistically high, committing the state to future raises that had not been budgeted. Management proposed raising the pay of 66 of the most underpaid classifications; the union wanted increases for 82 classifications. Both used the modal job evaluation score for a sample of jobs in current job classifications to identify the targeted classifications. Management proposed raising some jobs by two salary grades and others by one, in a step-to-step implementation. A secretary, for example, who had been in Salary Range 9—Step 3, would now be in Salary Range 11—Step 3. In this approach workers who got a two-range increase would see their salaries go up by 10 percent and workers with a one-range increase would get a 5-percent raise. In the management proposal, there was no attention to any goal of raising wages to an equity target.

The union proposed raises that would bring the undervalued jobs up to a salary range located on the average payline. Earlier in the discussion of implementation, the union had agreed to use the average payline for calculating the 1987 equity increases. Management had argued vigorously for the average line based on all wages paid by the state, maintaining that use of the *male* average line to calculate the amount of inequity was not rational. Too many male-dominated jobs would fall below that line and an argument could be made for raising their pay. Having given on that point, the union wanted an implementation that would bring wages up to or close to the average line. Thus, for many jobs, the union suggested moves into higher salary ranges than those found in the management proposal. The dollar raises in the union proposal would have been only a little higher than the dollar raises that management put forward, because the union proposed raising workers to higher ranges, but to lower steps in those ranges. The location of a job in a higher salary range meant that there would be automatic increases down the line, committing the state to higher wage costs in subsequent years. In the union's view, this would be a beginning of a phase-in of equity pay, even if the standard was only the average payline, pulled down by the historically low wages of women.

Management opposed not only increasing the state's future wage bill, but argued that the union wanted raises for some workers who were not among the most undervalued. This was true. For example, the union proposed a raise for administrative assistants, whose pay was only 13 percent below the male trend line, in contrast to the definition of underpaid as falling 15 percent or more below that line. As discussed above, these workers often have some supervisory responsibilities for other clerical workers whose increases would bring them very close to the pay of administrative assistants. Thus there was a reasonable argument for including them, even though technically they were not the most undervalued. The union may also have taken into consideration the desirability of maintaining unity and a sense of fair play among all clerical workers, who are an important part of their membership.

In sum, management proposals would spend pay equity

money to relieve the poverty of the lowest paid, but were not linked to any plan to achieve equity. As the union leader said, "Is this what four years of work have boiled down to? This could have been done four years ago. I don't trust that we will have another shot at equity and I want to get some start on it now." Nevertheless, the management proposal, supported by the opinions of the fact-finder prior to the strike, was accepted in the settlement by the union and was implemented. Although in 1987 pay equity had been treated as poverty relief, the potential existed in the new law for redefining it as equitable pay in future years.

The Future of Oregon Pay Equity

The final assessment of the Oregon pay equity effort must wait, for only with the legislative session in 1989 will it become clear whether the 1987 Pay Equity Fund was a one-time poverty relief intervention or a down payment on future equity. The main actors were cautious about the future. Spokespeople for the Executive Department recognize that there may still be some undervaluation that will not be corrected with the 1987 equity increases. But they are not completely consistent, for some also express a belief that most of the undervaluation will have been taken care of. Management expects that the unions will argue that there has only been the first step. This is certainly the position of the OPEU, although they are not optimistic about actually achieving a phase-in to a closer approximation of pay equity.

One reason for lack of optimism is a clear understanding of how difficult the implementation of a new job classification system will be. The hard decisions implicit in this process were postponed until 1989. The state administration still seems committed to a new classification system, but they have encountered essentially the same implementation problems faced by the previous administration. In the opinion of the Personnel Director, the state will not be able to have "one great big system" in which the point-factor scores all have a consistent relationship to each other. She does anticipate that the internal structuring of occupational categories can be done with point scores. This suggests that, at least in her view, a consistent assessment of comparable worth across job families cannot be achieved. This, of course, has important implications for the ultimate fate of the concept of "true" comparable worth.

Because the new administration involves agencies more integrally in the process of change than did the old administration, because they are attempting to demystify the process of job evaluation, because they will not force agencies to accept job classifications that cut across agency lines when these are not acceptable to the agencies—implementation of a new system probably has a better chance. In addition, Personnel plans to design a new compensation system that would be more flexible than the old one, widen the ranges, and increase the number of steps. If there is more flexibility in the compensation plan, this will help in implementation.

However, the Personnel Director was pessimistic about the chances of implementation through collective bargaining. "We can build a perfect system on paper and . . . we'll get stuck right there in negotiating with the union, because while they may agree that some classes are undervalued and need to go up, the current status of the negotiations now indicate that even when everything is going up, we can't agree. The ultimate wage rate and the implementation plan is where the issues are. If there are some red lines and overvalues, they won't agree. . . . You can say, give me a window [legislative suspension of bargaining] to implement but that's not been popular with a labor-dominated legislature. So, we've got some hard times. If we can educate folks, they may see the need for it [legislative intervention]. Otherwise, we just sit there and don't implement new classes. Or we wait until the contract expires and implement unilaterally management's last offer, and you don't do that without disruption, a strike probably" (Interview with Director of Personnel and Labor Relations, July, 1987).

The union's assessment of the probable future was equally tentative. In the view of OPEU's comparable worth leader, management would be unable to bargain hundreds of new classes with redlining of the "overvalued" without the active support of the union. "They will have to bring it to the table if they are going to freeze someone's wages. . . . There's going to be a trade-off, you can have these go up only if these go down. And that's a situation we can't afford to get into. So, we have to fight the thing now. We're going to be very wary of all their classification proposals because they have said loud and clear that we're not going to implement new classes now because we can't downgrade." She thought that there would have to be some changes in the classification system, but that the state was not going about it in the right way: "The longer the state thinks they're going to do it all at once, the big bang theory of classification development, the more likely they are to fail. I think the way to do it is to partially implement. You get modal evaluations for current classes and new evaluations for ones you want to implement and you slowly change over. That's what works. The other approach doesn't work. You can have the nicest constructs and the most beautiful system and the correct intellectual and technical approach and it means absolutely nothing if it doesn't get implemented. So you have to pay attention to implementation or you've wasted time and money and frustrated thousands of people. Implementation is the key."

Conclusion: True Comparable Worth and the Politics of the Possible

Oregon's first effort to implement comparable worth failed in 1985. In 1987, its second effort partially succeeded, distributing $22 million to 6,000 workers. In addition to immediate wage increases, the law provided for legislative oversight and required that all state agencies study and report on their progress toward pay equity every two years, thus creating the conditions for ongoing efforts to achieve changes closer to the goals of comparable worth. Moreover, a large part of the work on a new classification system had been completed and its contours were acceptable to both unions and management.

The political process was very different in 1987 than in 1985, accounting for much of the difference between disaster and progress. Two differences seem most important: First, the political mobilization of women was more effective, and second, pragmatic politics produced a plan that threatened no one's status or pay.

Success was the culmination of the efforts of the OPEU comparable worth leader, political mobilization of women both in the Oregon Public Employees Union and in the women's movement, and the vigilance of women legislators. Workers who would benefit most were informed and involved in the campaign. In addition, more effective political action on the part of union, legislative, and women's movement feminists, as well as their male allies, kept scarce funds from being allocated to other purposes as conflicts between management and labor were worked out.

A pragmatic approach on the part of OPEU comparable worth leadership and a state executive less determined to quickly achieve a new classification system muted many of the conflicts that had undermined true comparable worth in 1985. There was no attempt at system change and wage increases were modest, going mostly to those with poverty level incomes, masking the fact that a 10-percent raise for some workers and not for others amounts to some redistribution of the wage. Consequently, there was no opposition to this particular pay equity plan from state employees or state agencies and no interunion battles to confound the issue and dilute support.

The 1987 political compromise enacted an operational definition of comparable worth that was very different from the true comparable worth of 1985. By the time the 1987 bill was passed, everything that might upset either management or the unions was removed, as a comparison of the two plans shows (Figure 5.1). First, the effort to achieve a single wage plan for all state workers was abandoned. This was an inevitable consequence of a second change insisted upon by the unions, the implementation of all pay equity adjustments through collective bargaining rather than legislative intervention: A single wage plan could not be achieved if pay equity adjustments were bargained by nine different unions. Third, no changes in either classifications or wage ranges were in the 1987 plan, only wage increases within the existing pay and classification structure. Management decided to postpone any system changes because the unions would not agree to redlining or reducing the grade level of any job classes, moves that management held to be essential for the achievement of a rational classification structure.

Opposition to redlining, the unions' bottom line, colliding with management's insistence on redlining led to several other inter-related changes in the 1987 plan. Management demanded that no protections against redlining be included in the bill, in

Figure 5.1
Provisions of Oregon Comparable Worth Plans, 1985 and 1987

*1985 Provisions**	*1987 Provisions*
One wage plan.	Many wage plans.
Implementation through legislation.	Implementation through collective bargaining.
Review and grievance procedure.	No review and grievance procedure.
Strict relationship of points to dollars.	Points used only to identify undervalued.
Male line as goal and basis for increases.	Average line as goal, but not used to calculate increases.
Complete system change—classification and pay.	No system change.
All undervalued raised.	Only most undervalued raised.
Partial redlining—no salaries reduced.	No mention of redlining—no salaries reduced.
One-time implementation.	Phasing not specified.
Maintenance—pay equity a primary consideration in all wage setting; reporting.	Maintenance—reporting and legislative oversight.
Point factor system to be used in determining comparability.	A neutral and objective method to be used in determining comparability.

*Provisions of the original 1985 bill, expressing the concept of true comparable worth. The bill finally passed in 1985 was closer to the 1987 bill in its focus on the most undervalued.

effect reserving for themselves the possibility, already existing in state law, of withholding wage increases or reducing the wages of certain job classifications. In response, the union demanded that requirements for the use of a point-factor job evaluation system to determine comparability be deleted from the bill, on the grounds that without protection against redlining, management might use point-factor comparisons to reduce rather than raise wages. Similarly, and partly because 1987 changes did not include a new wage plan, the calculation of wages on the basis of evaluated points was not in the 1987 plan. Job evaluation points were to be used only to identify undervalued jobs, not to set wages. Finally, the bill eliminated clear future constraints on bargaining, such as amendments to collective bargaining and arbitration laws requiring that pay equity should be a primary consideration in all wage setting, and substituted a general directive that equity should be an important consideration in compensation and classification matters.

In sum, management retained the possibilities of gaining further control over the classification system, while labor avoided any restrictions on bargaining and immediate threats of lower wages to achieve equity. The women's movement, however, had to take considerably less than they had wanted to achieve. Instead of a point-factor job evaluation system as the basis of identifying inequities, they had to settle for a "neutral and objective method" for doing the same thing.[6] Moreover, the bill that passed and was implemented was a long way from other ideal standards for doing comparable worth. There was no target line, no plan for a phased-in implementation, and no controls to keep management and unions from returning males to their position of wage superiority. In fact, this plan did not bring women up to any standard of equity, although it raised the lowest wages by about 10 percent and undoubtedly reduced poverty.

In 1987, class/gender conflicts were still important in shaping the outcome. Indeed, perhaps more than in the 1985 process, there were clear class and gender divisions in the course of working out the final compromise. The new management, no less than the old one, seemed to take a position similar to the current stance of many managers in the private sector, attempting to regain as much control as possible from the territory won in the past by the unions. New management, like the old, used comparable worth implementation to that end.

From a management perspective, attempting to increase control over promotion and seniority rights, for example, was just rational management practice, necessary to build a well-functioning organization with the most competent people. As management sought to keep its flexibility to manage as it saw fit, it first decided not to implement any new classes, then that it couldn't live with any limitations on its right to redline job classifications. Finally, management would not come to an agreement with the state's largest union on a new contract, leaving to the union whether to accept what management offered or to strike.

Pay equity was, once again, the at least temporary victim of the drive on the part of management to weaken organized labor. The result was a strike.

Unions, for their part, continued to deal with pay equity as one part of their overall efforts to represent their members' interests. For the Oregon Public Employees Union, pay equity became a central issue and a major organizing tool that made an important contribution to the successful strike. Yet, the union had to balance the conflicting interests of its members in regard to comparable worth, seeking to avoid the risk of losing some active members, mostly higher-paid male workers, while trying to gain the maximum for low-paid women workers. The policies that would most help the women would undercut some of the men.

The question of what policies are in the best interest of working women divided feminists working for the union from some feminists in the women's movement. Union feminists could argue that opposition to redlining and to the consistent use of evaluated points in wage setting were strictly questions of general labor interests; resolute support of the wages of their own members was only good union policy and thus in the interests of all members, including women. Women's movement feminists could counter, and they did, that unions were still protecting men at the expense of women. There is some truth in both these claims, signaling an ambiguous and contradictory situation for working women and their unions.

Union feminists also argued that without labor unions, women workers cannot achieve comparable worth because an organized and collective voice of workers is necessary to win and protect any gains. Therefore, women workers must pay attention to union unity, even if this means, as in this case, some feminist policies are sacrificed. In the long run, union strength is the route to security and decent wages. However, movement feminists had reason to be skeptical of the claim that women could rely totally on the unions. Oregon unions before the comparable worth effort, with the possible exception of AFSCME discussed above, had not been energetic in bargaining up the wages of their women members. Male leaders of Oregon unions had not initiated the comparable worth effort in the state. This was the work of feminists, both inside and outside unions. Again, both positions have some validity.

Unions seem necessary for pay equity because in the struc-

ture of work organizations only management and unions have
access to decision-making processes and some possibility of ef-
fecting change. A benign management might initiate pay equity,
but this seems unlikely, particularly in periods of budget aus-
terity. In the public sector, legislators can pass laws and set up
task forces to initiate change, but without a strong supportive
coalition of people on the inside, involved in daily operations,
change efforts are easily undermined. Women's movement representatives outside the organization can lobby, testify at hearings,
and monitor the progress of comparable worth in coalition with
sympathetic legislators, but feminists from outside cannot directly enter the wage-setting process. For these reasons, union
representation is critical for women workers. However, if they do
not have power within unions, with women officers and staff who
work for women's interests, unions may just be another place
where gender disadvantages for women are maintained and a
gender-divided class structure reproduced.

However, even if feminists were powerful in labor unions
committed to pay equity, dilemmas would remain: Is job evaluation a good technique to obtain pay equity? Can comparable
worth be implemented without generating new feelings of disadvantage and opposition? So long as different jobs have different
wages, so long as there is no radical equalization of pay, some
implicit process of valuation will be part of wage setting, even if
wage setting is done through collective bargaining. Job evaluation
seems a more fair and open method of assigning relative value
than market or other types of power, such as that related to
gender or racial privilege. The difficult questions for feminists
and unionists are whose values are represented in the evaluation
system and who controls it: Does job evaluation put more power
over wage setting in the hands of management? The implementation dilemma is also difficult. The Oregon experience indicates
that the most politically successful approach is a gradual implementation that does not openly undermine the status and pay of
any workers. Equity is not possible without redistribution, but
somehow workers must see it as legitimate. For this reason,
poverty relief may be more acceptable than equity arguments.

Management actions often complicate the problem of deciding what policies are in the best interests of women workers.
The idea of comparable worth opens up for management the

possibility of a new basis on which to oppose wage increases for traditionally well-paid working-class male-dominated jobs. Management can appeal to what is rational and reasonable to demonstrate that some wages should be lowered, while some should be raised. It is hard for a management committed to service to argue that employees should continue to be paid so little that they must seek social benefits to supplement their wages from the very employer who also supplies the benefits. But in an era when blue-collar men are being forced to give back wages, even the state as employer may look for ways to take advantage of that downward pressure on wages. Arguments for the comparability of work and wages tied to points serve that purpose.

Thus, women workers and feminist advocates of comparable worth are caught in a bind. The very strategy that seems to promise a solution to the historic undervaluing of women's work can be turned back upon them to become a way of undermining the strength and unity of unions that are necessary for the achievement of pay equity. Management has not been slow to understand this and to act upon this understanding, at least in the state of Oregon. The union strategy was to look for a way to achieve comparable worth that would not undermine union strength. That meant abandoning "true comparable worth" for a more pragmatic substitute. A plan that cannot be implemented is, finally, no plan at all.

CHAPTER SIX

Doing Comparable Worth
Theorizing Gender and Class

Why is gender inequality so persistent and how is it continually reconstituted in new forms in the process of broad social and economic change? I began this study with that question in mind because, in spite of a flood of scholarship, our answers are still unsatisfactory. I was convinced that at least a small part of the answer depends on a better understanding of the connections between gender and class, for women's situations are not just the product of strongly held gendered beliefs and long-established habits of living, but are rooted in the economic realities of survival. I also believed that ties between class and gender are deeply embedded in what we have usually theorized as gender-neutral organizational and class processes. I hoped that a close observation of an effort to achieve pay equity reform, which deals with both gender and class inequality, would illuminate some of the ways that this happens.

The words I have used to designate the central theoretical question have shifted throughout this discussion, indicating indecision about how to best conceptualize the issue (see, for example, Harding, 1986b). Should we talk about gender *and* class, gender/class, or gendered class relations? Gender *and* class implies more autonomy of processes and relations than I intend, while gendered class seems to mean that class relations are fundamental although affected by gender. Gender/class captures more nearly the way that, in my opinion, we should be thinking about these processes. However, a certain conceptual flexibility may be helpful as we come to more completely understand that gender is an integral part of the organization of social life, not something to be confined to the family or to relations between women and men.

I have tried to see gender and class in their dynamic inter-relation, believing that a theory of gendered class relations should illuminate "the processes of creation and re-creation of class and gender relations [as they] take place simultaneously and involve both material and ideological dimensions" (Beneria and Roldán, 1987:165). Our emerging understanding will not produce a tightly argued, abstract theory of determinations, but will stay close to the concrete, historical, and detailed reality. The goal of a general and rigorous explanatory system is antithetical to a feminist project that must have room for many realities, including many manifestations of gender/class, even as it attempts to connect those realities to the global and local processes of capital accumulation.

Doing comparable worth provides a way of looking at connections between gender and class from two different angles: first, from the view of political process, where conflicting interests and unequal power tend to reproduce gender and class relations even as attempts are made to alter them; and second, from an underlying angle where gender/class relations are seen as embedded in organizational and ideological processes. These two angles of vision focus on the same ongoing re-creation of social relations. The political process both grows out of and is part of the reconstitution of the underlying gender/class relations.

Gender and Class in the Political Process of Doing Comparable Worth

Comparable worth, in some respects, is not very radical, in spite of the fears of some business groups. Using an established management tool, it seeks changes within the boundaries of certain accepted assumptions about legitimate power, such as that hierarchy of some kind is inevitable in large organizations. However, the great difficulty in carrying out this reform in Oregon and elsewhere suggests that it is, at the same time, a challenge to some political and economic interests. Here I summarize how those interests were manifested in the Oregon experience, emphasizing the ways that class and gender conflicts acted to delay and alter the meaning of comparable worth. While there are many elements in this case that are specific to Oregon, similar class/gender processes can be found elsewhere.

Doing comparable worth in Oregon extended from 1981 to 1987, going through three stages, each with a different definition of comparable worth, and each marked by somewhat different conflicts around gender and class. In the first 1981 stage, a pay equity bill was directed toward all employers in the state and would have required almost all to pay comparable wages for work of comparable value. What this meant was not spelled out in the bill and the potentially large consequences for employers were unclear. However, employers' interests were implicit in the lack of support from legislators for this bill; it failed to pass in either house of the legislature.

The second comparable worth bill passed in 1983 after two years of feminist mobilization around the pay equity issue that produced a broad coalition of women's groups and labor unions. Initially opposed by the state as the employer, this time the bill passed easily, at least partly because it contained a different definition of comparable worth. In the altered definition, the group that would be affected was much narrower than the groups targeted by the 1981 bill; the state of Oregon was the only employer slated for reform. This focus on the state mitigated possible opposition from private employers, but reduced the possible gains for women workers. Comparable worth, as defined in the 1983 bill, was a single, bias-free, sex-neutral job evaluation system applied to all state jobs to rank-order jobs and set salaries. The bill mandated a study, using this definition, of both the compensation and job classification systems of the state, and set up a Task Force to carry it out. Potential class and gender conflicts were temporarily held at bay by a coalition among the state administration, the Oregon Public Employees Union, and feminists in the Task Force and the community around the goals of this study. The employer and the male leadership of the OPEU would get a new job classification system; feminists and women workers would get a new and equitable wage system. A new classification system seemed essential to an equitable pay system, so that all would reach their goals. Only the smaller unions had reservations about the possible class effects of this plan.

A number of issues, related essentially to class and gender, plagued the project from the beginning, undermined its legitimacy, and eventually culminated in its failure. These were the operational definition of comparable worth, whether primary emphasis should be on pay equity or job classification, how to combine collective bargaining and wage setting through job evaluation, who would control the project, how to achieve legitimacy of the comparable worth plan, and the timing and scope of the project. Each of these issues was related to the others.

"True" comparable worth emerged as the project's goal. This was to be a comprehensive and equitable wage system covering all jobs in the state, based upon point-factor scores determined through the application of a sex-neutral, unbiased job evaluation system. True comparable worth was consistent with feminist goals and acceptable to both the state administration and the Oregon Public Employees Union.

However, true comparable worth presented the possibility to management to strengthen its power over the labor unions in wage setting. The more closely wages are tied to evaluated points, the fewer the issues that must be resolved in management-union negotiations. If management controls the job evaluation process, unions have even less influence. The attempt to achieve one pay policy for the state and to assure the future maintenance of equitable pay also suggested limitations on collective bargaining, and thus a change in the present balance of power between the employer and the unions in the direction of more power for the employer. Thus the feminist proposal to eliminate gender inequity exacerbated class conflict, threatening to place feminists on the side of management, even though the most broad-based support for comparable worth outside the women's movement came from organized labor. All of this was not immediately evident because the largest union bargaining with the state supported true comparable worth until almost the end. Interunion disagreements marked the project and the lack of a unified labor perspective undermined the project: Unanimous union support was necessary for success but the unions could not reach agreement.

Feminist/labor Task Force members and management fought for control of the project. Unions and feminists saw the Republican administration as anti-labor and anti-comparable

worth and thus sought to control the study and the recommendations. Management protected what it saw as its rights to control
personnel practices and succeeded in maintaining control over
the study process and in establishing its aim to achieve a new job
classification system as the *de facto* goal of the project, displacing
pay equity as the primary focus of technical work.

"True" comparable worth implied a comprehensive system
change in both job classification and compensation. The magnitude of these changes led to severe time pressures and to problems in maintaining the legitimacy of comparable worth in the
eyes of workers for the state of Oregon. The more widespread the
changes, the greater the likelihood that workers will feel that
their status or pay position has been undermined and their place
in the internal stratification of the organization threatened. The
need to preserve the legitimacy of the project was understood by
all the participants and had partly guided a number of significant
decisions, such as hiring Hay Associates as the project consultant.
However, the array of competing interests, many of them linked
to class and gender, was too great to maintain legitimacy in the
eyes of everyone. Legitimacy became an ever greater problem as
the project proceeded.

As these pressures were mounting, the project went forward. Using the Hay Associates Guide Chart–Profile Method of
Job Evaluation, the Task Force and state management docu-
mented the content of and evaluated all jobs in state employment. In this process, and in the process of building a proposed
new classification system, technical issues repeatedly had political implications for the maintenance of the subordinate situation
of women workers. For example, consultants opposed even slight
technical modifications to reduce gender bias in the evaluation
system because such changes might disturb a reasonable hierarchy; measured undervaluation of women's work was minimized
by several technical decisions. The study, on the whole, reproduced the existing class hierarchy, but made some important
changes in the gender hierarchy among working-class jobs, showing undervaluation of many low wage women-predominant jobs;
approximately 10,000 workers would need wage increases to
erase the undervaluation.

Two problems with the study prevented implementation of
those increases. First, management was unable to construct an

acceptable classification plan in the time alloted, severely under-mining the project's legitimacy. Second, organized labor opposed the Task Force implementation plan, which included a one-time intervention in collective bargaining, redlining, or a temporary restraint on higher wages, and some comparable worth standards for collective bargaining.

The first problem grew out of management's intent to retain exclusive control over the project, to completely revise the classi-fication system, and to use the comparable worth effort as a mechanism to gain more centralized and rationalized bureau-cratic control over collective bargaining and state agencies, even at the expense of low-wage women workers. The second problem grew out of the Task Force's commitment to the most fully consistent interpretation of true comparable worth, even if this involved some restraints on labor, and labor's opposition to any legislated restraints on bargaining, including the strict use of job evaluation points to set wages, even if those were intended to improve the wages of some union members.

Both problems show how class processes can undermine women's interests. However, women workers needed a strong labor movement that could support their demands, giving them good reasons to favor labor's opposition to restraints on bargain-ing. Thus women workers and their feminist advocates faced a contradictory gender/class reality, a new and fair *system* was neces-sary to reverse historically existing wage inequities, but what appeared necessary to get such a system threatened to undermine the very organization that had been absolutely central in the campaign for equity. This contradiction was difficult to resolve.

A partial resolution came in a compromise bill that redefined comparable worth from a comprehensive wage system based on principles of equity to a strategy for raising to an equity target the wages of undervalued jobs, but leaving the system as a whole unchanged. This satisfied both feminists and labor unions, but not the governor and his administration. He vetoed the 1985 compromise comparable worth bill essentially on class grounds: The new law did not provide a new classification system that management wanted and did not put constraints on collective bargaining that, according to management, were essential for the combination of bargaining with wage setting using job evalua-tions. The interests of women workers were thus marginalized in conflicts over class issues.

The third stage in Oregon's comparable worth effort followed the 1985 defeat, as the groundwork for a 1987 bill was laid by feminists in the Oregon Public Employees union, feminist legislators, and the state administration. A new bill defining comparable worth as a strategy to raise undervalued jobs toward an equity target through collective bargaining and to begin phasing in a new classification and wage system, also through bargaining, was repeatedly modified as management, labor, and feminist representatives negotiated their differences. By the time a new bill was passed and its implementation negotiated, comparable worth had a new operational definition as poverty relief for the most undervalued. Again, management-labor differences shaped the outcome, although it was management that forced the final, poverty relief definition.

A new Democratic state administration still seemed focused on increasing control over unions, insisting on management's right to lower wages of "overvalued" jobs in the implementation of any new classification system. Labor would not accept this, and to protect workers against being identified as overvalued, insisted that the new law not require point-factor job evaluation to determine the comparability of jobs. Although this meant that the women's movement's bottom-line demand was deleted, feminists felt that the new comparable worth bill was a real achievement. The new law gave raises totaling $22 million to nearly 6,000 workers, most of whom were women, and required that the state reassess every two years its progress in raising wages of undervalued jobs. However, it did not establish a new equitable wage *system*, although that was still a future goal of both management and unions.

In summary, between 1981 and 1987, no one ever argued against the justice and necessity of higher wages for low-wage women's jobs. However, conflicts between management and labor resulted in the successive redefinition of comparable worth—from a comprehensive equitable pay system, to equity for undervalued jobs, to poverty relief—as unions and management would not give up what each defined as fundamental positions on the implementation of a comparable worth plan. Union women kept the comparable worth demand alive, so that it had to be dealt with by a management that still held the greatest power and could, in large measure, decide the outcome. The issues had to do with the balance of power in the wage-setting process and

redistribution of the wage. There was little working-class solidarity across gender and occupational status lines to support
redistribution of the wage through a temporary wage restraint on
higher-paid jobs (redlining). Management would not relinquish
any of its power to control the wage and classification system by
agreeing to protections for the wages of more highly paid workers
during a period of transition to a new and more equitable system.
To achieve some gains for low-wage jobs, women leaders of the
Oregon Public Employees Union mediated these conflicts between the interests of their own members while negotiating to
protect their union against the demands of management, even
though this sometimes brought them into conflict with middle-
class community feminists.

To return to the questions with which I started this review of
the politics of doing comparable worth in Oregon, we can conclude that it was so difficult to achieve this reform because management attempted to use it for its own ends and the process became an arena of conflict between unions and management. In
addition, pay equity threatened the status and wage interests of
some workers who would not gain from the reform. Women workers and their advocates did not have the power to control management or to disregard the interests of other state employees,
even temporarily. Consequently, the politics of class and gender
turned out to be much more important in doing comparable worth
than the problem of sex bias in job evaluation, which many of us
saw as the central issue in the beginning. Even an evaluation
instrument that contains managerial and gender-biased assumptions showed that much women's work is undervalued, but to
correct undervaluation by constructing a new classification and
wage system on the basis of job evaluation scores was politically
impossible. Thus, poverty relief replaced true comparable worth.

This concrete and complex interplay of gender and class
politics has implications for feminist theories. Writers on patriarchy have sometimes asserted that the primary cause of wom-
en's oppression is the interests of men in maintaining the subordination of women. Critics point out that such theories assume
inaccurately that all men, as men, have similar interests, but that
reality is more complicated. This study suggests that such formulations may be too abstract and too static, as well as too simple, to
be useful in understanding how women's subordination is re-

created. In the Oregon pay equity process, the interests of managers and male workers were at odds. Male-dominated unions would not undercut the interests of male members, but this sometimes meant supporting women's interests and sometimes opposing them, as Milkman (1987) also observes. Moreover, it is too simple to speak of "women's interests" for these contained internal contradictions and were also not the same for all women. When we look at gendered class processes, we see a reality that is complex and variable, but at the same time permeable, open to change.

Gender and Class in Organizational and Ideological Processes

The specific class and gender conflicts that helped to shape the fate of comparable worth in Oregon both emerged from, and helped to re-create, a gendered substructure of organizational class processes. My strategy for finding a way into this substructure, as I outlined in Chapter 1, was to examine the main points of opposition in the change effort, on the grounds that oppositions might indicate some of the important processes and locations of the reproduction of gendered inequality and signal the simultaneous creation of gender and class.

By oppositions I mean conflicts or disagreements which may not even focus on the main objective of change—achieving equity—but which arise in the course of working toward that goal. The content of the disagreement, as well as the gender, class, and organizational identities of those who disagree, may reveal how and where gender is embedded in class and organizational processes. Because I observed oppositions in only one large organizational change effort that used only one management technique, the Hay system, it is reasonable to ask what theoretical conclusions can be drawn. The state of Oregon is much like other public bureaucracies; the Hay system is still very widely used (ILO, 1986). Therefore, the processes identified here probably exist in many other places.

The primary oppositions in the Oregon project were around the structure and interpretation of the Hay Guide Charts, around the structure and implementation of a new classification system, and around the rights of management versus the rights of labor. These conflicts were often fought out over the wording or inter- pretation of documents, such as the job evaluation instrument, job descriptions, proposed legislation, or union-management contracts. The construction, manipulation, and interpretation of these texts, often containing organizational rules that are the accretion of past practices and struggles, are one arena of contests over power and the control of concrete organizational practices.

Such textual disputes in the Oregon project revealed that both class and gender are reproduced in efforts to protect the existing organizational hierarchy and the integrity of the instru- ments for the re-creation of hierarchy, as well as in the obscuring of skill and complexity in lower-level female-dominated jobs. Gender is also reproduced in what are often identified as class processes, union-management conflict over wage redistribution or over bargaining rules, issues not always explicitly dealing with women's interests, but marginalizing those interests. In addition, a close examination of the interpretations of job evaluation docu- ments by management and management consultants reveals an underlying logic of organization in which gender inequalities are embedded. This logic is accepted by workers, unions, and man- agement, and constitutes some of the fundamental ground upon which organizational structures and practices are created and women's and men's gendered situations are reproduced.

The Integrity of Organizational Hierarchy

The production of a reasonable organizational hierarchy and the protection of its integrity, making sure that the allocation of rights, responsibilities, and rewards do not get out of line with the formal order expressed in the organization chart, is an ongoing effort. Its concrete forms, bureaucratic personnel techniques, including the proliferation of job classifications, the vertical and horizontal ordering of the classifications, the specification of lev- els of responsibility and lines of authority are all elements in managerial control (for instance, Edwards, 1979) that character- ize capitalist class societies and that help to maintain the class structure as they subdivide and control the labor process and structure the relations between workers and employers. The same practices order these relations along lines of gender. Gender is so built into the techniques and the hierarchy that to change evaluations of women's jobs is to risk upsetting the hierarchy, particularly the worker-manager hierarchy.

The embeddedness of gender was shown in the resistance to more than minor changes in organizational hierarchy that emerged early in the Oregon project. When Task Force feminists proposed altering the Hay Human Relations Scale and adding a measurement of stress to the Working Conditions Scale, the consultants put together an impressive opposition to these suggestions. When the Task Force did not accept the consultants' arguments (see Chapter 3), and insisted on expanding human relations scoring, the consultants made sure that this scoring would not be used in the actual job evaluations by formulating instructions for the job evaluators in such a way that the revisions could seldom be used. Management representatives on the project consistently supported the consultants on this issue.

The consultants were worried, as they repeatedly pointed out, that increasing human relations points to lower-level female jobs would distort a "reasonable," in their eyes, hierarchical structure and that, in particular, this change would result in a relative undervaluation of managerial jobs. In other words, the distance measured in points and eventually in wages between managers and women workers would be reduced. Hierarchy itself would be compressed. The state of Oregon would have to be committed to compressing the hierarchy, that is, to greater overall equality, if such changes in the evaluation of and wages for female jobs were to be made.

This was true for the state of Oregon using the Hay system, but we can infer that other managerial systems have similar characteristics, although they may not be so clearly articulated and rationalized. Thus, we can argue that to recognize value in previously hidden aspects of women's work requires a general reduction in organizational hierarchy (see also Kanter, 1977). This reduction is not only between female- and male-dominated jobs, but also across what could be considered class boundaries between workers and managers. The maintenance of "rational" class boundaries, then, is intrinsically involved in the undervaluation of female-dominated low-paid jobs. The ideological undervaluation of women's work, which then gets translated into, or used as a justification for, low pay, is built into the organizational authority structure that also is part of maintaining class relations and class boundaries.

The preservation of hierarchy may have more to do with class than with gender from the point of view of managers and consultants. For example, management consistently supported the consultants when they expressed concern about the compression of the hierarchy at the upper levels, which is reflected in much lower salaries for top management in the public sector than in the private sector. Management and consultants favored the expansion rather than the contraction of hierarchical distance to attract and keep "good" managers. Their push to expand hierarchy would, of course, increase the overall inequality and especially affect the relative positions of women and men. Since there were no female-dominated job categories and almost no women employees at the upper level, only men would gain, and all women (and many men) would be made more unequal.

Management and consultants also seemed more concerned to protect hierarchy across the worker-manager line than to maintain the existing gender ranking among working-class jobs. They strenuously pushed for a reduction of gender ranking in working-class jobs through reducing men's wages, arguing for redlining, and even for the right to reduce the salary ranges of whole job classifications. As the preceding chapters show, this led to opposition from unions wanting to protect male members. Thus management mobilized potential conflict between women and men workers while pursuing its own interests.

The setting up of the job evaluation committees by Hay Associates suggests some of the complexities of gender and class connections and how these may be used and maintained. Blue-collar workers and lower-level clerical and service workers were compared to each other, while managers and supervisors were compared with other managers and supervisors. Conflicts between blue-collar men and white-collar women could become open in this structure, while conflicts between lower-level white-collar women and upper-level white-collar men were not so likely to emerge. Thus, a class/gender divide was not made an issue, but was recognized and preserved in the structure of job evaluation, while gender divisions between working class jobs were built into the process. This can be seen as a move to preserve the integrity of both gender/class hierarchy and class boundaries.

The exclusion of certain professionals from participation in the 1985 project and the resistance of others to the outcomes of that comparable worth effort reflect stratifying processes that maintain hierarchy, and thus, the gendered class structure. Doctors, lawyers, judges, college professors, and highway patrolmen, all male-dominated occupations, were not included in the comparable worth study. Such professional and occupational groups are so powerful and well organized that their superior status appears as natural, unassailable. These, at least in the United States, are always groups whose members are overwhelmingly white and male. They occupy high or special positions in the internal stratification of organizations. The fact that their status is inviolate reduces the possibility of altering hierarchy within particular occupational families and in the larger structure of an organization.

Other professionals working for the state of Oregon opposed the new classification and wage plan because it either undermined their status or did not adequately recognize the undervaluation of their work. Their reactions illuminate the role of professionalization in the maintenance of hierarchy (Larson, 1977; Glazer, 1988). The ongoing struggle for professionalization affects the internal structuring of public bureaucracies. As workers take on new tasks, they find new bases for identifying their professional competence, for their difference from other workers, and for better pay and respect. Women as well as men workers strive for professionalization and recognition.[1] Pay and status differences exist between middle strata and working-class jobs, and any reduction in these differences is resisted by both women and men professionals. Women as well as men participate in the preservation of hierarchy, and thus, participate in preservation of a gendered class structure. Class differences between women are also evident in the objections of supervisors of clerical workers to any reductions in the differences in pay between them and the people they supervise.[2]

Management consultants also have an interest in hierarchy and the tools for its re-creation, and as a consequence, help to perpetuate gender/class processes. The skill, time, and attention that the consultants devoted to circumventing Task Force feminists' decisions may indicate that management consultants' interests were threatened by efforts to change hierarchy through revaluing human relations and working conditions. Management consultation is a large, multinational business. Consultants' products are valuable and the integrity of their job evaluation instruments is important. The legitimacy of their product rests upon their claims that it fairly and consistently represents the judgments of many managers and, in the sizable pay equity market, that it is not sex biased. To accept the Task Force amendments would be to admit that their instrument was sex biased and also to give their stamp of approval to job evaluation factors which, in fact, did not represent the accumulated judgment of managers. The very basis for their business may have been in question. Thus, the interests of consultants and other experts seems invested in a particular view of reality which they reproduce in their consulting and advising activities. These activities are an important element in the proliferation of similar management techniques of control to multiple locations, helping to assure that gendered class patterns are similar in many places.

In sum, the processes that maintain and reproduce the internal hierarchies of organizations also maintain and reproduce class/gender relations. The devalued position of many female-predominant jobs is embedded in the organizational class structure in such an integral way that to "revalue" such jobs is to threaten the present contours of the structure and the interests of those who gain by maintaining its legitimacy. The processes include bureaucratic personnel practices and professional differentiation, both carried out through the creation and interpretation of documents, such as job classifications, that impose an order of authority on the ongoing work process and define the boundaries of wage claims. Textual interpretation is a skill and a resource that enhances management power in the everyday work of running organizations. Personnel practices and professionalization are usually conceptualized as gender-neutral processes, but are some of the ways that gender-based inequality is embedded in social structure. Class and gender processes cannot be separated; at the same time, class differences between women exist, and women as well as men participate in the construction of processes that subordinate women.[3]

Hidden Skills in Women's Work
or the Active Production of Invisibility

The goal of comparable worth is to make visible and equitably reward the previously hidden skills demanded in many female-predominant jobs. One of the reasons that this goal is difficult is that it is not simply error that keeps skill unseen.

Invisibility is embedded in interests and processes of both class and gender. Managers' and management consultants' opposition to reducing hierarchy involved refusal to give job evaluation points to certain skills, such as caring for and relating to people, found in many female-dominated jobs (see also Barker, 1986). The maintenance of hierarchy rests partially on the obscuring of skill.

The resistance of male job evaluators to female evaluators' perceptions of skills in women's work points to other ways that women's skills are hidden. In Oregon, tasks and associated skills, such as mediating office relationships or caring for mentally retarded "students," were rendered invisible in the job evaluation instrument and in the evaluation process. Insisting on the reality of such skills and tasks created controversy between women and men job evaluators. Contending for control over definition of what is true, job evaluators revealed how invisibility is actively produced.

The active production of invisibility is an ideological process, grounded in the material reality of class and gender inequality and with clear material consequences for both women and men. A number of researchers have made important contributions to understanding how this process helps to build gender into class relations. These include comparable worth researchers (Remick, 1984; Steinberg and Haignere, 1987), investigators of the labor process (for example, Braverman, 1974; Feldberg and Glenn, 1977; Knights and Willmott, 1986), and researchers concerned with gender and skill (Phillips and Taylor, 1986; Cockburn, 1983, 1985; Game and Pringle, 1984).

Such studies suggest a number of ideological processes that create invisibility, all of which are confirmed in the Oregon case. These include, first, the belief that certain knowledge and skills are natural to or inborn in women, while real skill is something that is acquired through training. Second is the equation of women's skills with what anyone can do with only a basic education. Third is the identification of skilled work with masculinity and unskilled work with femininity (Cockburn, 1983, 1985, 1986). In addition, observation of Oregon pay equity efforts suggests an additional process, the definition of skills in a way that is consistent with the position's placement, rather than the determination of its placement in a way that is consistent with skills.

The types of knowledge perceived as natural to women have to do with caring, nurturing, mediating, organizing, facilitating, supporting, and managing multiple demands simultaneously. In the Oregon study, women job evaluators had difficulty in making these job skills visible to the men. Other researchers have also identified such skills, and their unvalued and hidden nature (for example, Davies and Rosser, 1986; Sacks, 1984; Remick, 1984).[4]

"Anybody who has been to school can do it" is a way of hiding the more technical skills necessary in lower-level clerical and service jobs. These include, for example, composing letters and other documents, dealing with requests for information, resolving conflicts between workers, and arranging meetings. This belief is supported by the lack of formal training for many service and clerical jobs, while many male-predominant jobs require apprenticeship or formal on-the-job training.

Connections between definitions of skill and masculinity are, I think, most significant in the intertwining of gender and class processes. In this study of comparable worth, such processes were revealed when male blue-collar workers could not believe that women's jobs required troubleshooting or could reach journeyman levels; both these concepts are proxies for skill. Social processes defining masculinity, femininity, and skill supported the refusal to believe that women's jobs could be skilled, for male evaluators did not want other men to know that they might have agreed to define the secretary or administrative assistant as a skilled job.

The involvement of gender in the social and ideological production of skill is complex: The identification of feminine with unskilled hides the skills in women's jobs, while the same identification may justify the exclusion of women from other skilled jobs (Phillips and Taylor, 1986). Men have organized to protect their jobs and their skills, and have done this through excluding women (Cockburn, 1983). Faced with deskilling through the introduction of new technology, men have sometimes held on to the illusion of skill by maintaining their jobs as preserves of masculinity (see Game and Pringle, 1984). New jobs created by new technology emerge as sex segregated (Cockburn, 1985; Strober and Arnold, 1987). Men and masculinity have much to do with this process. As Cockburn sums it up, "Men form friendships through, and thrive upon, the mutual exchange of knowledge and a humorous competitiveness concerning technology. A great deal of their enjoyment of work derives from this style of relationship with colleagues and clients. Men continually define women as *not* technological. By this dual process they create a highly masculine-gendered social environment and a woman who cannot fit into it" (1986:77).[5]

The practice of defining a position's skills in terms of its hierarchical placement, rather than determining placement on the basis of skills, is a bureaucratic way of creating invisibility. For example, in the Oregon job evaluation process, when doubt existed about the level of skill required by a particular job, the placement of the job in the organizational chart was often used as additional information to resolve the matter. The grouping of positions in job classifications can obscure skills while implicitly defining them in terms of hierarchical placement. For example, in Oregon, four clerical categories contained over 7,000 positions, approximately half of all workers in female-dominated jobs.[6] These positions differed widely in job content, complexity, and level of knowledge required, yet, for practical purposes such as authority and pay, within each of the four classifications, the most skilled of these positions could be equated with the least skilled. At the same time, most of the considerable number of single incumbent jobs were held by men. With single incumbent jobs, particular skills and capacities have maximum visibility and a greater chance of "appropriate" reward.[7]

The perceptions of women and men, masculine skill and feminine natural qualities, are formed and re-created in the workplace, but in a process that extends beyond office and factory doors, providing one of the links with gender and class processes in the community and the home.

Opposition to Redistribution of the Wage or the Active Production of Wage Inequality

Severe opposition to redistribution in the Oregon project was implicit in the objections to reducing hierarchy and to acknowledging certain skills in female-dominated jobs, but open and explicit in opposition to suggestions that present wage shares might be reduced for purposes of redistribution. Rejection of redistribution came from many workers, blue-collar, professional, and supervisory, who thought that disproportionate salary increases for a disadvantaged group might come from money that otherwise would go to them. Income differentials are tangible supports for status and respect and for that reason are defended. However, in Oregon more material reasons fueled fear of redistribution, for most of those who might be affected had modest incomes themselves. In addition, at the time of the study, Oregon had been in a recession for several years, and state employees had not had wage increases of any size for some time. In the private sector, unionized workers had been forced to accept pay cuts.

The redistribution monster, as one union leader called it, was kept at bay by union protests against any attempt to redline wages or reduce the wages of any job classification in implementing changes in the system. Unions also opposed strong pay equity wording in legislation regulating future bargaining on the grounds that such wording would reduce flexibility in negotiating members' wages. Behind this lay concerns about managing adverse reactions to redistribution. The failure of unions to coalesce around an implementation plan in 1985 was a failure to agree about how to deal with (male) members' concerns about redistribution. In 1987, this issue lay behind union-management conflict that prevented implementation of new job classifications. All of this points to opposition to redistribution and to the anchoring of unions' claims to legitimacy in the present wage distribution. Since the existing distribution is the outcome of past battles to raise wages, its symbolic and practical importance to union members and leaders is understandable. However, the existing patterns favor those with the most power, male workers. As those patterns are protected, wage inequities are re-created.

Management also resists redistribution if their own relative wages are at stake, but, in Oregon at least, they supported redistribution from men to women workers when it might have increased management's control over wage setting. Management's support of redistribution from men to women was strictly limited to attempts to reduce the wages of some blue-collar jobs, and thus no threat to class-based income distribution. In effect, management's attempts to manipulate redistribution served to preserve more of the gender-based wage inequality. Existing wage differentials reinforce beliefs about what is a reasonable hierarchy. Resisting wage redistribution supports class/gender differences and is an intrinsic part of ongoing organizational class processes.

Struggles Over Authority and Control or the Active Production of Marginality

Union-management controversy about pay equity implementation and Task Force–management controversy over project control point to another process in which class and gender are linked and through which women's subordination is solidified: the active production of marginality. The controversies that reveal the underlying process were about authority and control, often over wage setting, but also involving other issues. The actions and arguments that constituted the controversies effectively defined what was important, often leaving out women and their needs and, as a result, marginalizing those needs.

Many of the controversies in the project apparently had nothing to do with gender. They had to do with management's right to define and decide, and with unions' attempts to prevent management from infringing on labor's rights, as well as with differences between unions about what union strategy should be. These were class and bureaucratic issues, but they were not gender neutral. They were built upon a gendered organization of what is most important, and, of course, the consequences were not gender neutral.

Marginalization is not simply a pushing to the side, a failure to pay attention, or carelessness, but an active process of creating what is most urgent, interesting, or significant. Marilyn Frye (1983) has used the metaphor of a stage to talk about this process.[8] Following that idea, we might observe that management's insistence on its power and prerogatives against the attempts of unions to increase their own territory of control is at the center of the stage, and other things, such as women workers' needs, are peripheral. Women are not in the main action; theirs is a role backstage where they do what is necessary to keep the play going. If those who move the scenery and press the costumes come on stage and criticize the play, they are inappropriate as well as disruptive.

Comparable worth attempts to criticize the play, but it

meets already organized, ongoing definitions of relevances and interests (Smith, 1987b). In the Oregon case, the shifting of the project's *de facto* goal was a clear case of marginalization through the power to decide what is most important. In addition, the historically created class and gender interests of men seemed so welded into the structure of union-management relations that practical proposals to legislate improvements in women's relative situation appeared to undermine general working-class interests, such as the principle that trade unions must not allow lowering of members' wages or restricting of the right to bargain.

Labor relations are structured in such a way that women's interests may appear as "only" gender interests, which are devalued and displaced. Men's interests, on the other hand, are often seen, and acted on, as representing general class interests. If practical class interests are defined in terms of the content of ongoing negotiation, conflict, and agreement, this picture may be accurate, but it incorporates the marginalization of women. When women organize effectively within unions, as in the Oregon case, their issues can start to become part of the main dialogue. Marginalization is reversible, but it is also pervasive.

Organizational Logic and Its Gendered Substructure

An organizational logic[9] that gives form to and justifies bureaucratic structures became visible in project discussions about job evaluation and job classification restructuring. Gender is a fundamental, but hidden, constitutive element in this logic. Hay consultants give instructions in this logic as they sell their products, but this is instruction based on what they have previously learned from managers in both the public and the private sectors. Because Hay Associates have built their job evaluation system through many years of working with managers of diverse organizations to determine what job components are valuable to them, the system is a residue of those managerial judgments, which constitutes a set of decision rules that, when followed, reproduce managerial values.

Organizational logic and these decision rules are also the imagery out of which managers construct and reconstruct organizations. This is not just ideology, but the underlying logic of organization that supports a blueprint for structure. This logic has a concrete material form in the instruments of job analysis and evaluation which include job specifications and the guidelines for evaluation that describe compensable factors and how levels of complexity of factors are to be determined. Thus, these documents contain the symbolic indicators of structure and the guidelines for daily actions that produce structure.

Dorothy Smith (1987) identifies these practices, procedures, and documents as part of the abstract, intellectual mode of ruling. As Smith argues, such textually mediated processes are part of the relations of managing and organizing that are conceptually constructed from the standpoint of men in ruling positions. From that standpoint, women and their work have been invisible, simply assumed, even though women create the physical and psychological conditions that make the abstract, intellectual mode possible. Without women, gender, which is relational, is also invisible. Thus, the abstract, rationalizing mode is posited on a gendered substructure in which women are erased and the male is taken as the general human. Bureaucratic documents used in structuring hierarchy appear as objective, gender neutral, their gender subtext invisible. However, traces of this subtext may appear, as in the case of organizational logic.

Hierarchy is the first principle in organizational logic. The principal of hierarchy is taken for granted; only the particular ranking is an issue. That ranking must be reasonable, rational, and make sense. Repeatedly, management consultants and managers invoked rationality, common sense, and "what everyone knows" to justify a particular ranking or a particular decision. Hierarchy must make sense to managers, but it also must make sense to workers, if it is to contribute to orderly and efficient working relationships. Workers are assumed to believe that hierarchy is reasonable and inevitable. Hierarchy is based on abstract differentiations that appear to be gender neutral.

Another element in organizational logic is the job, the basic unit in the hierarchy, a description of a set of tasks, competencies, and responsibilities with a location within an organizational chart. As Hay consultants frequently emphasized, a job is separate from the person who fills it. It is an empty slot, a reification that must continually be reconstructed. The rationale for evaluating jobs as devoid of actual workers reveals further the logic—the intent is to assess the characteristics of the job, not incumbents who may vary in skill, industriousness, and commitment. Human beings are to be motivated, managed, and chosen to fit the job. The job exists as a thing apart.

Organizational logic assumes a congruence between responsibility, job complexity, and hierarchical position. For example, a lower-level position, the level of most jobs filled predominantly by women, must have low levels of complexity and responsibility. In addition, the logic holds that two jobs at different hierarchical levels cannot be responsible for the same outcome. As a consequence, for example, tasks delegated to a secretary by a manager will not raise her hierarchical level because such tasks are still his responsibility, even though she has the practical responsibility to see that they are done. Levels of skill, complexity, and responsibility, all used in constructing hierarchy, are conceptualized as existing independently of any concrete worker.

The job in organizational logic is an abstract category that has no occupant, no human body, no gender. Such a job can exist, can be transformed into a concrete instance, only if there is a worker; behind the abstract job is a disembodied worker who exists only for the work. A worker suited to the job cannot have other imperatives of existence which impinge upon the job, for these may alter the very notion of the category. At the very least, outside imperatives cannot be included within the definition of the job. Too many obligations outside the boundaries make a worker unsuited for the position. The closest this disembodied worker comes to a real worker is to a man for whom work is full-time and life-long and who has his material daily survival needs and children tended to by a woman.

Thus the disembodied worker doing the abstract job is actually a man. Gender images are implicit in the understanding of the job as a disembodied, abstract thing.

A job is implicitly a gendered concept, even though organizational logic presents it as gender neutral. "A job" already contains the sex-based division of labor and the separation between the public and the private domains and assumes a particular organization of domestic life and social production. Hierarchies are gendered because they also are constructed on these underlying assumptions. In addition, principles of hierarchy, as exemplified in job evaluation systems, have been derived from already existing structures in which gender is one of the bases for allocating real people to positions and for defining jobs themselves, and in which women workers have always been clustered in the lowest status and the worst-paid jobs. The concrete value judgements in a system such as the Hay system are designed to replicate such gendered structures.

Partly because the abstract job is gendered, jobs are often invented and constructed with the gender of the occupant in mind. Female jobs are often described and justified on the basis of women's identification with domestic life, and for this they are devalued because women are assumed to be unable to conform to the demands of the abstract job. Perhaps ironically, job evaluation is a useful technique for identifying undervaluation of women's concrete jobs precisely because it attempts to be gender neutral.[10] The claim to gender neutrality is actually a directive to assess women's jobs as though they were jobs of men. This does not erase, but reaffirms, the underlying gender organization of the abstract job.

To summarize, organizational logic is both ideology and a material factor in the ongoing construction of large work organizations. Gender is invisible in organizational logic in practice: Gender is never mentioned in discussing the rating and ranking of jobs by complexity, and the job itself is a category without a sexed human body. Nevertheless, images of gender, of a differentiated feminine and masculine, are implicit in the concepts. Recognition that the underlying image of the job is tied to a particular historical meaning of masculinity may lead to more radical conclusions than those that arise from a pay equity strategy—that the very form of the job, and the hierarchy in which it is the unit, must be transformed if male domination is to be eliminated.

Summary and Implications

I have tried to show some of the processes in which gender and class are created and re-created in one large, complex public-sector work organization, arguing that these processes also characterize other bureaucratic organizations. Large work organizations, as many social theorists have pointed out (for instance, Burawoy, 1979; Edwards, 1979), are one of the places that class relations are concretely lived and reproduced. Gender relations are also embedded in organizational processes, often in the same processes that constitute class. Thus, work organizations and class processes are fundamentally gendered. In the ordinary activities of doing work, organizing and dividing it into jobs and positions, and setting wages, sex segregation and the gender wage gap, as well as class divisions, are maintained and reproduced.

The processes identified here are first, the ongoing recreation of organizational hierarchy. The undervaluation of low-wage women's jobs is an integral part of the hierarchy that organizes work and locates class boundaries. These processes are visible primarily as gender-neutral bureaucratic practices or as professionalization. The documents and procedures that structure the processes are expressed in abstract, genderless terms. Women as well as men may be those who organize bureaucratic measures and strive for professionalism (Glazer, 1988). In the process, it is unnecessary to evoke images of special female capacities or incapacities to perpetuate the hierarchical location and the low wages of women's sex-segregated jobs; only an appeal to the rational and the reasonable is needed.

Hierarchy is reinforced through the obscuring of certain skills and competencies in many female-defined jobs. The invisibility of some skills in typical women's work is actively created in a number of ways, while in contrast, the visibility of other skills, traditionally identified with masculinity, is also actively produced. The definition, control, and transformation of skill are central to work and class; their allocation and recognition on the basis of gender indicates a profound connection between gender and class.

Related to both hierarchy and invisibility of skill is resistance to wage redistribution, which is reinforced by management, by unions responsive to male workers, and by the way that even small differences in pay are linked to status and respect in the finely graded internal stratification of work organizations.

Marginalization processes cast women's concerns to the edges of management and labor union frames of vision, relegating women's issues to the realm of the unimportant. Thus the class situations of women workers are continually reproduced as subordinate in confrontations and negotiations between management and labor.

Finally, underlying the other processes is a hidden ideological and material construction of both gender and class in a logic of organization in which concepts of hierarchies and jobs implicitly assume a gendered division of labor and society. Women are excluded from this ostensibly gender-neutral discourse on work and organization that lies beneath and informs the way that ordinary practices are put together and change.

Can Comparable Worth Change the Gendered Class Structure?

What prospects does comparable worth hold for change in the gendered class structure?[11] Does it have any radical implications? Writers on comparable worth take different positions on this issue. Heidi Hartmann (1987:257) argues that it will have little impact on class, that it will not change the basic nature of the capitalist labor market, essentially agreeing with the critics (for example Blum, 1987; Brenner, 1987) who argue that the comparable worth strategy assumes the hierarchical division of labor and differentiation of wages of the capitalist labor market. Comparable worth has been justified on the basis of neoliberal economic theory. For example, Barbara R. Bergmann (1987) argues that comparable worth will reduce the poverty of women, but is nothing to be alarmed about because "pay equity is an attempt to approximate the result of a free market in which discrimination is absent" (p. 47); and "pay equity job evaluations . . . are in harmony with the orthodox idea that in a non-discriminatory market, each occupation's wages would over the long run depend mainly on the human capital required to perform that occupation" (p. 47). All of this "can move us toward a more rationally run and efficient labor market than we have now" (p. 51). Whether or not comparable worth can eliminate some of the irrationalities of capitalist labor markets and confirm the validity of human capital theory, let us grant that it assumes the wage relation and thus does not present an alternative or a present threat to the capitalist economy.

On the other hand, Hartmann contends, "comparable worth nevertheless has revolutionary implications for gender relations. . . . Women whose wages are raised would receive increases in the neighborhood of 10 to 30 percent" (p. 257; see also

Sorensen, 1986). These women would be better able to support themselves, less dependent upon the family wages of men, and consequently more powerful in their personal relationships. However, these effects may be limited because there are a number of other causes for women's economic inequality that will not be remedied with pay equity. For example, Smith (1987:238) cautions that, even as comparable worth is having some success, the structure of employment is changing radically in ways that may undermine comparable worth as a strategy. Work is being decentralized through franchise systems, smaller production units, and home-based industrial work. These trends remove work from the organizational structures amenable to job evaluation and pay equity comparisons (p. 238). Although such changes are occurring, large organizations are not likely to go away very soon and comparable worth will remain a possible strategy for improving women's wages.

However, higher wages, although desperately needed by many women, are not likely to basically alter the gendered substructure of work organizations and class relations, as my analysis, above, of the embeddedness of gender within class suggests. Sweden is a case that supports this contention. There the wage gap between women and men is considerably lower than in any other country, the achievement of a policy of wage solidarity in the labor movement. But sex segregation of occupations and work organizations is high, caregiving work is undervalued compared to other types of work, women do the repetitive and routine work, men are overwhelmingly in control of the top positions in powerful institutions (Acker, 1988). Gender is still firmly entrenched within the organization of power.

Nevertheless, comparable worth does have some radical implications for gender/class processes,[12] as both Feldberg (1984) and Steinberg (1986) also point out. I think that we need to put this reform within its historical context to assess its impact and its potential. First of all, the strength of the comparable worth movement attests to the continuing vitality of the women's movement. The fact that doing comparable worth reveals that there are conflicts of interest between women in different occupational and class situations, and between women and men in similar class situations, should not lead to a conclusion that this reform is headed in the wrong direction. On the contrary, comparable worth does not cause these conflicts, and in an historical perspective, it may be seen as one of the processes through which these contradictions were brought to visibility in a public arena in which they could be confronted, if not resolved. It seems to me that such conflicts must be dealt with if there is to be a broad social movement that can work to change the overall organization of ruling.

Of course, we do not know whether bringing such underlying conflicts of interest into public controversy will result in some resolutions that strengthen the labor movement and build better ties between the women's movement and the labor movement. Within the present organization and control of work, divisions could just as well be magnified. Management can use comparable worth to divide organized labor and to weaken it. On the other hand, I think that history will show that comparable worth was part of the process of ending the marginalization of women in the U.S. labor movement and, as a consequence, a factor in strengthening it.

Comparable worth for the first time brings women's issues into labor unions and establishes them as central class issues. This is true, I believe, even though most unions are still male-dominated and relatively uninterested in pay equity (Bureau of National Affairs, 1984; see also Freeman and Leonard, 1987; and Needleman and Tanner, 1987). Other issues, conventionally defined and excluded as women's issues, such as child care and health implications of working at video display terminals, also enter union dialogue along with pay equity. The interests of women workers are class interests around which union organization can prosper. This is clear in the Oregon case, in which organizing around comparable worth contributed greatly to the success of a strike and to the building of an active union. Female top leadership was an important factor in this outcome, which led to further strengthening of female leadership. If the U.S. labor movement is to revive, it may be because women become active around such issues. Feldberg emphasizes the mobilizing potential of comparable worth: "Working for pay equity offers new insight to workers in male- as well as female-dominated jobs because it makes explicit and challenges many employment practices" (1987:250).

Historically, comparable worth may also turn out to have

been part of the process of eliminating the family wage for men. The idea that men should be paid more than women because it is they who support the family hangs on as ideology even as it declines as actuality. This ideology of the male family wage has been an important support for the gender/class system, linking masculinity to the necessity to work for a wage and justifying the gender-based wage gap. Of course, men have also justified their higher wages on the grounds of greater skill. Comparable worth challenges both these claims. The family wage, to the extent that it has actually existed for working-class men, is also under attack from pressures to reduce high wages in unionized industries. Comparable worth, if it is paid for from male wages, could hasten the process. Employers push for this. As Bergmann (1987: 49) suggests, pay equity money can come from funds that otherwise would increase men's salaries: "It would be unrealistic to expect to get all or even a large part of the pay equity adjustment money out of the share of national incomes going to profits." This approach to pay equity, as the Oregon case suggests, is very divisive for unions whose male members may force a defensive policy that maintains relative wages. However, given the low level of unionization in the United States and the rapid restructuring of the economy, it is possible that most men will have no such defenses, and that the family wage for men in working-class jobs will be eliminated through the lowering of men's wages, not through the raising of those of women.

Historically, comparable worth may be most important not as an end in itself, but as part of a process of taking apart and questioning the legitimacy of the ideologies of ruling and the technical tools that embody and implement the ideologies. The radical challenge emergent in comparable worth may lie in its potential to expose the "social values and priorities underlying the wage hierarchy" (Feldberg, 1984: 324; see also Steinberg, 1987: 469), to reveal the centrality of power in the setting of wages, and to even question the legitimacy of hierarchy. These potentialities were evident, I think, in the Oregon project at the moments of opposition which, at the same time, provided clues to the process of reproducing gender and class. However, our distance from the potential is suggested in the outcome: poverty relief rather than an equitable wage system.

Poverty relief was more politically feasible than pay equity because it does not directly challenge either the hierarchical structure of managerial power or the ideological connections between both masculinity and professional status and attributions of skill and competence. Poverty relief reduces the wage gap as it gives proportionately larger increases to low-paid workers, but it hides this redistribution under an appeal to alleviate the suffering of the poor. Men are saved from having to confront the possibility that their work is not more valuable than the work of women in women's jobs. Management is saved from scrutiny of the legitimacy of the bases of its authority. Professionals are protected from the possibility that their skills are shared with those lower in the hierarchy. In these ways poverty relief sidesteps the issue of how work is valued, evaluated, and organized into structures of dominance and subordination. These are the very questions that may result from equity demands, for such demands can open to scrutiny the bases and mechanisms that actually underlie the wage. This is the radical potential of this liberal reform, to reach its goals it may be pushed beyond the limits of its original intent. [13]

Notes

Chapter One

1.   The term pay equity is sometimes used as a less politically loaded term than comparable worth. I use the terms as synonyms.

2.   The comparable worth literature contains a number of discussions of the definition of value. Helen Remick (1984) argues that employers' values are embedded in job evaluation. Melissa Barker (1986) discusses at length the problem of definition of value in job evaluation, concluding that the values are those located in an inadequate theory of the organization.

3.   Here I refer to the point-factor approach to job evaluation, commonly used in comparable worth projects. Other methods are described by Treiman (1979).

4.   See Steinberg (1984) for a similar history of comparable worth.

5.   At the time of this study, all minorities were about 5 percent of the state's population. Blacks only began to come into the state during World War II. As late as the 1950s, some Oregon towns had "Sundown Laws"—minority people who came into town had to leave by sundown or be ushered out by the local law enforcement officers.

6.   As Morgan and Taylorson (1983) point out, "In the actual analysis of day-to-day relationships at work the two factors (together with other factors such as age) overlap and mutually influence each other" (p. 5).

7.   Marxist class analysis is, of course, only one of the approaches to class. Writers in other perspectives have also debated about women, class, and gender. These discussions, which engaged mainstream sociologists in debates with feminist sociologists, occurred primarily in Britain, not in the United States. See Crompton and Mann (1986), Goldthorpe (1983), Stanworth (1984).

8.   The political economy of housework is an attempt to do this. For an exposition and critique of this debate see Seccombe (1974), Molyneux (1979), Hamilton and Barrett (1986).

9.   See, for example, Kuhn and Volpe (1978), Eisenstein (1979), Hartmann (1976, 1981), and Barrett (1980).

10.   I am oversimplifying by implying that structural Marxism always argues for empty places in a simplistic way, and by implying that there are only two Marxist ways of thinking about class, although various interpretations can be loosely grouped in this way. See Connell (1983) for a critique of structural Marxist class analysis.

11.   For other recent discussions of the concept of gender see Harding (1986), and Flax (1987).

12.   Implicit in this argument is that complex organizations, whether in the private or public sector, are the practical locations of class. Complex organizations are also a location for the reproduction of gender. Another implicit assumption I make is that the work force in state organizations can be talked about with the language of class. The extensive discussion of the role of the state in capitalist societies can be put aside, I think, with the observation that "there is little objective difference between state employees and non–state employees" (Clegg and Dunkerley, 1980:483–489; see also Crompton and Jones, 1984: 214–215) in their tasks, the conditions of their work, or their dependence on a wage. The relations between state managers and state workers can be taken as class relations.

13.   For a different approach to the same problem of understanding how women's positions in work organizations are reproduced as subordinate, see Reskin and Roos (1987).

14.   Sociologists and economists conventionally approach wage setting with theories about independent variables that cause variation in the dependent variable, wages. Examples are human capital theories, supply and demand theories, segmented labor market, and dual economy theories. The approach I am taking is different, arguing that wage setting must be understood as concrete practices and actions in which pay and power differentials are the outcomes.

15.   Radical and socialist feminists, as well as other radicals, sometimes argue for increased wage equality related to need. The adoption by feminists of the essentially liberal argument for wages based on the "value" of work could be problematic because the argument could be used to support larger, rather than smaller, wage differences.

Chapter Two

1.   Both interests and power are complex concepts, encompassing different meanings and variously defined by a long list of social theor-

ists (see Lukes, 1974, 1987). Here I understand power in the three-dimensional sense formulated by Lukes. To exercise power is to prevail over the preferences of others, to control the issues that come up for decisions, and to shape the beliefs and desires of others so that their interests may be obscured. See also Connell (1987) for an excellent discussion of gender and power.

2. Edwards (1979) describes the job classification and wage grades at Polaroid as basic to bureaucratic control. With 300 job titles, 14 pay grades with seven steps in each for 6,397 workers, Polaroid had similarities to the state of Oregon. All large public jurisdictions have similar systems.

3. Rynes and Milkovich (1986) examine the notion of the "market wage" and find that there are a range of pay levels for any particular type of work within and across geographical regions. They further find that wage surveying is a subjective process. "Indeed, judgment enters into virtually every step of the wage survey process, and each successive judgment may modify the eventual results" (p. 78).

4. The gender wage gap is lower in the public sector than in the private sector. Freeman and Leonard's (1987) discussion of unions and women workers suggests that unions in the public sector may have been more successful in raising women's wages relative to those of men than unions in the private sector.

Chapter Three

1. There are, of course, other interpretations of the emergence and nature of hierarchical organizational design, particularly those that see it as an emergent feature of all attempts to organize complex activities on a large scale (for instance, Abrahamsson, 1985) or as necessary for efficiency under those conditions. I obviously am more convinced by the analyses that emphasize the control aims of these organizational forms.

2. A survey of British employers in 1976 (Thakur and Gill) confirmed that this is one of the purposes employers have in mind when they institute job evaluation. Asked why they had introduced job evaluation, almost all employers replied, "to get a fair pay structure." Fifty-five percent used job evaluation "to establish a system of job hierarchy" (1976:14).

3. See Barker (1986) for a thorough discussion of the history of the Hay system.

4. See Lichtenstein (1984) and Barker (1986) for an analysis of the implicit weights in the Hay Guide Charts.

5. See Lichtenstein (1984) for further analysis of the effects of levels and numbering patterns in the Hay Guide Charts.

6. The impact of a factor on the total score is determined by the

number of levels that are actually used in evaluations (Aaron and Lougy, 1986). If only two levels in Freedom to Act were actually all that were ever used, it would contribute less to the total variance of scores than Human Relations if all three levels were used.

7.   I observed 81 of the 355 benchmark evaluations and, in addition, listened to sore-thumbing sessions and group discussions on evaluations. In the pretest evaluations, I was a member of an evaluation team that discussed or evaluated 32 jobs. Most of my observations were of the blue-collar clerical team.

8.   A recent British study confirms this finding (Rose, Marshall, Newby, and Vogler, 1987). Using a sample survey of the economically active population, they report that 14 percent of employees without managerial or supervisory status report supervisory or managerial responsibilities.

9.   This discussion is based on material from Acker (1987).

10.   The argument that beliefs about gender form part of the ideology of capitalism is widespread. See, for example, Harding (1986) and Acker (1988a).

11.   For an interesting description of this process see Barbara Garson, *All the Livelong Day.*

Chapter Four

1.   Another interesting example was the road maintenance worker. To keep a steady crew with year-round employment, road maintenance workers were assigned to a variety of tasks throughout the seasons. They might be digging ditches at one time or driving complex machinery at another. Consequently, their questionnaires revealed a variety of tasks at widely different levels of complexity and skill. Hay consultants initially thought that there had been a mistake in writing the job composite, viewing this job design as undesirable because it meant that workers would sometimes be paid higher salaries than the complexity of the tasks required.

2.   This discussion and that in the next section depends heavily on the Oregon Task Force Final Report and the statistical analysis in the report and its appendices. The report was written and the statistical analyses done by Margaret Hallock.

3.   These estimates based on regression equations underestimate the wage gap at particular Hay point levels. For example, women in entry-level jobs at 100 Hay points earned 32 percent less than men in entry-level, 100-point jobs, while the wage gap predicted from the regression equations was only 25 percent. The regression equations represent a

line of best fit based on the overall distribution of scores, while separate calculations of average wages at particular point levels represent only the distribution of wages at a particular point score.

Chapter Five

1.   During 1985 there was a terminological shift in Oregon from comparable worth to pay equity. This had symbolic significance for management, which was distancing itself from the disastrous classification plan that they identified with comparable worth. For the unions, the term pay equity emphasized equity rather than comparability, which to many union members had come to indicate the lowering as well as raising of wages.

2.   According to union leadership, the Personnel Director had agreed to these negotiations, but then withdrew, saying that she hadn't realized that negotiations meant being bound by the rules laid down in the law. She was willing to discuss, but not to negotiate formally.

3.   The State's low offer was made even more unpalatable by the fact that 10 of the top managers, including the Director of the Executive Department and the Director of Personnel and Labor Relations, were getting hefty wage increases, justified partly on the grounds that these increases would open up the top of the wage scale and increase the possibilities for also raising the wages for middle-level managers and professionals.

4.   A coincidental event may have marked a new turn in labor-management relations in the public sector in the state of Oregon. The preceding spring there had been a bitter teachers' strike in the public schools in another town. Management refused to bargain on permissible issues and the teachers' union responded by refusing to settle wages until other issues were also settled. The management consultant advising the school board on this strategy was the brother of the new governor.

5.   Another dispute between management and OPEU illustrates management attempts to use comparable worth to undermine the union, although, of course, that was not the stated motive. A week before adjournment, Executive requested that equity increases for employees not represented by unions go into paychecks on July 1, 1987. At the same time, there was no contract between the Executive Department and the Oregon Public Employees Union and it was unclear when union members would get their increases, since pay equity was part of bargaining, which was still in process with no agreement in sight.

OPEU was outraged. "This is a union initiative, a coalition of

women and union. Without the union, it would not have happened."
And to allow early wage increases to people who did not belong to a
union, who had been indifferent to the issue, was something the union
could not tolerate. Top administrators, on the other hand, saw themselves as on the side of women. "I didn't think it was responsible for me
not to come forward and advocate the distribution of the money to
people who deserve it. There were 904 women (management and
unrepresented, who were among the most undervalued and thus targeted for equity increases) out there. . . . here I was arguing from the
Executive Department that we should give the money and I was being
opposed by the very people who previously were saying we should
distribute the money" (Interview with Director of Executive Department, July, 1987). To the Director of Personnel, "It was inconceivable
that they would hold these folks up." Legislators understood the union
argument and gave a last-minute directive that none of the equity funds
be distributed until a major union had settled with the state.
6.　The objective and neutral method was likely to be the Hay Guide
Chart—Profile Method of job evaluation, according to the Director of
the Personnel Division.

Chapter Six

1.　In Oregon, for example, new imperatives to deal with sexual
abuse of children have produced new tasks and new claims to special
expertise among some groups of social workers.
2.　Differences in organizational power between first-line clerical supervisors and clerical workers are often so minor that to call these class
differences may be inaccurate. This is a concrete example of the problems of fitting women into conventional molds of class analysis (see
Crompton and Jones, 1984:10).
3.　Others have pointed to the importance of hierarchy for women's
subordination in work organizations, most notably Rosabeth Moss Kanter (1977), who argued that women's organizational behavior could be
best explained as a function of their particular locations within organizational structure, and that a flattening of hierarchy would greatly enhance
the possibilities for women to have better jobs. The processes that
maintain hierarchy and women's lower-level jobs in white-collar bureaucracies have implications for class, as Crompton and Jones (1984)
point out; the mobility prospects of white-collar men are greatly en-
hanced by the fact that women workers will not be promoted, thus
minimizing the number of competitors for advancement. Any study of
mobility in industrial societies that is only a study of male mobility, and

this characterizes most mobility studies, thus fails to grasp properly an essential aspect of contemporary gender/class structure.

4.   For example, the female office management function is described by Davies and Rosser (1986) as one type of gendered jobs, "which capitalise on the skills women have by virtue of having lived their lives as women" (p. 109). These jobs serve to coordinate, communicate, and facilitate the work of various units in the British National Health Service. They are typically filled by mature women, which is important for the demands of the jobs, as these call upon skills acquired in the organization and management of a home and family, comprehensive knowledge of the work organization's procedures and personnel, and human relations skills necessary for smooth operation (p. 110). Similar jobs exist in Oregon and elsewhere (for instance, Sacks, 1984). Whether or not such jobs require particularly female experience, they are usually filled by women, and the complexity of the tasks and the level of practical knowledge involved is often differently assessed by those doing the jobs and by outside observers, whether managers or male job evaluators, as in this study.

5.   The gendering of jobs through masculine control of technology may be linked to broader issues of masculinity (Hacker, 1989). Connell, for example, maintains that masculinity is defined in a combination of strength and skill, focussed in the early development of the person on the development of the body. "What it means to be masculine is, quite literally, to embody force, to embody competence. Genital potency is a specific organisation within this pattern" (1983:27). As Connell also notes, "Physical masculinity has been reasonably successfully integrated with machinery" (p. 31). But force and competence are also terms for organizational power and knowledge, which are still monopolized by men. Thus, one aspect of the gendering of jobs may well be a defense of masculinity that includes a defense of masculine sexuality. In sum, we need to look for the implications of sexuality in fully explicating how jobs are gendered and why there is resistance to recognizing the mediating, organizing, supporting, and facilitating skills needed in female-defined jobs.

6.   In apparent contradiction, Glenn and Feldberg (1979) found that in one insurance company there were 350 job classifications for 2,000 clerical workers. This may point to some differences between the public and private sectors in the use of job classification. At least it suggests that the definition of jobs varies from employer to employer and that there may be various gendered ways that classifications are used in bureaucratic control processes.

7.   This suggests that the most equitable approach to pay setting might be to assess the value of each position individually, a logical

extension of the idea of pay equity through job evaluation. Some organizational theorists (for example, Kanter, 1987) now recommend such an approach as a way to fairly reward productivity rather than hierarchical position under new conditions of competition and changing technology. Individual wage setting is unlikely to be good for women because it would provide no way to make public and visible the hidden assumptions about women and their work that researchers and activists have identified, and it would undermine the collective strength of unions, leaving workers individually vulnerable.

8.   Dorothy Smith (1987b) uses a similar metaphor in a recent, as yet unpublished, paper. She talks about "the main business," or managing, organizing, and ruling the process of capital accumulation and how women and gender are outside the main business, even though it is built upon a gendered substructure. Smith's intent is to understand why it has been so difficult to talk about women within the theoretical discourse of political economy.

9.   The term "organizational logic" has been used by others and in different ways (Abrahamsson, 1985; Clegg and Dunkerley, 1980). I appropriate it here because it so succinctly captures the way of thinking I wish to describe.

10.   This was suggested to me by Lynda Ames.

11.   In this discussion I draw upon a number of excellent analyses of the possible impact of comparable worth, while not repeating all of their arguments. These include Steinberg (1984; 1986), Hartmann (1985; 1987), Feldberg (1984), and Brenner (1987).

12.   It is interesting in relation to this claim that in 1987 Swedish women in the labor unions began to take up the idea of comparable worth as a possible strategy to help them deal with small but intractable and relatively invisible wage inequalities between women and men.

13.   Feldberg (1984) makes a similar point. See also Eisenstein (1981) for an earlier argument along these lines and the origin of the idea that liberal feminist reforms contain a contradiction that may push them in radical directions.

Bibliography

Aaron, Henry J., and Cameran M. Lougy. 1986. *The Comparable Worth Controversy*. Washington, D.C.: The Brookings Institution.

Abrahamsson, Bengt. 1985. "Form and Function in Organization Theory." *Organization Studies* 6, no. 1: 39–53.

Acker, Joan. 1973. "Women and Social Stratification: A Case of Intellectual Sexism." *American Journal of Sociology* 78: 936–945.

———. 1980. "Women and Stratification: A Review of Recent Literature." *Contemporary Sociology* 9: 25–39.

———. 1987. "Sex Bias in Job Evaluation: A Comparable Worth Issue," in Christine Bose and Glenna Spitze (eds.), *Ingredients for Women's Employment Policy*. Albany: State University of New York Press.

———. 1988a. "Class, Gender, and the Relations of Distribution." *Signs* 13, no. 3: 473–497.

———. 1988b. "A Contradictory Reality: Swedish Women at Work in the 1980s." Paper presented at Society for the Advancement of Scandinavian Studies Annual Meeting, April, 1988.

Acker, Joan, Kate Barry, and Joke Esseveld. 1983. "Objectivity and Truth: Problems in Doing Feminist Research." *Women's Studies International Forum* 6, no. 4: 423–435.

Atiyeh, Victor. 1985. "Statement re: veto of Senate Bill 59." Salem: State of Oregon Archives.

Barker, Melissa. 1986. "An Organizational Perspective on Job Evaluation Methods: Implications for Comparable Worth Approaches to Pay Equity." Ph.D. Dissertation, Department of Sociology, University of Oregon.

Baron, James N., Frank R. Dobbin, and P. Devereaux Jennings. 1986. "War and Peace: The Evolution of Modern Personnel Administration in U.S. Industry." *American Journal of Sociology* 92, no. 2: 350–383.

Barrett, Michelle. 1980. *Women's Oppression Today.* London: Verso.

Beatty, Richard W., and James R. Beatty. 1984. "Some Problems with Contemporary Job Evaluation," in Helen Remick (ed.), *Comparable Worth and Wage Discrimination: Technical Possibilities and Political Realities.* Philadelphia: Temple University Press.

Beechey, Veronica. 1987. *Unequal Work.* London: Verso.

Bell, Deborah E. 1985. "Unionized Women in State and Local Government," in Ruth Milkman (ed.), *Women, Work and Protest.* Boston: Routledge & Kegan Paul.

Bellak, Alvin O. 1982. *The Hay Guide Chart–Profile Method of Job Evaluation.* Chicago: The Hay Group. Also chap. in *Handbook of Wage and Salary Administration*, 2nd ed., Milton L. Rock (ed.). New York: McGraw-Hill, 1983.

Benería, Lourdes, and Martha Roldán. 1987. *The Crossroads of Gender and Class.* Chicago: University of Chicago Press.

Bergmann, Barbara R. 1987. "Pay Equity—Surprising Answers to Hard Questions." *Challenge* (May–June): 45–51.

Bernard, Jessie. 1973. "My Four Revolutions," in Joan Huber (ed.), *Changing Women in a Changing Society.* Chicago: University of Chicago Press.

Bielby, William T., and James N. Baron. 1987. "Undoing Discrimination: Job Integration and Comparable Worth," in Christine Bose and Glenna Spitze (eds.), *Ingredients for Women's Employment Policy.* Albany: State University of New York Press.

Blum, Linda M. 1987. "Possibilities and Limits of the Comparable Worth Movement." *Gender and Society* 1, no. 4: 380–399.

Blum, Linda, and Vicki Smith. 1988. "Women's Mobility in the Corporation: A Critique of the Politics of Optimism." *Signs* 13, no. 3: 528–545.

Braverman, Harry. 1974. *Labor and Monopoly Capital.* New York: Monthly Review Press.

Brenner, Johanna. 1987. "Feminist Political Discourses: Radical Versus Liberal Approaches to the Feminization of Poverty and Comparable Worth." *Gender and Society* 1, no. 4: 447–465.

Burawoy, Michael. 1979. *Manufacturing Consent.* Chicago: University of Chicago Press.

Bureau of National Affairs. 1984. *Pay Equity and Comparable Worth: A BNA Special Report.* Washington, D.C.: Bureau of National Affairs.

Clegg, Stewart, and David Dunkerley. 1980. *Organization, Class and Control.* London: Routledge & Kegan Paul.

Cockburn, Cynthia. 1983. *Brothers: Male Dominance and Technological Change*. London: Pluto Press.

———. 1985. *Machinery of Dominance*. London: Pluto Press.

———. 1986a. "The Material of Male Power." in Feminist Review (ed.), *Waged Work: A Reader*. London: Virago.

———. 1986b. "The Relations of Technology: What Implications for Theories of Sex and Class?" in Rosemary Crompton and Michael Mann (eds.), *Gender and Stratification*. Cambridge: Polity Press.

Collinson, David, and David Knights. 1986. "Men Only: Theories and Practices of Job Segregation in Insurance," in David Knights and Hugh Willmott (eds.), *Gender and the Labour Process*. Aldershot, Eng.: Gower.

Connell, R. W. 1983. *Which Way Is Up? Essays on Class, Sex, and Culture*. Australia: George Allen & Unwin.

———. 1987. *Gender and Power*. Stanford, Calif.: Stanford University Press.

Cook, Alice. 1983. *Comparable Worth: The Problem and States' Approaches to Wage Equity*. University of Hawaii at Manoa: Industrial Relations Center.

———. 1985. *Comparable Worth: A Case Book of Experiences in States and Localities*. University of Hawaii at Manoa: Industrial Relations Center.

———. 1986. *Comparable Worth: A Case Book of Experiences in States and Localities. 1986 Supplement*. University of Hawaii at Manoa: Industrial Relations Center.

Crompton, Rosemary, and Gareth Jones. 1984. *White-Collar Proletariat: Deskilling and Gender in Clerical Work*. Philadelphia: Temple University Press.

Crompton, Rosemary, and Michael Mann. 1986. *Gender and Stratification*. Cambridge, Eng.: Polity Press.

Davies, Celia, and Jane Rosser. 1986. "Gendered Jobs in the Health Service: a Problem for Labour Process Analysis," in David Knights and Hugh Willmott (eds.), *Gender and the Labour Process*. Aldershot, Eng.: Gower.

Dex, Shirley. 1987. *Women's Occupational Mobility*. London: Macmillan.

Duster, Troy. 1981. "Intermediate steps between micro- and macro-integration: The case of screening for inherited disorders," in K. Knorr-Cetina and A. V. Cicourel (eds.), *Advances in Social Theory and Methodology: Toward an Integration of Micro- and Macro-sociologies*. Boston: Routledge & Kegan Paul.

Edwards, Richard. 1979. *Contested Terrain*. New York: Basic Books.

Eisenstein, Zillah, ed. 1979. *Capitalist Patriarchy and the Case for Socialist Feminism*. New York: Monthly Review Press.

————. 1981. *The Radical Future of Liberal Feminism*. New York: Longman.

Elizur, Dov. 1987. *Job Evaluation and Comparable Worth*. Aldershot: Gower.

Epstein, Cynthia. 1983. *Women in Law*. New York: Basic Books.

Farnquist, Robert L., David R. Armstrong, and Russel P. Strausbaugh. 1983. "Pandora's Worth: The San Jose Experience." *Public Personnel Management* 12: 358–368.

Feldberg, Roslyn L. 1984. "Comparable Worth: Toward Theory and Practice in the United States." *Signs* 10: 311–328.

————. 1987. "Comparable Worth: The Relationship of Method and Politics," in Christine Bose and Glenna Spitze (eds.), *Ingredients for Women's Employment Policy*. Albany: State University of New York Press.

Feldberg, Roslyn, and Evelyn Nakano Glenn. 1977. "Degraded and Deskilled: The Proletarianization of Clerical Work." *Social Problems* 25: 52–64.

Firestone, Shulamith. 1969. *The Dialectic of Sex*. New York: Bantam.

Flax, Jane. 1987. "Postmodernism and Gender Relations in Feminist Theory." *Signs* 12, no. 4: 621–643.

Foucault, Michel. 1980. *History of Sexuality*, Vol. I. *An Introduction*. New York: Vintage.

Freeman, Richard B., and Jonathan S. Leonard. 1987. "Union Maids: Unions and the Female Work Force," in Clair Brown and Joseph A. Pechman (eds.), *Gender in the Workplace*. Washington, D.C.: The Brookings Institution.

Frye, Marilyn. 1983. *Politics of Reality: Essays in Feminist Theory*. Trumansburg, N.Y.: The Crossing Press.

Gamarnikow, Eva, David H. J. Morgan, June Purvis, and Daphne E. Taylorson. 1983. *Gender, Class and Work*. London: Heinemann.

Game, Ann, and Rosemary Pringle. 1984. *Gender at Work*. London: Pluto Press.

Garson, Barbara. 1975. *All the Livelong Day*. New York: Doubleday.

Glazer, Nona Y. 1988. "Overlooked and Overworked: Women's Unpaid and Paid Labor in the American Health Services 'Cost Crisis,'" *International Journal of Health Services*, 18, no. 1: 317–339.

Glenn, Evelyn Nakano, and Roslyn L. Feldberg. 1979. "Degraded and Deskilled: The Proletarianization of Office Work," in A. Zimbalist (ed.), *Studies on the Labor Process*. New York: Monthly Review Press.

Gold, Michael. 1983. *A Dialogue on Comparable Worth*. Ithaca, N.Y.: Cornell University, ILR Press.

Goldman, Robert, and Ann Tickamyer. 1984. "Status Attainment and the Commodity Form: Stratification in Historical Perspective." *American Sociological Review* 49: 196–209.

Goldthorpe, J. H. 1983. "Women and Class Analysis: In Defence of the Conventional View." *Sociology* 17, no. 4: 465–488.

Gottfried, Heidi, and David Fasenfest. 1984. "Gender and Class Formation: Female Clerical Workers." *Review of Radical Political Economics* 16: 89–103.

Gouldner, Alvin W. 1965. *Wildcat Strike.* New York: Free Press.

Grune, Joy Ann. 1980. *Manual on Pay Equity.* Washington, D.C.: Committee on Pay Equity and the Conference on Alternative State and Local Policy.

Hacker, Sally L. 1989. *Gender, Technology and Cooperation.* Winchester, Mass.: Allen & Unwin (forthcoming).

Hallock, Margaret. 1987. "Working Poor Push for Pay Equity." *Unison Magazine*, pp. 14–16.

Hamilton, Roberta, and Michele Barrett. 1986. *The Politics of Diversity.* London: Verso.

Harding, Sandra. 1986a. *The Science Question in Feminism.* Ithaca, N.Y.: Cornell University Press.

———. 1986b. "The Instability of the Analytical Categories of Feminist Theory," *Signs* 11, no. 4: 645–664.

Hartmann, Heidi. 1976. "Capitalism, Patriarchy and Job Segregation by Sex," in Martha Blaxall and Barbara Reagan (eds.), *Women and the Workplace: The Implications of Occupational Segregation.* Chicago: University of Chicago Press.

———. 1981. "The Family as the Locus of Gender, Class and Political Struggle: The Example of Housework." *Signs* 6, no. 3: 377–386.

———. 1987. "Comparable Worth and Women's Economic Independence," in Christine Bose and Glenna Spitze (eds.), *Ingredients for Women's Employment Policy.* Albany: State University of New York Press.

Hartmann, Heidi, ed. 1985. *Comparable Worth: New Directions for Research.* Washington, D.C.: National Academy Press.

Hartmann, Heidi, and others. 1981. *The Unhappy Marriage of Marxism and Feminism.* London: Pluto Press.

———. 1981. "The Unhappy Marriage Between Feminism and Marxism," in Heidi Hartmann and others, *The Unhappy Marriage of Feminism and Marxism.* London: Pluto.

Hartmann, Heidi, Patricia A. Roos, and Donald J. Treiman. 1985. "An Agenda for Basic Research on Comparable Worth," in H. Hartmann (ed.), *Comparable Worth: New Directions for Research.* Washington, D.C.: National Academy Press.

Hartsock, Nancy. 1983. *Money, Sex and Power.* New York: Longman.

Hearn, Jeff, and P. Wendy Parkin. 1983. "Gender and Organizations: A Selective Review and a Critique of a Neglected Area." *Organization Studies* 4: 219–242.

Holter, Harriet. 1984. *Patriarchy in a Welfare Society.* Oslo: Universitetsforlaget.

Hooks, Bell. 1984. *Feminist Theory: From Margin to Center.* Boston: South End Press.

Hutner, Frances C. 1986. *Equal Pay for Comparable Worth.* New York: Praeger.

ILO. 1986. *Job Evaluation.* Geneva: International Labour Office.

Janes, Harold D. 1979. "Union Views on Job Evaluation: 1971 vs. 1978." *Personnel Journal* 52, no. 2: 80–85.

Jagger, Alison M. 1983. *Feminist Politics and Human Nature.* Totowa, N.J.: Rowman and Allenheld.

Jones, Maxwell. 1976. *Maturation of the Therapeutic Community: An Organic Approach to Health and Mental Health.* New York: Human Sciences Press.

Kanter, Rosabeth Moss. 1977. *Men and Women of the Corporation.* New York: Basic Books.

———. 1987. "From Status to Contribution: Some Organizational Implications of the Changing Basis for Pay." *Personnel* (January): 12–37.

Knights, David, and Hugh Willmott. 1986. *Gender and the Labour Process.* Aldershot, Eng.: Gower.

Kuhn, Annette, and Anne Marie Volpe. 1978. *Feminism and Materialism.* London: Routledge & Kegan Paul.

Larson, Magali Sarfatti. 1977. *The Rise of Professionalism.* Berkeley: University of California Press.

Lewis, Jane. 1985. "The Debate on Sex and Class." *New Left Review,* no. 149 (January/February): 108–120.

Lichtenstein, Sara. 1984. "Comparable Worth as Multiattribute Utility." Talk given at Judgment and Decision Making Society Meeting, San Antonio, Texas.

Lukes, Steven. 1974. *Power: A Radical View.* London: Macmillan.

Lukes, Steven, ed. 1987. *Power.* New York: New York University Press.

McAdams, Kenneth G. 1974. "Job Evaluation and Classification." *Journal of American Water Works Association* 66, 7: 405–409.

McArthur, Leslie Zebrowitz. 1985. "Social Judgment Biases in Comparable Worth Analysis," in H. Hartmann (ed.), *Comparable Worth: New Directions for Research.* Washington, D.C.: National Academy Press.

MacKinnon, Catherine. 1982. "Feminism, Marxism, Method, and the State: An Agenda for Theory." *Signs* 7, no. 3: 515–544.

Milkman, Ruth. 1987. *Gender at Work: The Dynamics of Job Segregation by Sex During World War II.* Urbana: University of Illinois Press.

Mills, C. Wright. 1956. *White Collar.* New York: Galaxy.

Molyneux, Maxine. 1979. "Beyond the Domestic Labour Debate." *New Left Review* 116: 3–28.

Morgan, David H. J., and Daphne E. Taylorson. 1983. "Introduction: Class and Work: Bringing Women Back In," in Eva Gamarnikow, David Morgan, June Purvis, and Daphne Taylorson (eds.), *Gender, Class and Work.* London: Heinemann.

Morgan, Gareth. 1986. *Images of Organizations.* Beverly Hills: Sage.

Mouzelis, Nicos. 1967. *Organization and Bureaucracy.* London: Routledge & Kegan Paul.

Needleman, Ruth, and Lucretia Dewey Tanner. 1987. "Women in Unions: Current Issues," in Karen Shallcross Koziara, Michael H. Moskow, and Lucretia Dewey Tanner (eds.), *Working Women: Past, Present, Future.* Washington, D.C.: Bureau of National Affairs.

O'Farrell, Brigid, and Sharon L. Harlan. 1984. "Job Integration Strategies: Today's Programs and Tomorrow's Needs," in Barbara F. Reskin (ed.), *Sex Segregation in the Workplace.* Washington, D.C.: National Academy Press.

Phillips, Anne, and Barbara Taylor. 1986. "Sex and Skill," in *Feminist Review* (ed.), *Waged Work.* London: Virago.

Pierson, David, Karen Shallcross Koziara, and Russell Johannesson. 1984. "A Policy-Capturing Application in a Union Setting," in Helen Remick (ed.), *Comparable Worth and Wage Discrimination.* Philadelphia: Temple University Press.

Pollert, Anna. 1981. *Girls, Wives, Factory Lives.* London: Macmillan.

Remick, Helen. 1979. "Strategies for Creating Sound, Bias-free Job Evaluation Plans," in *Job Evaluation and EEO: The Emerging Issues.* New York: Industrial Relations Counselors.

———. 1981. "The Comparable Worth Controversy." *Public Personnel Management Journal* 10: 371–383.

———. 1984. "Major Issues in *a priori* Applications," in Helen Remick (ed.), *Comparable Worth and Wage Discrimination.* Philadelphia: Temple University Press.

Remick, Helen, and Ronnie Steinberg. 1984. "Technical Possibilities and Political Realities: Concluding Remarks," in Helen Remick (ed.), *Comparable Worth and Wage Discrimination.* Philadelphia: Temple University Press.

Reskin, Barbara F., and Patricia A. Ross. 1987. "Status Hierarchies and Sex Segregation," in Christine Bose and Glenna Spitze (eds.), *Ingredients for Women's Employment Policy.* Albany: State University of New York Press.

Rose, David, Gordon Marshall, Howard Newby, Carolyn Vogler. 1987. "Goodbye to Supervisors?" *Work, Occupations and Society* 1: 7–24.

Rubery, Jill. 1980. "Structured Labour Markets, Worker Organization and Low Pay," in Alice Amsden (ed.), *The Economics of Women and Work.* Harmondsworth, Eng.: Penguin.

Rynes, Sara L., and George T. Milkovich. 1986. "Wage Surveys: Dispelling Some Myths About the 'Market Wage.'" *Personnel Psychology* 39: 71–90.

Sacks, Karen Brodkin. 1984. "Computers, Ward Secretaries, and a Walkout in a Southern Hospital," in Karen Brodkin Sacks and Dorothy Remy (eds.), *My Troubles Are Going to Have Trouble with Me.* New Brunswick, N.J.: Rutgers University Press.

Schwab, Donald G. 1980. "Job Evaluation and Pay Setting: Concepts and Practices," in E. R. Livernash (ed.), *Comparable Worth: Issues and Implications.* Washington, D.C.: Equal Employment Advisory Council.

———. 1985. "Job Evaluation and Research Needs," in H. Hartmann (ed.), *Comparable Worth: New Directions for Research.* Washington, D.C.: National Academy Press.

Scott, Joan W. 1986. "Gender: A Useful Category of Historical Analysis." *American Historical Review* 91: 1053–1075.

Seccombe, Wally. 1974. "The Housewife and Her Labour Under Capitalism." *New Left Review,* no. 83 (January–February): 3–24.

Sen, Gita. 1980. "The Sexual Division of Labor and the Working Class Family: Towards a Conceptual Synthesis of Class Relations and the Subordination of Women." *Review of Radical Political Economics* 12: 76–86.

Sennett, Richard, and Jonathan Cobb. 1973. *The Hidden Injuries of Class.* New York: Vintage.

Smith, Dorothy E. 1979. "A Sociology for Women," in Julia A. Sherman and Evelyn Torton Beck (eds.), *The Prism of Sex: Essays in the Sociology of Knowledge.* Madison: University of Wisconsin Press.

———. 1987a. *The Everyday World as Problematic.* Boston: Northeastern University Press.

———. 1987b. "Feminist Reflections on Political Economy." Unpublished manuscript.

Smith, Joan. 1987. "Comparable Worth, Gender and Human Capital Theory," in Christine Bose and Glenna Spitze (eds.), *Ingredients for Women's Employment Policy.* Albany: State University of New York Press.

Sokoloff, Natalie. 1980. *Between Money and Love.* New York: Praeger.

Sorensen, Elaine. 1986. "Implementing Comparable Worth: A Survey of Recent Job Evaluation Studies." *AEA Papers and Proceedings:* 364–367.

Spradley, James P. 1979. *The Ethnographic Interview*. New York: Holt, Rinehart and Winston.

Stanworth, M. 1984. "Women and Class Analysis: a reply to John Goldthorpe." *Sociology* 18, no. 2: 159–170.

State of Oregon. 1985. *Task Force on State Compensation and Classification Equity Final Report*. Salem: State of Oregon Archives.

Steinberg, Ronnie J. 1984. "A Want of Harmony: Perspectives on Wage Discrimination and Comparable Worth," in Helen Remick (ed.), *Comparable Worth and Wage Discrimination*. Philadelphia: Temple University Press.

———. 1986. "The Debate on Comparable Worth." *New Politics* 1: 108–126.

———. 1987. "Radical Challenges in a Liberal World: The Mixed Success of Comparable Worth." *Gender and Society* 1, no. 4: 466–475.

Steinberg, Ronnie, and Lois Haignere. 1987. "The Undervaluation of Work by Gender and Race: The New York State Comparable Pay Study," in Christine Bose and Glenna Spitze (eds.), *Ingredients for Women's Employment Policy*. Albany: State University of New York Press.

Stellman, Jeanne, and Mary Sue Henifin. 1983. *Office Work May Be Dangerous To Your Health*. New York: Pantheon.

Strober, Myra H., and Carolyn L. Arnold. 1987. "Integrated Circuits/ Segregated Labor: Women in Computer-Related Occupations and High-Tech Industries," in H. Hartmann (ed.), *Computer Chips and Paper Clips: Technology and Women's Employment*. Washington, D.C.: National Academy Press.

Task Force Minutes. 1985. State of Oregon. *Task Force on State Compensation and Classification Equity Minutes*. Salem: State of Oregon Archives.

Thakur, Manab, and Deirdre Gill. 1976. *Job Evaluation in Practice*. London: Institute of Personnel Management.

Thompson, E. P. 1963. *The Making of the English Working Class*. Harmondsworth, Eng.: Penguin.

———. 1978. *The Poverty of Theory*. London: Merlin Press.

Thompson, Paul. 1983. *The Nature of Work*. London: Macmillan.

Thorne, Barrie, and Judith Stacey. 1985. "The Missing Feminist Revolution in Sociology." *Social Problems* 32, no. 4 (April): 301–316.

Treiman, Donald J. 1979. *Job Evaluation: An Analytic Review*. Interim Report to the Equal Employment Opportunity Commission. Washington, D.C.: National Academy of Sciences.

Treiman, Donald J., and Heidi Hartmann (eds.). 1981. *Women, Work and Wages: Equal Pay for Jobs of Equal Value*. Washington, D.C.: National Academy Press.

Westwood, Sally. 1985. *All Day, Every Day.* Urbana: University of Illinois Press.

Wilkinson, Frank (ed.). 1981. *The Dynamics of Labour Market Segmentation.* London: Academic Press.

Willis, Paul E. 1977. *Learning to Labour.* Saxon House, Eng.: Teakfield Limited.

Wright, Erik Olin. 1985. *Classes.* London: Verso.

Young, Iris. 1981. "Beyond the Unhappy Marriage: A Critique of the Dual Systems Theory," in Heidi Hartmann and others, *The Unhappy Marriage of Marxism and Feminism.* London: Pluto.

Zinn, Maxine Baca, Lynn Weber Cannon, Elizabeth Higginbotham, and Bonnie Thornton Dill. 1985. "The Costs of Exclusionary Practices in Women's Studies: Viewpoint." *Signs* 11, no. 2: 290–303.

Index